T0137455

The Work of Art in a Digital Age: Art, Technology
and Globalisation

Melissa Langdon

The Work of Art in a Digital Age: Art, Technology and Globalisation

 Springer

Melissa Langdon
University of Notre Dame
Australia

ISBN 978-1-4939-4531-3 ISBN 978-1-4939-1270-4 (eBook)
DOI 10.1007/978-1-4939-1270-4
Springer New York Heidelberg Dordrecht London

Printed on acid-free paper

Springer is part of Springer Science+Business Media (www.springer.com)

Preface

Globalisation is one of the most important phenomena of our times, and yet one of the least understood. In popular and critical discourse there has been a struggle to articulate its human affects. The tendency to focus upon macro accounts can leave gaps in our understanding of its micro and particular experiences. This book argues that globalisation's spatial, temporal, and kinetic changes are impacting upon individual bodies and consciousnesses.

Digital art is introduced as a platform of articulation: a style borne of globalisation's *oeuvre* and technically well-equipped to converse with its flows. Digital art works are explored through an historical lens to show how they share similar discursive functions with earlier art forms. The capacity to re-centre globalisation around the individual is explored with reference to sensory works that encourage subjective and experiential encounters.

By exploring globalisation through digital art, this book moves away from universal and totalising approaches, in favour of personal and affective accounts. It shows how digital art can offer individual expressions of globalisation. Through discussing a wide array of international artworks that feature immersive, interactive, haptic and responsive technology, digital art's tools of articulation are examined. This book reveals how digital art works can facilitate new articulations of globalisation: as enactments and modes of expression.

*The amazing growth of our techniques,
the adaptability and precision they have
attained, the ideas and habits they are
creating, make it a certainty that profound
changes are impending in the ancient craft
of the Beautiful.*[1]

Walter Benjamin

---

[1] Walter Benjamin, 'The Work of Art in The Age of Mechanical Reproduction', in H. Arendt (Ed.), *Illuminations,* Fontana, Collins, 1970.

Acknowledgements

This book would not have been possible without the involvement of a number of key people.

I am extremely grateful to all the artists that provided me with permission to share their works. In particular, I would like to thank: Marnix De Nijs, Elaine O'Hanrahan on behalf of Desmond Paul Henry, Christian Moeller, Joachim Sauter, Wolfgang Ammer, Justine Cooper, Ross Mawdsley, ®™ark, The Yes Men, Neil Brown, Dennis Del Favero and iCinema, Nicholas Golebiewski, Shoba, Nicholas Golebiewski, PHAT, Beat Streuli, Tom Otterness, Andy Diaz Hope, Abbey Williams, Cristian Alexa, Brian Alfred, Josephine Starrs, Leon Cmielewski, Blast Theory, Justine Cooper, Marnix de Nijs, Kaho Abe and Jung Sin, Joanna Berzowska, Kevin Macdonald, Ibrahim Hamdan, Lara Baladi, Forest and Kim Starr.

The feedback received from David Savat and Ian Saunders, during the completion of my doctorate informed a number of the approaches and ideas that were later developed in this text. Thank you for this support. My editor Hector Nazario also provided valuable input and guidance, which made for a far more lucid and readable text.

This book has been written over endless cups of coffee. Thank you to the cafés that allowed me to sit writing at their tables, sometimes for hours: *Gertrude and Alice Book Café* and *Paris Le Go Café* in Bondi NSW, *The Reid Library Café* at the University of Western Australia, *Bookplate Café* at the National Library, ACT and *Greens and Co* in Leederville, WA.

My family have given the greatest support, particularly Tom who has provided invaluable input and suggestions throughout the writing process. To you, my love and thanks. From sourcing articles to debating ideas, my father John was an inspiration. I dedicate this book to him—for giving me a lifetime of education—and an education for life.

Contents

Chapter 1
Introduction: Towards New Understandings

Introduction

Globalisation and digital art are complex phenomena. Because of their historical coincidence, they can be used to inform understandings of each other, with each having the potential to function as an affective and experiential construct. Conceptualisations of globalisation have dramatically changed in response to the rise of digital technology. Writers have engaged with the spatial and temporal conditions of what has been variously termed the 'network society'.[1] This book explores these altered conditions and posits that new languages are required to articulate globalisation's individual affects. It reveals how digital art can function as a loupe for observing and expressing globalisation, as a human phenomenon (Fig. 1.1).

The presentation of globalisation as a human and 'felt' phenomenon is a critical breakthrough in the understanding and conceptualisation of globalisation. It is important because it provides new ways of accessing difficult concepts often discussed in large-scale, systemic and intangible ways. In popular media and texts, globalisation is often expressed in terms of the expansion of financial markets, the proliferation of Western capitalism, the growth of global consumption and the rise of Americanisation. As Jonathon Xavier Inda and Renato Rosaldo argue, there is a strong pattern of thinking about globalisation 'principally in terms of very large-scale economic, political, or cultural processes.'[2]

Many popular readings present globalisation as being synonymous with Americanisation and the rise of advanced capitalism. These articulations are often centered upon the idea that 'the United States is the dominating global nation, powerful to a degree and to an extent never before seen.'[3] As Clark Judge claims in the *Hoover In-*

---

[1] See: Manuel Castells, *The Rise of the Network Society,* Cambridge, Mass., Blackwell Publishers, 1996.

[2] Jonathon Xavier Inda and Renato Rosaldo (Eds.), *The Anthropology of Globalisation: A Reader,* Malden, Blackwell Publishing, 2002, p. 5.

[3] Clark S. Judge, 'Hegemony of the Heart: American cultural power threatens old orders worldwide,' *Hoover Institution Policy Review,* No. 110, Vol. Dec-Jan, <http://www.hoover.org/publications/policyreview/3462301.html>, 2002, (accessed 12 October 2008).

M. Langdon, *The Work of Art in a Digital Age: Art, Technology and Globalisation,*
DOI 10.1007/978-1-4939-1270-4_1, © Springer Science+Business Media New York 2014

Fig. 1.1 Marnix De Nijs,
Beijing Accelerator, 2006.
(Image courtesy of the artist,
2006)

stitution Policy Review: '[a]gain and again in everything from the pronouncements of statesmen to the chants of anti-globalization demonstrators to the manifestos of terrorists, a fourth factor of American power keeps coming up … This elusive factor is American cultural power.'[4] A core assumption underlining this view is that Americanisation underpins globalisation.

Equally, the term 'globalisation' is often interchanged with Western capitalism. As *BBC News* reported, the debate on whether globalisation is simply 'capitalism at its most evil or a promising way to reduce poverty is now raging wherever world leaders gather to discuss trade or economic issues.'[5] However, both positions are underscored by senses of globalisation as an economic transformation, occurring after the post-Second World War boom came to an end.[6] Several writers, such as Robert Went, present it as a distinctly new stage of capitalism.[7] Yet, the categorisation of globalisation in macro economic terms draws the focus away from micro experiences and articulations.

The reduction of globalisation to a series of generalised, systemic impacts overshadows the contradictions and iterations of human encounter, experience, memory, and response. This text challenges meta-narrative approaches of globalisation that have inhibited understandings of personal and individuated experiences. Influenced by Fredric Jameson and Masao Miyoshi's reluctance to define or delimit

---

[4] Clark S. Judge, 'Hegemony of the Heart,' <http://www.hoover.org/publications/policyreview/3462301.html>.

[5] No author, BBC News,'Globalisation: Capitalist Evil or a Way Out of Poverty?' *BBC News: Talking Point,* 6 February 2002, <http://news.bbc.co.uk/1/hi/talking_point/1791105.stm>, 2002, (accessed 12 October 2008).

[6] Robert Went, *The Enigma of Globalisation: A Journey to a New Stage of Capitalism,* London, Routledge, 2002, p. 93.

[7] Robert Went, *The Enigma of Globalisation,* p. 93.

globalisation,[8] it seeks find new ways of 'knowing' this 'unclassified topic'[9] by presenting the phenomenon as a series of flows rather than a single system.

When understood in this way, globalisation necessitates a method that is fluid in its facilitation of different voices and expressions, as reflected by the diverse artworks selected. This approach is sympathetic to Okwui Enwezor's notion that the 'value of the global paradigm for me—if it means serious interaction with artists and practices that are not similarly circumscribed—is its allowance for greater methodological and discursive flexibility.'[10]

A key rationale in writing this book is to facilitate more personalised understandings of globalisation. By exploring how different artworks engage participants in conversations with globalisation, it seeks to provide far less totalising accounts, framed by notions of engagement and affective experiences. To this end, the book will explore perceptual and intuitive approaches to art and technology, which might facilitate what Shauna M. MacDonald terms 'new modalities of reflection.'[11] In a review of Susan Kozel's *Closer: Performance, Technologies, Phenomenology*,[12] MacDonald engages with more nuanced and cross-disciplinary approaches to experiential digital works. She observes how Kozel, in particular, is able to effectively mediate 'multiple, complex concepts (i.e., flesh, the virtual) of (sometimes) divergent thinkers from diverse disciplines (i.e., dance, philosophy, performance, art, robotics, feminism) and even paradigms (i.e., art, science, technology).'[13]

The aim of this book is to encourage open and flexible discussions around globalisation's human impacts, which counter universalist approaches. International digital artworks will be explored in terms of how they express these micro affects through interactive, immersive and responsive media. This book will show how digital art, as a practice shaped by globalisation, has an ability to express its human impacts, and to present it as a dynamic cultural phenomenon.

In the following chapters globalisation will be discussed in terms of how it influences the way we think about and respond to the world. Globalisation's spatial, temporal and kinetic flows will be described in terms of personal experiences and articulations. Articulation in this context is used to refer to the dual processes of voicing and connecting, or as Alison Kooistra expresses, 'of joining together and in the sense of speaking out'.[14] Kooistra argues further that an 'anatomical articulation—the joining together or "membering" of distinct parts to form a larger whole—is accomplished through a verbal articulation—speaking out, claiming a

[8] See: Fredric Jameson and Masao Miyoshi (Eds), *The Cultures of Globalization*, Durham, Duke University Press, 1998.

[9] Fredric Jameson and Masao Miyoshi (Eds), *The Cultures of Globalization*, p. xi.

[10] Okwui Enwezor, 'Global Tendencies: Globalism and the Large-Scale Exhibition', in *Art Forum International*, Vol. 42, No. 2, November 2003, p. 154.

[11] Shauna M. MacDonald, 'Book Review: *Closer: Performance, Technologies, Phenomenology*', Vol. 5, Issue. 1, 2007, *Liminalities: A Journal of Performance Studies*, <http://liminalities.net/5-1/rev-closer.html>, 2007, (accessed 16 March 2012). This link is no longer active.

[12] Susan Kozel, Closer: *Performance, Technologies, Phenomenology*, Mass., MIT Press, 2008.

[13] Shauna M. MacDonald, 'Book Review', <http://liminalities.net/5-1/rev-closer.html>.

[14] Alison Kooistra, 'Speaking into Sight: Articulating the Body Personal with the Body Politic', *Explorations in Anthropology*, Vol. 8, No. 1, 2008, p. 1.

label or banner, or constructing a coherent narrative.'[15] This book introduces digital art as a style that shares an intimate history with globalisation, and one that is technologically equipped to facilitate new understandings of the phenomenon. Digital art will be located in continuity with—not in rupture from—earlier art forms. This marks a shift in the consideration of digital art, and challenges the tendency in digital art criticism to locate these works as essentially 'new media' works distinctly borne of the new millennium period.

As 'art of the times' digital art can provide lens for the viewing and contemplation of globalisation. In historical terms, it is well placed to comment upon the particular conditions and human responses brought about by globalisation. It also operates as an instance of globalisation, emerging from its flows of media and technology. Unlike other forms of static art, it is technically equipped to emulate globalisations dynamic spatial, temporal and kinetic affects. Digital artists are converting passive art spectators into active users. Through tactile, interactive and responsive media, participants experience globalisation's replicated and at times, contradictory effects: temporal dislocation, human connection, sensory overload, urban acceleration, remembrance of home and a sense of global action and citizenship. In this way, digital art might be seen to serve a similar function to Situationist works that used their particular social and historical locations and palettes of techniques to chronicle the times.

Key works from around the world will be used to show how digital art can reveal individual enactments of life under globalisation. To this end, digital art will be read as both an expression, and an element, of new global flows. Its ontological and affective qualities that connect it to the realm of art will be seen as creating new ways of understanding the external world, and articulating happenings and responses to globalisation. At the same time, this book contends that meta-narrative accounts are unable to account for the subjective nature of art production and human experience. The same partiality is reflected in the way that works are approached and interpreted by the author in this book.

The Approach

This text is constructed as a two-way conversation between globalisation and digital art. The objective of this book is not to provide categorical definitions for these terms, but to generate conversations around these concepts, informed by digital art examples. In keeping with this open and flexible approach, each chapter will draw upon discourses from cultural studies, media theory, communications and art history, framed by the sense that some of the more illuminating accounts have emerged from cross-disciplinary enquiry, with writers such as Okwui Enwezor, Marc Augé, Arjun Appadurai and Saskia Sassen employing eclectic discourses and approaches in their explorations of globalisation.

---

[15] Alison Kooistra, 'Speaking into Sight', p. 1.

Historical analysis will be used to contextualise digital artworks and their methods of production. While the nature of globalisation's impacts has historical precedents, the book will argue that the scale is unprecedented. By focusing upon the new millennium period, this text will suggest a need to address key changes in the style of digital art production in connection with the consciousness of globalisation and its histories. Senses of *fin-de-siècle* before and after the Millennium's turn, and the heightened awareness of globalisation and digitisation's cultural, political, technological, ideological, and economic impacts will be explored. By confronting the eclecticism and vibrancy of digital art, the book aims to offer new insights into why digital art operates as an affective platform for describing responses to globalisation.

A case study approach is used to enable the artworks to be sequenced historically, and to draw attention to key dialogues that are informing understandings of globalisation and digital art.In its purest form, case study research involves an iterative process of collection, contexualisation and analysis. By its nature, digital art lends itself to this form of induction. Given the unique ways in which individuals experience and describe art, the scope for generalist or constructivist theories seems limited. The artworks will be presented as individual constructions rather than general accounts, and will be examined in terms of the different perspectives offered on globalisation's human impacts and their moments of production.

Each chapter explores digital art in terms of a particular theme emerging from current discourses, for example, art and cultural commentary; political protest; or space, time and speed. The examples have been deliberately chosen and sequenced to reveal an historical and stylistic progression in the practice of digital art, and new conecptualisations of globalisation. They will be explored in terms of their production methods and references to other art practices. Artworks from diverse locations, employing eclectic media, and constructed in different cultural contexts will be discussed. In this way, the book aims to provide a more critical and readable account of digital art and its development in connection to globalisation. Ultimately, this book poses the question: what understandings of globalisation can digital art provide?

This text will also contest the claim that digitisation produces only detrimental affects: an assumption that underscores fears that the 'unremitting flood of numbers, codes, letters'[16] is 'replacing real bodies and real persons, threatening to make both obsolete',[17] as conceptualised by Anna Munster and also expressed by Jean Baudrillard in terms of the real being 'no longer real, but of the order of the hyperreal and of simulation'.[18] In her text *Materializing New Media: Embodiment in Information Aesthetics,* Munster posits that '[t]hought about the body and actual sensory par-

---

[16] Anna Munster, 'Low-Res Bleed: Congealed Affect and Digital Aesthetics', in *Australian and New Zealand Journal of Art,* Volumes 2–3, 2001–2002, p. 82.

[17] Anna Munster, 'Low-Res Bleed', p. 82.

[18] Mark Poster (Ed.), *Selected Writings by Jean Baudrillard,* Stanford, Stanford University Press, 2001, p. 175.

ticipation and engagement must be re-examined in our analysis of digital culture.'[19] This book will contend that these generalised readings offer reduced or simplistic understandings of globalisation's variable and often contradictory human affects.

This text will also disrupt the notion that digital media is hostile to the body or necessarily borne of a hard, masculine and de-sensitising technology. Or as Munster expresses, new media technologies are held to be responsible for privileging consciousness over embodiment in virtual environments, or for favouring the human over the machine in the design of 'computer interfaces.'[20] It will explore the rejection of the idea that 'in its obsession with developing a "machine" aesthetic digital artwork might stand accused of neglecting affective, aesthetic experience',[21] and instead show how many digital artists are engaging with sensory, perceptual and bodily experience in their art. Artists like Joanna Berzowska, Jung Si, Kaho Abe and iCinema will be discussed in terms of their use of technology to present qualities of softness, tactility, sensuality and femininity. As such, digital art will be shown to have the means to generate affective and particular critiques of globalisation.

In using the term 'affect' this book focuses upon subjective and bodily responses to globalisation and art. Affective approaches create space for the shifts, iterations and contradictions of human responses, in ways that counter static, universal or objective methods. To this end, we might use Gilles Deleuze and Félix Guattari's 'rhizomatic' languages to account for the 'variation, expansion, conquest, capture, [and] offshoots'[22] of affective encounter, as a construct that is 'always detachable, connectable, reversible, modifiable, and has multiple entryways and exits and its own lines of flight.'[23]

Simon O'Sullivan converses with Deleuze's conceptualisations by arguing '[w]hat we're interested in, you see, are modes of individuation beyond those of things, persons or subjects.'[24] In his article 'The Aesthetics of Affect', O'Sullivan explores Deleuze's notion further that '[t]his is art's function: to switch our intensive register, to reconnect us with the world.'[25] He contends that the spectator might become an active participant that is engaged with an artwork at the level of representation. To this end, we are 'involved in a dance with art…and art does what is its chief modus operandi: it transforms, if only for a moment, our sense of our "selves" and our notion of the world.'[26] O'Sullivan similarly engages with Félix Guattari's notion

---

[19] Anna Munster, *Materializing New Media: Embodiment in Information Aesthetics*, Dartmouth College Press, New Hampshire, 2006, p. 10.

[20] Anna Munster, *Materializing New Media*, p. 10.

[21] Anna Munster, 'Low-Res Bleed', p. 78.

[22] Gilles Deleuze and Félix Guattari, *A Thousand Plateaus*, Trans. Brian Massumi, Minneapolis, University of Minnesota Press, 1987, p. 21.

[23] Gilles Deleuze and Félix Guattari, *A Thousand Plateaus*, p. 21.

[24] Simon O'Sullivan, 'The Aesthetics of Affect: Thinking Art Beyond Representation', *Angelaki: Journal of the Theoretical Humanities*, Vol. 6, No. 3, 2001, p. 128.

[25] Simon O'Sullivan, 'The Aesthetics of Affect', p. 128.

[26] Simon O'Sullivan, 'The Aesthetics of Affect', p. 128.

Fig. 1.2 Forest and
Kim Starr, *Chick with
Marine Debris at East-
ern Island: Midway
Atoll,* 2008. (http://www.
starrenvironmental.com/
images/image/?q=080605-
6576&o=birds)

that 'by allowing individuals access to new materials of expression, new complexes
of subjectivation become possible...In such a pragmatic, and aesthetic, reconfiguration one creates new modalities of subjectivity in the same way an artist creates new
forms from a palette.' This is the function of aesthetic affect. To this end, digital art
might facilitate affective encounters with globalisation, as an interactive mode of
articulation (Fig. 1.2).[27]

Digital Art as a Critical Language

A further objective of this book is to offer new understandings of digital art, as an
expressive language that can be contextualised in terms of art history. Digital art
has been variously termed net.art, new media art, media art and new media, with
each category re-orienting the practice according to technical, aesthetic or stylistic
concerns. Whether we see digital art as being evolutionary to or revolutionary from
earlier art styles, what is clear is the need to develop a means for locating it. This
is particularly so if we agree with Mark Hansen that the formal traditions of art
theory and criticism have limited application for the articulation of digital works.[28]
Arguably, the intimate and experiential natures of digital artworks can provide challenges for those seeking to locate them. Formal categorisations of art governed by
strict notions of authorship, aura and originality, seem to preclude an art characterised by replica, misappropriation, freedom of access and anonymity.

In contesting these formal tenets, digital works often subvert conventional requi-
sites for production, artistry, and display. Digital artists often oppose formal notions

---

[27] Simon O'Sullivan, 'The Aesthetics of Affect', p. 131.

[28] Mark B.N. Hansen elaborates on this idea in his text *New Philosophy for New Media,* Cambridge Mass., MIT Press, 2004, p. 3.

of artistry with its makers 'biologists, engineers, designers, and hackers rather than the newest crop of fine-arts graduates.'[29] As Joline Blais and Jon Ippolito observe, '[f]ar from the traditional epicentres of artistic production and distribution, creative people sitting at computer keyboards are tearing apart and rebuilding society's vision of itself.'[30] These writers question whether the boundaries have 'become irrelevant in an age when art and science, commerce and fashion are whipped together in the global culture blender we call the Internet?'[31] While the practice of defining art may seem problematic or irrelevant, the function of digital art still serves a critical purpose.

This book shows that there are strong grounds for locating digital works as art, for they creatively converse with the external world in ways that are reminiscent of earlier practices and styles. Digital art's ability to critically reflect upon social, political, and historical phenomena—and generate new ways of seeing—is an essential characteristic of social art. Rather than abandoning the category of art or placing digital works on the outer, we might expand the field to account for different and emergent modes of expression. This step has been a necessary process for all novel and revolutionary styles throughout history, ranging from Modern cinema to Dada performance. In the face of formalist dissent, artists have engaged with the backlash and incorporated the criticism into their works. It is this engagement and resistance that has often made works understandable as art, and provided grounds for applying understandings from art history.

In choosing the term 'digital art' this book seeks to provide less a definition and more a language for locating creative works mediated by digital technology in one of three ways: as the product, process or subject thereof. Digital artworks incorporate eclectic media from interactive film and video to gaming and wearable technology. As a broad category of classification, digital art incorporates any expression mediated by digital technology. The computer, it will be argued, is central to production, operating as an interface, facilitator and/or canvas for display. However, unlike technological determinist accounts it will be contended that digitisation influences rather than determines the message. Digital art will be located in continuity with—and not in rupture from—earlier artistic discourses and styles.

Chapter Summary

Through a case study approach that features diverse artworks from around the world, the book will elaborate on how digital art is technically, philosophically and historically apposite to critique globalisation's flows. It will link this expressive platform to the realm of affect and show how digital artists can facilitate subjective interpretations and bodily responses, and voice diverse experiences and perspec-

---

[29] Joline Blais and Jon Ippolito, *At the Edge of Art,* London, Thames and Hudson, 2006, p. 7.

[30] Joline Blais and Jon Ippolito, *At the Edge of Art,* p. 7.

[31] Joline Blais and Jon Ippolito, *At the Edge of Art,* p. 7.

tives on globalisation. Each chapter will engage with different digital art works and explore the possible intentions of the artists. In challenging universal accounts, this book will uncover particular and differentiated artistic accounts of globalisation. Each chapter will feature works that engage with current dialogues on globalisation and digital art practice. The introduction of each chapter will also provide an explanation of why the art has been chosen, and how it might inform understandings of digital art and globalisation

Chapter 2: Digital Art and Cultural Commentary, shows how digital art can offer sensory, affective and particular articulations of globalisation. It explores digital art's emergence in connection to earlier interventions in art and technology. Through re-tracing previous practices, digital art's capacity to offer novel forms of cultural commentary and critique will be analysed. Art's expressive and affective qualities will be explored, in relation to how reactions might be generated in response to social and political phenomena as well as conceptualisations of affect. Through engaging with writers such as Walter Benjamin, Lev Manovich, and Darren Tofts, the platform of digital art will be explored, located and contextualised. In doing so, this book will argue that digital art forms a continuation with earlier art discourses and practices. Through examining preceding styles a comparative framework of analysis will be introduced and an argument established for locating digital art in continuity with earlier expressions.

Chapter 3: Globalisation and the Crisis of Articulation provides cultural and political contexts for framing key examples of digital art. In examining some of the difficulties associated with the articulation of globalisation, this book will discuss different readings and engage with Appadurai's construction of globalisation as a series of flows.[32] In Chap. 2, the conversation on globalisation will be opened up with the suggestion made that new means of articulating the phenomenon are required. Chapter 3 builds upon the previous chapter, which shows how digital art might operate as that critical voice.

The fourth chapter of this book examines some of these more radical articulations. Through a focus on 'Digital Art and Political Revolt', it analyses protests to globalisation by early digital artists such as Ross Mawdsley, ®™ark and The Yes Men, who works are seen to represent these expressions. In this chapter, the use of digital tactics to oppose Western political leaders, Non Government Organisations (NGOs) and multi-national corporations are examined. The artists' use of Internet, television, and street campaigns to generate global revolt will be discussed, as will their strategic infiltrations of virtual and physical spaces. Ross Mawdsley, ®™ark, and The Yes Men's art are situated and contextualised in terms of earlier expressions of resistance, with critical questions posed such as: how is digital technology being used in backlash to globalisation? And, what are the discourses that inform these accounts? The legitimacy of tactics such as spoofing, hacking, impersonation and sabotage will be examined. This chapter also discusses local enactments of global movements and critiques of 'glocalised' political campaigns.

---

[32] Arjun Appadurai, 'Disjuncture and Difference in the Global Culture Economy', *Theory, Culture, and Society,* Vol. 7, 1990, pp. 295–310.

Chapter 5: 'Global Space, Time and Speed: T_Visionarium II and Beijing Accelerator moves forward from the idea of political revolt to examine spatial and temporal enactments of globalisation in digital art. It considers iCinema and Marnix de Nijs' interactive installations as key works that converse with global flows of space, time and speed. This chapter explores the role that graphical user interfaces (GUI) can play. Both installations feature transcriptive narratives, which enable the participant to simulated spatial, temporal and kinetic flows. Affective, responsive and participatory technologies engage users on bodily levels. Both artworks are contextualised in terms of the dialogues on globalisation and digital art, established in Chaps. 2 and 3.

The sixth chapter *Metropolis: Imagining the Global City* continues the conversation established in the previous chapter through exploring a key space: the global city. This chapter will argue that the global city operates as an important site for the manifestation of urban change, influenced by the rapid movements of people, ideas, ideologies and finance. Using the exhibition *Metropolis* as an indicative point of reference, eight artists' perceptions of life within North American cities will be examined. The artworks discussed are: Shoba's *Blowing Zen* (2003), Nicholas Golebiewski's *This is Where I Live* (2003), Tom Otterness' *Nine Eleven* (2003), Cristian Alexa's *Ten-Second Couples* (2000), Abbey Williams' *YES* (2002), Andy Diaz Hope *Financial District Infiltration: Everybody is Somebody's Terrorist* (2004) PHAT's *Harlem: The* Ghetto Fabulous (2004).

In some of the works, such as Diaz Hope's *Financial District Infiltration: Everybody is Somebody's Terrorist* (2004), the global city is seen to intensify senses of alienation. In others, such as PHAT's *Harlem: The Ghetto Fabulous* (2004), the city is shown to localise ethnic difference: offering opportunities for solidarity and revolt. The *Metropolis* artists punctuate their works with human responses to globalisation, underscored by themes such as the nature of individuality in a globalised world, human flow and dispalcement, social fragmentation and suspicion, and belonging and connection. Constructed as private and intimate articulations of globalisation, these works implicitly counter universal or totalising accounts of globalisation through offering disparate and at times contradictory accounts by diverse international artists.

Chapter 7: In the Line of Flight: Changing Practices in Digital Art will examine a global exhibition held in synchrony with a symposium in Beijing. One of the reasons that it has been included in this book is to showcase how digital artworks are being exhibited, and to explore curators' perspectives on digital art, and how it might offer new perspectives on globalisation. To this end, the inclusion of *In the Line of Flight* and its sequencing in the book is designed to enable direct comparisons to be made to the *Metropolis* exhibition discussed in Chap. 6. Secondly, this chapter highlights the eclectic approaches that have informed the conceptualisations of digital art that are explored in Chap. 3. The exhibition featured an eclectic array of digital art formats, from video games to responsive garments and haptic installations. The exhibition reflects the different degrees to which artists are identifying changing practices in art, and engaging with those realities in their works will be examined. Lastly, the organisation of the exhibition was itself a global endeavour.

Through incorporating artists and participants from around the world, it exemplifies the new ways that art is being made, shared and exhibited in a global age.

The eight examples that this chapter focuses on reveal divergent perceptions of globalisation's flows. These include Blast Theory's *Can You See Me Now?* (UK, 2001–2007), Justine Cooper's *Transformers* (Australia, 2002), Marnix de Nijs' *Run Motherfucker Run* (Netherlands, 2004), Joanna Berzowska's *Intimate Memory Shirt* and *Feathery Dresses* (Canada, 2004), Jung Sin and Kaho Abe's *Haptic Glove* (USA, 2004), and Leon Cmielewski and Josephine Starrs' *Floating Territories* (Australia, 2004).

The artworks presented in the exhibition *In the Line of Flight* raise questions about the nature of art collaboration, production and display under globalisation. Themes explored: the cultural influence of North America and the West, the movement of individuals globally, the virtualisation of communities, and the rise of the global city, as a cultural manifestation of globalisation. Each example raises questions about the politics of art display, and the role of digital technology in facilitating creative communication, collaboration, and construction. '*In the Line of Flight:* Changing Practices in Digital Art', reflects upon shifting digital art practices and promotes new understandings of globalisation's human impacts, as subjectively interpreted by different artists.

Chapter 8: A Brave New World: Digital Art and Social Engagement moves beyond the previous chapters to explore global digital artworks produced between 2009 and now. Kevin Macdonald's 2011 film *Life in a Day,* Ibrahim Hamdan's 2011 film *Images of Revolution, Lara Baladi's 2012 installation Alone, Together… In Media Res, and Chris Jordan's 2009-current Midway series is* discussed in terms of social, political and environmental issues that they raise. The chapter explores how artists are using their works to put out 'calls to action'. The question of how digital art can effect real change in the physical world will be examined.

Chapter 2
Digital Art and Cultural Commentary

Introduction

This chapter establishes grounds for perceiving digital art as a critical voice—one that can facilitate both personal and affective responses to globalisation. It posits that digital art is borne of a turbulent era, sharing an intimate history with globalisation. This chapter shows how art can function as a platform for cultural commentary. It also provides means for considering and contextualising the digital art case studies presented within the text (Fig. 2.1).

The first part of this chapter foregrounds the emergence of digital art through discussing art's capacity to articulate and respond to, technological change. Digital art is contextualised in terms of earlier styles of expression, ranging from Modern cinema to 1960s technological art. The impacts of digitisation and the Internet upon artistic production, experience and display are then examined. This chapter explores how digital art both challenges—and confirms—earlier artistic practices and discourses. It also shows how digital technology can be used to generate diverse styles of art, with varying levels of interactivity and immersion.

Art and Technological Change

Some seventy years before the advent of digitisation, Walter Benjamin observed how 'the work of art of the Dadaists became an instrument of ballistics. It hit the spectator like a bullet, it happened to him, thus acquiring a tactile quality.'[1] Their art generated affective responses to emotive subjects such as war, class conflict and political change. Feelings of shock and repulsion were often conjured by Dadaism and Situationism. These movements continue to influence digital works of art, with disjunction and self-reflexion often apparent.

---

[1] Gene Youngblood, 'A Medium Matures: Video and Cinematic Enterprise', in Timothy Druckrey (Ed.), *Ars Electronica: Facing the Future,* Cambridge Mass., MIT Press, 1999, p. 63.

M. Langdon, *The Work of Art in a Digital Age: Art, Technology and Globalisation,*
DOI 10.1007/978-1-4939-1270-4_2, © Springer Science+Business Media New York 2014

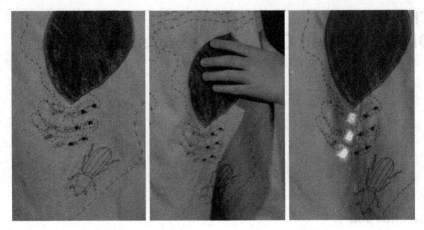

Fig. 2.1 Joanna Berzowska, *Intimate Memory Shirt,* 2005. (Image courtesy of the artist)

As cultural theorist Frederic Jameson observed, Modern expression presented 'fragmented senses of the world.'[2] One Modernist technique that features strongly in digital art is montage. Montage emerged as a form of cultural backlash in its critique of conservative bourgeois tastes. It was deliberately 'ugly, dissonant, bohemian, sexually shocking'.[3] Using irony and irreverence, many Modern artists countered the neo-Platonic ideals of their predecessors, namely the notion that art should capture aesthetic 'truth' and the sublime. Artists like Marcel Duchamp reflected this dissidence in his work through manipulating or destroying their art materials.[4]

As Lisa Saltzman writes, Modern art—like digital art—was irrevocably tied to its moment of production. The devastation of World War I produced some art that was 'driven in its acts of repression and denial to re-create itself according to an idealized notion of the past rather than create itself anew after acknowledging and mourning its losses.'[5] However, artists and filmmakers like Pablo Picasso and Fritz Lang used feelings of destitution despair as catalysts for innovation. Picasso's painting *Guernica* and Lang's film *Metropolis,* for example, appeared as what cultural theorist Guy Debord termed 'art in the epoch of its dissolution'[6] or 'the pure ex-

---

[2] Fredric Jameson, 'Postmodernism and Consumer Society', in H. Foster (Ed.), *The Anti-Aesthetic: Essays on Postmodern Culture,* Seattle, Bay Press, 1983, p. 114.

[3] Fredric Jameson, 'PostModernism and Consumer Society', p. 124.

[4] Lev Manovich, 'The Death of Computer Art', <http://www.thennetnet.com/schmeb/schmeb12.html>.

[5] Lisa Saltzman, 'Marketing Modernism in Fin-de-Siecle Europe—Book Review', *Find Articles,* <http://findarticles.com/p/articles/mi_m0422/is_n4_v78/ai_19178144/pg_6>, 1996, (accessed18 April 2007).

[6] Guy Debord, *The Society of the Spectacle,* (Trans. Black and Red), Detroit, Black and Red, 1983, p. 30.

pression of impossible change.'[7] In similar ways, many digital artists use Modern principles of disruption, civil disobedience, dislocation and juxtaposition create anti-aesthetics, which challenge traditional Academy art. Andrew Darley argues that digital technology 'tends much more to foreground itself as a technique within the work itself—thereby linking itself to anti- or counter-realist forms'.[8]

Another way that digital art responds to earlier practices is through the incorporation of political protest, and adaptation of popular media ranging from poster art to advertising, film and photography. Modern cinema, in particular, has strong resonances with digital art. Geraldine Pratt and Rose Marie San Juan contend that Modern cinema shows some of the earliest articulations of virtual, immersive and experiential affects. The writers see strong similarities between Modern film and digital expression, arguing that

> cinema and cyberspace produce comparable effects of dislocation and disembodiment, arguably privileging the visual as a way to simulate proximity without physical presence, and thus transforming the relationship between subject and object of viewing in particular ways.[9]

Michael Heim shares this view, in claiming that

> [e]xiting a movie theatre resembles somewhat the exit from a virtual world. After hours immersed in screen adventures, you emerge from the dark to blinding bright daylight. The sensory shock brings with it a residual emotional tone aroused by the film.[10]

While Pratt and San Juan describe digital impacts in terms of Modern film elements such as detached proximity and disembodiment, many digital artists show to the contrary, how digital technology can re-engage the body, through conjuring senses of physical immersion, interaction and intimacy. Joanna Berzowska's tactile and responsive garments—explored in detail in Chapter Seven—show digital technology to be personal, sensory and feminising.

Mark Nunes posits that the awareness of digitisation's spatial, temporal and kinetic impacts is comparable to earlier technological responses. In his text *Cyberspaces of Everyday Life,*[11] Nunes offers an analysis of analogue and digital technological affects. He compares the development of the British mail service to the rise of email, in terms of popular shifts in the cognition of nearness, distance and space.[12] Yet despite similarities, the scale of digital affects is unique. It is a key distinction to make, because it establishes one argument about the comparative nature of digital and analogue affects, and another about the level of impact.

---

[7] Guy Debord, *The Society of the Spectacle,* p. 30.

[8] Andrew Darley, 'The Digital Image in the Age of the Signifier', in Andrew Darley (Ed.), *Visual Digital Culture: Surface Play and Spectacle in New Media Genres,* London, Routledge, 2000, p. 131.

[9] Rose Marie San Juan and Geraldine Pratt, 'Virtual Cities: Film and the Urban Mapping of Virtual Space', *Screen,* Vol. 43, No. 3, 2002, p. 250.

[10] Michael Heim, *Virtual Realism,* New York, Oxford University Press, 1998, p. 54.

[11] Mark Nunes, *Cyberspaces of Everyday Life,* Minneapolis, University of Minnesota Press, 2006.

[12] Mark Nunes, *Cyberspaces of Everyday Life.*

The Modern concept of art 'happening' and generating physical responses is resonant with digital art. The digital collaboration iCinema, for example, employ earlier principles of space, time and narrative in their works, which are then reformulated through digital technology. In their installation *T_Visionarium II*, which is closely examined in 'Chapter Five', high levels of interaction, immersion and response confront the user. A generative surround sound system, tactile and responsive interface and evolving graphical system, which is sensitive to the user's line of sight, enables *T_Visionarium II* to transcend the limits of Modern cinema, through transforming the physically passive art spectator into an active user.

Digital Art Terminologies

Just as the isolation of digital expression from the field of art is problematic, so is the elevation of it to a separate domain. This action would reflect technological determinist assumptions, underscored by the sense that media art is fundamentally different or 'new'. This notion pervades the writings of Marshall McLuhan and Lev Manovich, and is evident in early net.art expressions, explored further in Chapter Four. As a formalist idea, technological determinism privileges digital form over content, valuing digital media for its own sake. It is shaded by the ideal that digital art is a novel and form of creative expression. Technological determinist accounts view analogue and 'old school' formats as static, outmoded and corrupt. Digital media triumphs as the vanguard technology: capable of exhilarating speeds.

Lev Manovich writes that 'those of us who work with digital art often debate another convergence – the convergence between art world and computer world'.[13] Manovich creates a binary between what he terms 'Duchamp-land' and 'Turing-land',[14] and argues that in Duchamp-land, an art object is defined by the criticism it provokes, which can be prompted by its 'literally destructive attitude towards its material, i.e., its technology'.[15] 'Turing-land', however, is diametrically opposed. It emphasizes the digital medium rather than the message. As opposed to Duchamp-land, Turing-land works tend to lack irony in their critique of art mediums, for 'objects in Turing-land take technology which they use always seriously'.[16]

In reflecting upon Technological Determinist productions, Patrick Lichty observes how they often harbour the assumption that 'the present is a bore, and it takes too long for projects to get out of beta. The acceleration of culture demands the con-

---

[13] Lev Manovich, 'The Death of Computer Art',< http://www.thennetnet.com/schmeb/schmeb12. html>

[14] Lev Manovich, 'The Death of Computer Art', <http://www.thennetnet.com/schmeb/schmeb12. html>

[15] Lev Manovich, 'The Death of Computer Art', <http://www.thennetnet.com/schmeb/schmeb12. html>.

[16] Lev Manovich, 'The Death of Computer Art', <http://www.thennetnet.com/schmeb/schmeb12. html>

sumption of ideas at their peak of freshness.'[17] To the digital determinist, the pure innovation and exhilaration of technology is the message in itself, with analogue technology rendered static, outmoded, and corruptible. In works such as Mawdsley's *Simian* series, digitisation triumphs as the vanguard technology: capable of excessive speeds as it cuts through space and time. However, the exhilaration of the media is often at the expense of the critical message.

Writers like Anna Munster and Geert Lovink, however, advocate approaches that negotiate divisions between subjects and objects. In conversation with Lovink, Munster perceives what she terms 'media art', as a fluid and distributed aesthetic. However, the contention that digital expression is not art—as indicated by Manovich's essay 'The Death of Computer Art'[18]—is problematic, for it prescribes what art is or should be. Such claims, argue Munster and Lovink, require 'a rethink of aesthetics beyond the twinned concepts of form and medium that continue to shape analysis of the social and the aesthetic.'[19] By removing digital art from its contexts of production, Technological Determinism isolates the medium from the message. Through simply claiming that the medium *is* the message, such theorists privilege digital form over content. In challenging Technological Determinist approaches, this book locates digital art in continuum with earlier art discourses and expressions. Globalisation is similarly conceptualised in relativist terms, which connect current conditions to previous moments in time.

Terms like 'new media' arguably wittingly sever art's ties in declaring that digital expression belongs to a different practice, discourse, time or technology. This 'newness' severs digital art from past expressions and aligns it with what Donna Haraway describes as a 'Twenty-first century technoscience and technoculture are nothing if not frontier practices, always announcing new worlds, proposing the novel as the solution to the old, figuring creation as radical invention and replacement, rushing toward a future that wobbles between ultimate salvation and destruction but has little truck with thick pasts or presents.'[20] Technological determinists often extol the innovation of digital technology, rendering analogue a redundant or obsolete format: static, outmoded and corruptible.

In his use of the term 'New Media',[21] Lev Manovich for example ascribes a distinct novelty to the form. Yet, as Richard L. Richards contends, '[m]ost new media have been developed in dialogue with existing "old" and established media forma-

---

[17] Patrick Lichty, 'Alpha Revisionist Manifesto', *Nettime,* <http://www.nettime.org/Lists-Archives/nettime-bold-0105/msg00391.html>, (accessed 01 July 2003).

[18] Lev Manovich, 'The Death of Computer Art', <http://www.thennetnet.com/schmeb/schmeb12.html>.

[19] Geert Lovink and Anna Munster, 'Theses on Distributed Aesthetics. Or, What a Network is Not', *Fibreculture eJournal,* Issue 7, <http://www.journal.fibreculture.org/issue7/issue_7munster_lovink.html>, 2005, (accessed 12 December 2005).

[20] Donna Haraway, 'Speculative Fabulations for Technoculture's Generations: Taking Care of Unexpected Country', *(Tender) Creature Exhibition Catalogue,* Alava, Artium, < http://www.patriciapiccinini.net/essay.php>, 2007, (accessed 16 March 2012).

[21] The term is used throughout Lev Manovich's text *The Language of New Media,* Cambridge Mass., MIT Press, 2001.

tions such as cinema and television'.[22] He argues that any examination of digital technology in light of 'previous models of technological change'[23] will 'blunt any facile notion of "newness"'.[24] By omitting the adjunct of 'art', Manovich's term locates digital expression outside the realm of art. Darren Tofts suggests, the term 'new media' favoured by Lev Manovich assumes that digital media 'lacks predecessors'.[25] Equally, the alignment of the medium to the message imposes a distinct causality, limiting the potential for digital art to be art as opposed to media. Hansen explains that it is not 'simply that the image provides a tool for the user to control the "infoscape" of contemporary material culture, as Manovich suggests, but rather that the "image" has itself become a process and, as such, has become irreducibly bound up with the activity of the body.'[26] An artist may use digital technology to convey a message but from there, the message may transcend the medium to express outside ideas such as the affects of globalisation upon the individual.

While Munster and Lovink use terms such as 'new media art' and 'new media theory', Tofts disengages with the notion of novelty. In his classification of digital media he omits the descriptor 'new' and chooses the phrase 'media art'.[27] In doing so, he creates possibilities for comparative artistic discourse while acknowledging new forms of art. Through contextualising digital expression in terms of earlier art discourses and strategies, Tofts provides a relative framework for articulation.

However, Tofts argues that the term 'digital art' is far too reductive in 'foregrounding the computer as the decisive factor in the art-making process'. Yet, clearly digital technology informs its production, experience, history and conceptualisation. 'Digital art' is consistent with other artistic terms that invoke a technology, such as video art, creative writing, printmaking and painting. One problem with his terminology, however, concerns his choice of the word 'media' in his classification 'media art'. 'Media' is a general term used to describe various mass communication formats, from television to radio and newspapers. The category of 'media art' also provides no way of distinguishing between digital and analogue works, for example. Some theorists question the value of that distinction, instead viewing digital technology as a continuation of earlier formats. Yet, the differentiation is critical, if we view digitisation as affecting the production, experience, and understanding of digital art.

---

[22] Richard L. Richards, 'Review of Dan Harries (Ed.), The New Media Book', *The Association of Moving Image Archivists,* <http://muse.jhu.edu/journals/the_moving_image/v004/4.1edwards. html>, 2004, (accessed 28 April 2006).

[23] Richard L. Richards, 'Review of Dan Harries', (accessed 28 April 2006).

[24] Richard L. Richards, 'Review of Dan Harries', (accessed 28 April 2006).

[25] Darren Tofts, *Interzone: Media Arts in Australia,* Melbourne, Craftsman House, 2005, p. 9.

[26] Mark B.N. Hansen, *New Philosophy for New Media,* p. 10.

[27] Darren Tofts, *Interzone,* p. 9.

Fig. 2.2 Marnix de Nijs, *Run Motherfucker Run,* 2004. (http://www.marnixdenijs.nl/run-motherfucker-run.htm)

Art and Cultural Critique

Installations like Marnix de Nijs' *Run Motherfucker Run* also engage with the idea of art responding to contemporary cultural and political events. To this end, digital works may be reminiscent of Frankfurt School art, which instigated new forms of creative opposition in seeking to tear down regimes and foster new ways of thinking. Under the auspices of Theodor Adorno, the Frankfurt School invoked Marxist discourses in seeking to unite art, politics and technology.[28] Writers such as Walter Benjamin, Max Horkheimer, Leo Lowenthal and Herbert Marcuse were concerned with the social, political and economic conditions that influenced and repressed, practices of art. In their expression of cultural phenomena, Frankfurt School theorists reflected dual senses of articulation: as both speaking about and connecting to the world. Through connecting art and cultural commentary, Frankfurt School artists and theorists negotiated artistic limits, and provided new modes of cultural critique (Fig. 2.2).

Walter Benjamin's notions of mechanical reproduction and industrial design also surfaced in Frankfurt School art. Corporate motifs were ironically used in their backlash against stifling political and economic conditions. Adorno's adaptation of Thorstein Veblen's theories of consumption reiterated Marx's analyses of Western capitalist political economies. He engaged with the idea that in an era of mass consumption, art is marred by constraints imposed by the cultural power brokers. In his critique of Aldous Huxley's Brave New World, Adorno highlights many of these tensions between mass culture and art production. Huxley's text, Adorno claims, exemplified the ways in which homogenisation was beginning to 'massify and destroy individual thought and action.'[29] Under these conditions, the principles

---

[28] John A. Walker, *Art in the Age of Mass Media,* Third Ed., London, Pluto Press, 1983, p. 3.

[29] Douglas Kellner, *Media Culture: Cultural Studies, Identity and Politics Between the Modern and PostModern,* London, Routledge, 1995, p. 75.

of 'Community, Identity and Stability',[30] Adorno notes, 'came to replace the three ideals of the French Revolution.'[31]

Art and cultural theories of the Marxist tradition challenged political and economic foundations. Schneider Adams observes how as 'early as 1857–1859, in his *Introduction to the Critique of the Political Economy,* Karl Marx argued for tying art to the culture that produced it',[32] based upon the premise that the production of art was influenced by social and political contexts. Marx's opposition to the formalist ideal of 'art for art's sake' was evident through his concern for production, and the social and economic contexts influencing content. As Schneider Adams states, '[f]or Marx, art did not belong in an ivory tower inhabited by aestheticians, but rather in the larger context of society and the economic historical process.'[33] This sense is apparent in the theatre of German playwright Bertolt Brecht. In emphasising the importance of the message over medium, he suggested that artists had a responsibility to provide cultural critiques, with art functioning as something more than just aesthetic form.[34] Marxist theorist Ernst Fischer also championed that 'art, if it is truthful, must also reflect decay. And unless it wants to break faith with its social function, art must show the world as changeable. And help to change it.'[35] This is one of the key tenets of Walter Benjamin's theory that art functions as a 'political commodity'.[36]

The Production of Art

Mechanical art's focus upon content—as opposed to form, aura and originality—is pertinent to digital art. In 'The Work of Art in the Age of Mechanical Reproduction', Benjamin shows how art produced through 'mechanical' or industrial means, might oppose formal assumptions of authorship, originality and aura. In making these claims, he suggests the capacity for technological expressions to be artistic and termed 'digital art', as opposed to 'graphic design', 'video' or 'multimedia'. Benjamin's understanding of mechanised forms of art is centred on the idea that once it is replicated through technological means, such as film or photography, it has the capacity to reach mass audiences and have unprecedented large-scale social and political impacts. By expanding the category of art to include new kinds of ex-

---

[30] Douglas Kellner, *Media Culture,* p. 75.

[31] Douglas Kellner, *Media Culture,* p. 75.

[32] Laurie Schneider Adams, *The Methodologies of Art: An Introduction,* Boulder, Westview Press, 1996, p. 59.

[33] Laurie Schneider Adams, *The Methodologies of Art,* p. 59.

[34] Laurie Schneider Adams, *The Methodologies of Art,* p. 60.

[35] Laurie Schneider Adams, *The Methodologies of Art,* p. 62.

[36] Laurie Schneider Adams, *The Methodologies of Art,* p. 63.

pression, Benjamin arguably 'detailed a shift in the function and ontology of art in the age of technical reproducibility'.[37]

Walter Benjamin's seminal essay 'The Work of Art in the Age of Mechanical Reproduction',[38] discusses the liberation of art from traditional concepts of aura, originality, authenticity, and authorship. By exploring mechanical art and the principle of replica, he subverts constructed formal boundaries of artistry, production and display. Through articulating art in terms of its surrounding cultural and political contexts, Walter Benjamin perceives mechanical art's capacities for self-reflexive critique. Through conversing with an industrial backlash to the 'academies' of Western Europe, Benjamin engages with wider questions concerning the nature of art, production, and cultural change. Benjamin's questions about the place of art in the industrial era are pertinent to the conceptualisation and location of digital art. As the following chapters show, digital artists are engaging with new technologies—as means of production—within their works.

In a return to Walter Benjamin's notion of the creative industrialist, digital artists are transcending formal categorisations and the traditional binary of artist/critic. Digital collectives such as Rhizome, ISEA, Critical Art Ensemble and Ars Electronica have also affected the practice by providing 'buffer zones' between art and discourse. New collaborations between artists, designers, programmers and academics challenge traditional notions of artistic production. In a return to the Benjaminian notion of the creative industrialist, Enwezor observes how 'on occasion artists are able to compete with computer researchers, rather than simply creating new demos for commercial software, thus functioning as "memes" for computer industry.'[39] Art and artistry, under these conditions, transcends the fixity of formal categorisations. The collaborative involvement of artists, designers, programmers and academics has also challenged traditional notions of authorship.

However, Okwui Enwezor claims it is 'the artist who decides what an object of art is or what it can be, not simply the progressive, formal, transformation of art inside of the medium of art.'[40]Enwezor proposes that the artist that should lead the interpretation of their work. This interpretation challenges the role of the Academy (or established galleries and academic institutions) in influencing aesthetics, values and taste, and determining what art is or may be. To this end, the notion of 'art as art' is valid when viewed purely as form, and in isolation from the realms of personal meaning, context, and experience. But according to Enwezor, when we perceive 'art as meaning', we gain a new language for expressing often inaccessible phenomena, such as globalisation and digitisation. However, we might also create space for art audiences to subjectively determine meanings. While art offers external languages derived from criticism and artists' intents, it also generates internal responses. The

---

[37] Mark B. Hansen, *New Philosophy for New Media*, p. xx.

[38] Walter Benjamin, 'The Work of Art in the Age of Mechanical Reproduction'.

[39] Lev Manovich, 'The Death of Computer Art', (accessed 03 June 2004).

[40] Okwui Enwezor, 'The Postcolonial Constellation: Contemporary Art in a State of Permanent Transition', *Research in African Literatures,* Vol. 34, Issue 4, 2003, p. 58.

perceptions and reactions of the experiencer are important. This is particularly so for tactile and interactive digital works, which seek to generate affective responses.

Art and Digital Technology

One way in which digital expression converses with earlier forms of art is through self-reflexive engagement with its moments of production. The conversations created by contemporary digital works reveal conflicting perceptions of the Internet, its origins and the cultural impacts of digital technology. While the emergence of the Internet is debated, it is often linked to Joseph Licklider's notion of a network formed of globally connected computers.[41] Licklider headed a computer research program in October 1962, which would form the basis of the United States' Advanced Research Projects Administration (ARPA) and the development of ARPA-NET in 1969.[42] The computer system was a complex network that would retain nuclear weapon control in the event of a Communist strike. ARPANET was designed so that if any element were destroyed, the remaining parts would retain operational autonomy for counter-attack.

While ARPANET is often attributed as the first global Internet, many of the ideas that influenced its inception can be found in earlier writings, to include Leonard Kleinrock's 1961 PhD proposal *Information Flow in Large Communication Nets*– a paper that describes connected communication networks.[43] Despite conflicting accounts of the Internet's origins, its association with the military administration ARPA may explain early perceptions of digital space as strategically structured, regulated and controlled. This sense underscores Rita Raley's notion that the computer is emblematic of a controlled society.[44] While this claim will be explored in relation to the art of Ross Mawdsley, ®™ark and The Yes Men in the following chapter, other artists have engaged with more open constructions of the Internet.

In challenging the formal structures of distribution, criticism, and display, some 1960s interventions in art and technology asserted critical independence through challenging the limits of art and technology. During this period, figures like Desmond Paul Henry were actively experimenting with art and digital technology. Henry created 'drawing machines' that produced early versions of digital art. The artistic group Fluxus were also mixing different technologies and exploring ideas of

---

[41] Vinton G. Cerf et al., 'A Brief History of the Internet', *Internet Society,* <http://www.isoc.org/internet/history/brief.shtml> n. d., (accessed 06 December 2007).

[42] Vinton G. Cerf et al., 'A Brief History of the Internet', <http://www.isoc.org/internet/history/brief.shtml>.

[43] Leonard Kleinrock, 'Information Flow in Large Communication Nets', *RLE Quarterly Progress Report,* Cambridge Mass., MIT Press, 1961.

[44] Rita Raley, 'Statistical Material: Globalisation and the Digital Art of John Klima', in *The New Centennial Review,* Vol. 3.2, 2003, p. 69.

Fig. 2.3 Desmond Paul
Henry, *Image 003 v.2*, 1961.
(Image courtesy of Elaine
O'Hanrahan on behalf of the
artist)

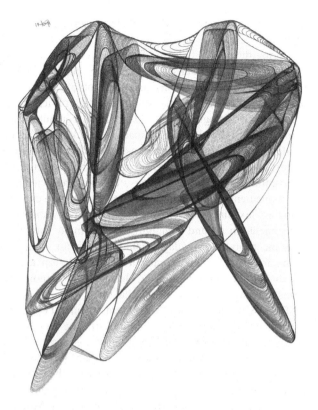

technological and artistic control. These artists explored the use of diverse technologies, and sought to legitimise mixed media works as art.[45]

Andreas Huyssen describes how the

> [i]mplicit dependence on a traditionally structured system…which is put under erasure by the Fluxus event, is perhaps best expressed in what Adorno called the increasing 'Verfransung der Kunste.'[46]

Adorno's concept of *Verfransung*—or entanglement of boundaries—disintegrated traditional structures and merged artistic practices, creating a 'sense of evolving dissolution, of aesthetic entropy, a reciprocal emptying out of traditions, a loss of form and truth content.'[47] By rebuking the formal structures of distribution, criticism, and display, 1960s interventions in art and technology re-asserted their critical independence through challenging the limits of art and technology. Huyssen contends that

---

[45] Andreas Huyssen, 'Back to the Future: Fluxus in Context', in Janet Jenkins (Ed.), *In the Spirit of Fluxus,* Minneapolis, Walker Art Center, 1993, p. 150.

[46] Andreas Huyssen, 'Back to the Future', p. 150.

[47] Andreas Huyssen, 'Back to the Future', p. to t.

the Fluxus 'intermedia work ultimately legitimised itself as a medium in its own right (Fig. 2.3).'[48]

During the 1980s, the rise of personal computers changed perceptions of information. Digitisation transforms data into numerical code, meaning, 'the original waveform is digitally encoded and the information in it represented by the presence or absence of pulses of equal strength, making it less subject to degradation than a conventional analogue signal.'[49]The digital computer was central to this shift, becoming 'the first widely disseminated system that offers the user the opportunity to create, distribute, receive, and consume audiovisual content with the same box.'[50]

Just as digital artists have engaged with Modern, Frankfurt School and 1960s interventions in art and technology, they have reflected upon 1980s art and technology movements. During the 1980s, artists began to experiment with domestic technologies: fax machines, cassettes, video players and televisions, invoking earlier experiments in art and technology. In a similar way, contemporary digital artists have incorporated everyday media into their art. Leon Cmielewski and Josephine Starrs, for example, incorporated a 1980s 'table-top' arcade game interface for their installation *Floating Territories.*This work is explored in Chapter Seven, in the terms of changing practices in digital art.

The 1980s also gave rise to the literary genre of cyber-punk, which has continued to influence the production of digital art. The OutlawTechnologists, the Eighties Wave and the Neuromantics, for example, experimented with themes of futurism, virtuality, and urban transcendence. William Gibson's 1984 text *Neuromancer,*[51], for example, was one of the first to conceive of the cyber city. That interest in virtual metropolises has influenced contemporary works of digital art, from Shoba's post-apocalyptic vision of New York in *Blowing Zen* to Marnix de Nijs' futuristic city in *Run Motherfucker Run.* Marnix de Nijs uses a treadmill in his installation to convey an altered sense of speed in a global-digital world. His art replicates feelings of psychological fragmentation elicited by globalisation's space-time affects.

In the following decade, artists began to engage with globalisation and new flows of time, speed and space. 1990s 'net.artists' experimented with new digital technologies, using connective devices and interactive media to articulate and even to simulate, globalisation's spatial, temporal and kinetic flows. Ross Mawdsley, ®™ark,and The Yes Men created works that dragged users across contexts, times and landscapes. Christian Moeller and Joachim Sauter's digital installation *Networked Skin* of 1994 also provided an early articulation of globalisation's alteration of space. The artists used the façade of a building to project their interactive digital work. By enabling multiple users in different locations to interact with *Networked Skin,* they positively engaged with global technologies (Fig. 2.4).

---

[48] Andreas Huyssen, 'Back to the Future', p. to t.

[49] Mark J. P. Wolf, *Abstracting Reality: Art, Communication, and Cognition in the Digital Age,* Lanham, University Press of US, 2000, 'Foreword'.

[50] Peter Lunenfeld (Ed.), *Introduction in The Digital Dialectic: New Essays on New Media,* Cambridge Mass., MIT Press, 1999, p. xix.

[51] William Gibson, *Neuromancer,* New York, Ace Publications, 1984.

Fig. 2.4 Christian Moeller and Joachim Sauter, *Networked Skin*, 1994. (http://www.christian-moeller.com/display.php?project_id=46)

However, critics like Jean Baudrillard and Paul Virilio express concern over the saturation of images and buzz of information in a technological age. According to their critiques, the hyper-intensification of space, time and speed negatively impacts upon feelings of connection and reality. Under these conditions, there is little time to contemplate or connect with others. A parallel might be drawn between the speed of digital technology and globalisation's rapid flows of finance, technology, people, ideas and ideology, or the overriding sense that living in a global/digital age is temporally and kinetically frenetic. The shift from an analogue to digital world has required adaption in terms of how we affectively relate to our environment and each other. To this end, Timothy Allen Jackson posits that digital art can create 'a rupture with our previous relationship to time and space as well as to previous conceptions of the real and to larger metaphysical issues'.[52]

Situationist Art

Early digital artists reflected a spirit of Situationism as they experimented with the new media and applications made available in the early 1990s. As a form of digital art, 'net.art' provided radical critiques of traditional art practice and cultural phenomena, such as globalisation. Digital artists such as This is Not Art, and Jodi.org, engaged with earlier artistic strategies like parody and mimicry, while incorporating the banal technical realities of digitisation into their works: computers crashing, pop-up banners, frozen screens, glitches, and hacker sabotage. Groups like ®™ark and The Yes Men on the other hand, used digital technology to construct 'corporate'

---

[52] Timothy Allen Jackson, 'Towards a New Media Aesthetic' in David Trend (Ed.), *Reading Digital Culture,* Oxford, Blackwell, 2001, p. 349.

web pages that parodied those of their opponents, namely global figures and institutions.

Throughout the late 1980s and early 1990s, digital artists were engaging with two contentious topics: consumption and technology. With the rising market economies of the Western world and the elaboration of a culture of consumption, artists used forms of mass communication, such as advertising, to articulate their concerns. Naomi Klein's text *No Logo* emerged as a powerful critique of Western commoditisation and the impact of the mass media. Texts such as Klein's came to inform artistic movements, alarmed by the West's reign of influence over other cultures. Art began to vocalise what Jameson terms, 'the inner truth of that newly emergent social order of late capitalism'.[53]

Digital artists like ®™ark re-situated corporate images and adopted Situationist principles of irony, juxtaposition and altered meanings. Their art was designed to challenge users' expectations and senses of authenticity and 'truth'. In creating an anti-realist aesthetic, these digital artists often integrated or parodied other works without acknowledgement, blurring the line between original and mass-produced art. Digital art from this period often conversed with controversial social, political and economic issues. In conjuring responses of anger, shock or disbelief from their audiences, these artists confirmed Jameson notion that 'there is very little in either the form or the content of contemporary art that contemporary society finds intolerable and scandalous.'[54] Jameson's claim might be used to describe the current digital economy, where only the unexpected, obscene or grandiose gestures succeed in attracting our attention.

The artistic interventions of ®™ark, explored in the following chapter, might easily be confused with the political gestures of governments and multi-national corporations. Digital artworks like these are also often 'accidentally' discovered on the Internet, which can make contexts for interpreting or locating them less evident than if they were situated in formal gallery spaces. Yet, even if their contexts are unclear, it still does not justify their severance from the realm of art, nor universalise the claim that digitisation produces 'a climate where the viewer cannot distinguish between the expressive and the canned effect'.[55] Like any new intervention in art, digital art simply calls for new languages of articulation.

---

[53] Fredric Jameson, 'PostModernism and Consumer Society', p. 114.

[54] Fredric Jameson 'PostModernism and Consumer Society', p. 124.

[55] Scott Weiland, 'Sense, Memory and Media', <http://www.digitalartsource.com/content/featur/feat17/feat17p1.html>, *Digital Art Source,* (accessed 14 May 2004). This link is no longer active.

Art and Attention Economies

While attention economies can produce innovation through the construction of larger-than-life works, Amy Scholder and Jordan Candall propose that 'it is not necessarily a very equal world. There remains only so much attention to go round.'[56] This sentiment is echoed by Critical Art Ensemble's contention that '[i]f the project does not possess monumental scale or volume, it's considered just the work of a common user.'[57] In their own practice, digital artists Critical Art Ensemble recognise the levels of global visibility that 'larger-than-life' campaigns—simultaneously staged in virtual and physical arenas—can attain. Their art strongly contests the traditional severance of art and politics, and assumptions of formal display.

Many early digital works presented high impact, yet didactic articulations. In Ross Mawdsley's *Journey into Darkness,* for example, the artist offers a rather simplistic account of globalisation. The slow, fatalistic crawl of a fly across a corporate logo emblazoned razor blade in the work, seems to overstate the death of individuality under globalisation. These links re-emerge in the artwork 'Revolt', where the presence of expressionless Lego™-style figures signals the absence of freedom and originality. The most concerning imagery however, concerns his presentation of disembodied black torsos, which show a kind of crude empathy for the 'other'. Mawdsley's focus upon grandiose Flash™ aesthetics and the digital 'medium' arguably compromises the depth of his message. Many of these early net.art works experimented with new forms and media, often at the expense of a critical message. The tension between form and meaning will be discussed in the following chapter: 'Digital Art and Political Revolt'.

The need for artists to compete with the 'attention economy' can also lead to the commercialisation of art. Julian Stallabrass contends that current digital art institutions like ZKM still 'set their agenda according to the pulse of Siemens and Deutsche Telekom; that is to say, they have to modify their levels of social criticism or "forget their deutschmarks."'[58] The ties between art and commerce arguably become stronger, when galleries and art institutions are forced to find private revenue in the face of government funding cuts. In the Australian context, 2008 Queensland Arts Minister Rod Welford has announced that 'the arts-as-business model [is] replacing the arts-as-welfare model',[59] and that the sector needs 'to fight aggressively to maintain funding.'[60] Galleries and art institutions have had to em-

---

[56] Jordan Crandall and Amy Scholder (Eds), *Interaction: Artistic Practice in the Network,* Distributed Art Publishers Inc, New York, 2001, pp. 71–72.

[57] Jordan Crandall and Amy Scholder (Eds), *Interaction,* p. 77.

[58] Julian Stallabrass, *Internet Art: The Online Clash of Culture and Commerce,* London, Tate Publishing, 2003, p. 117.

[59] Rosemary Sorensen, 'Ain't no sunshine when the grants are gone', *The Australian,* <http://www.theaustralian.news.com.au/story/0,,22875256-16947,00.html>, 2007, (accessed 6 December 2007). This link is no longer active.

[60] Rosemary Sorensen, 'Ain't no sunshine when the grants are gone', <http://www.theaustralian.news.com.au/story/0,,22875256-16947,00.html>.

brace what Rosemary Sorensen terms a 'shift in philosophical approach and that they had to change to compete. It was inevitable that, in terms of ranking, some were going to miss out.'[61]

Digital art can also be viewed by collecting institutions as less economically lucrative than traditional art, in terms of sponsorship, recognition, and visitation. Questions about archiving, classification and the location of digital works may have contributed to this issue. Some attempts by galleries to acquire digital works have also been met with criticism, from those who view such efforts as tokenistic. The purchase of digital works has sometimes been construed as no more than what Julian Stallabrass terms 'a relatively cost-effective way to appear contemporary, and especially to be seen to address issues of globalisation.'[62] These tensions, however, can add to the richness and critical complexity of the forms produced in a similar way to earlier styles.

Open Art

Some observers point to the open and democratic nature of digital formats, which is seen to oppose the strict constraints of the established art world. However, like all creative practices, digital art is also shaped by politics of elitism and exclusivity. Much of the language of new media criticism can be unnecessarily obscure. At forums and colloquia, many of the same names dominate. Equally, the production and experience of it is limited to those that have the necessary digital infrastructure and fluency. As Stallabrass notes, '[t]he character of online elitism is of a different kind from that found in the art world, which is embedded in location, architectural display and ownership of rare objects.'[63]

The Internet offers unprecedented levels of creative exchange. As globalisation's most powerful 'technoscape', the Internet enables new opportunities for collaboration. It also enables artists and audiences to overcome the previous constraints of physical distance, which effected the transportation, construction and display of art. The Internet offers new kinds of viewing spaces. It can enable artists to reach a far wider range of audiences, and increase the awareness of their works. It also give exposure not just to exhibitions taking place at well-known galleries, but at small and otherwise overlooked spaces.

Some argue that online exhibitions threaten the survival of physical galleries, or offer limited kinds of affective experiences, Countering this critique, Douglas Davis notes how with the rise television and video, there was the similar fear that 'a new, apparently dematerialized museum—i.e., the Web—will somehow drive us

---

[61] Rosemary Sorensen, 'Ain't no sunshine when the grants are gone', <http://www.theaustralian. news.com.au/story/0,,22875256-16947,00.html>.

[62] Julian Stallabrass, *Internet Art,* p. 118.

[63] Julian Stallabrass, *Internet Art,* p. 136.

all indoors, away from public spaces like theaters, movie houses or museums.'[64] Davis notes, however, how the opposite in fact occurred, with 'access leading to a hunger not only for more but for going out in search of different forms of art creation.'[65]Digital art has the capacity to become a more accessible and 'familiar' format, than traditional art forms such as sculpture or painting. It can be made and experienced via such banal digital devices as the mobile phone, laptop or tablet. While digitisation enables eclectic media forms to be borrowed, juxtaposed and overlaid, digital art borrows from a medley of historical and theoretical traditions.

The recombinatory nature of digital art can also allow it to transcend the traditional boundaries of genre, artistry and production. The use of open source content, connective media and banal devices to make and share digital art, might however, render it a more collaborative and participatory form of expression. As exemplified by many of the works explored in this book—such as iCinema's *T_Visionarium II* and Blast Theory's *Can You See Me Now?*—many people are often involved in the creation of digital works. One artwork can involve several collaborators, ranging from film makers to graphic designers, academics, programmers, sound designers and audiences. In crowd sourced and collaborative works, traditional principles of originality, artistry and authorship are challenged.

Many digital works feature misappropriated content, which is ironically remediated to offer a form of cultural commentary. This evident in ®™ark's interventions discussed in Chapter Four and Brian Alfred's film *Overload*, discussed in Chapter Six. Jodi.org have actively embraced a spirit of anti-ownership, by enabling their art to be altered, downloaded or distribution by users. Digital art collectives such as ®™ark,Jodi and Critical Art Ensemble disrupt traditional notions of originality and authorship, in making it difficult to ascertain who the artist is, and who owns the intellectual property. The artist Barbara Kruger incorporates advertising emblems in her works, often without reference. Her actions reflect a spirit of anti-authorship, which is reminiscent of Situationist techniques. iCinema's artwork *T_Visionarium II*, explored in Chapter Five, also converses with questions surrounding Digital Rights Management (DRM). As iCinema suggest, the issue is not just about copyright protection, it is whether its enforcement opposes the sense of the Internet as open, collaborative and essentially, democratic.

Following on from 1970s and 1980s electronic art—which experimented with technologies such as television, camcorders, stereos, computer games and video players—from the 1990s through to the new millennium, artists began experimenting with portable media players, personal digital assistants, smart phones, laptops, global positioning systems and wireless technologies. In doing so, they explored new forms of artistry and modes of production, begging the question of what art might have become in the digital age? If digital technology was altering art production, then it was also transforming the ways in which it could be shared, produced and understood. In the 2000s, the the ubiquity of digital technologies with enhanced

---

[64] Douglas Davis, 'The Museum of the Third Kind', *Art in US,* Vol. 93, Issue 6, New York, 2005, p. 75.

[65] Douglas Davis, 'The Museum of the Third Kind', p. 75.

production capabilities, means that more and more people are using smart devices to make and share content online. Jay David Bolter and Richard Grusin observe how

> [f]or the first time in history users have greater accessibility to such technological processes as film editing, web-page creation, mp3 sampling, and online communication; all of which have been facilitated through digital infrastructures.[66]

Just as the popularisation of production might challenge traditional notions of the 'artist', digital duplication, appropriation, crowd sourcing and collaboration have the potential to rebuke ideals of aura, authenticity and originality. Digital art can disrupt the traditional demarcation and 'distance' between the artist and spectator. Yet, rather than alienating audiences, Darren Tofts notes how this reconfiguration of the relationship can actually attract and empower audiences, through offering more accessible (and less intimidating) spaces to experience it.[67] The interchanges between production and experience are exciting elements of digital art.

Interactivity and Criticism

While immersive principles are present in earlier forms, interactive digital art can enables users to transcend the limits of space, time and speed. While heightened levels of interactivity and responsiveness can differentiate digital art from earlier expressions, Stallabrass notes how '[t]he spectrum of interaction on offer shades from the minimal choice involved in clicking through a set sequence of pages to permitting users to create the work themselves'.[68] Janet Murray argues that '[l]inear media such as books and films can portray space, either by verbal description or image, but only digital environments can present space that we can move through.'[69] In extending this idea, Dennis Del Favero notes in relation to iCinema's *T_Visionarium II* how 'persons present become protagonists in a set of ever evolving interactive narratives. Central to all these innovations is the reformulation of narrative itself.'[70] Unlike traditional cinematic works, the images that unfold are generated at random, without a linear time horizon. The art evolves in response to the user's movements and directions. Under these conditions, digital narrative becomes navigable. To this end, principles of interaction, immersion and participa-

---

[66] Jay David Bolter and Richard Grusin, 'Immediacy, Hypermediacy and Remediation', *Remediation: Understanding New Media,* Cambridge, Mass., MIT Press, 2000, p. 31.

[67] Julian Stallabrass, *Internet Art,* p. 61.

[68] Julian Stallabrass, *Internet Art,* p. 61.

[69] Janet Murray, *Hamlet on the Holodeck: The Future of Narrative in Cyberspace,* Cambridge Mass., MIT Press, 1997, p. 79.

[70] Dennis Del Favero, 'Digitally Expanded Forms of Cinematic Narration', in Dennis Del Favero and Jeffery Shaw (Eds.), *(dis)Locations,* Karlshruhe, ZKM, Centre for Art and Media/Centre for Interactive Cinema Research, Sydney, University of New South Wales, 2001.

tion can make interfaces seem natural and inviting. *T_Visionarium II* is explored in detail in Chapter Five.

The most effective works from the 1990s showed high levels of nuance in their uses of digital technology to generate interactivity and negotiate the binaries of media and message. Jodi.org for example, actively conversed with operational issues, incorporating technical glitches, frozen screens, quitting applications and pop-up spam into their art. They ironically engaged with these technological realities, and in doing forged an iterative relationship between content and form. However, some theorists like Alexei Shulgin argue that interactivity is often manipulative, for it is 'always the author with his name and his careers behind it, and he just seduces people to click buttons in his own name'.[71] As discussed in Chapter Four, some examples of early net.art were heavily directed. However, more recent expressions give the user greater scope to influence the narrative direction of works, often in real time. These developments suggest new approaches to digital art, with the emergence of works that are self-reflexive and confirm Thomas McEvilley's sense that 'a hybrid object attempts to incorporate into itself its own counterweight or critique—its other.'[72]

In Chapter Seven, artworks that traverse the boundaries between artist/spectator are explored. It creates a distinction between works that simply 'use' digital technology as a means, and those that use it to generate particular messages. In order to create these kinds of 'interfaceless' experiences, Bolter and Grusin argue that the interface needs to 'be one that erases itself, so that the user is no longer aware of confronting a medium, but instead stands in an immediate relationship to the contents of that medium.'[73] This idea might actualise Richard Wagner's concept of the 'total art-work'[74]—where the artist comes to 'dominate, even overwhelm, flooding the spectator/hearer with sensory impressions of different kinds. It is not meant as information but as experience.'[75]

While a user must have some basic digital skills to negotiate pop-up boxes, navigate their way through hyperlinks and manipulate the interface, as digital artist Hisham Bizri states, it is not necessary for the user to be aware of every intended effect. Digital art, he argues should be the product of subtle iterations

> between the artist, the viewer, society, history, and art itself. In other words, it functions in human experience making everything relevant: its form, the artist's intention, the social and historical ideal of the times, the scientific spirit of the age, all these are part and parcel.[76]

[71] Julian Stallabrass, *Internet Art,* p. 61.

[72] Thomas McEvilley, *Art and Discontent: Theory at the Millennium,* Documentext, New York, McPherson and Company, 1991, p. 76.

[73] Jay David Bolter and Richard Grusin, *Remediation,* p. 23.

[74] Adrian Henri, *Total Art: Environments, Happenings, and Performance,* New York, Praeger, p. 10.

[75] Adrian Henri, *Total Art,* p. 10.

[76] Hisham M. Bizri, *Hisham M. Bizri,* <http://www.hishambizri.com/artistic.html>, 2004, (accessed 07 December 2004).

According to Bizri, individual experience is just as important as the artistic intent, when it comes to art meaning. A user does not require the same technical or aesthetic understandings as the artist, to have a meaningful encounter with their art.

Affective Art

Digital art has the capacity to engage the user at an affective and bodily level, and offer readings of globalisation centred upon the particularities of human encounter. Heightened levels of interactivity, responsiveness, and immersion are key elements that separate digital from conventional art forms. While these qualities alter the physical experience of works, they also have symbolic implications for the understanding of what art may be. As Hansen contends,

> if the hypostatization of the formal act of framing reality vacates the artwork of its Romantic trappings (specifically the autonomy and its objective status as the bearer of truth of the idea), and if the shock-effect relocates the impact of the work squarely in the domain of experience, this is all in the service of redemption of embodied experience.[77]

Digital art's focus on particular encounters, rather than universal aesthetics, arguably leads to 'a renewed investment of the body as a kind of converter of the general form of framing into a rich, singular experience.'[78] It is this language, which might be used to inform understandings of globalisation.

Key works of digital art offer affective expression of globalisation. As Merleau-Ponty elucidated, in a discussion of phenomenology and affect, 'the perception of a work, more than its author or history, was primary because it engaged viewers and readers in their own response to meaning.'[79] His argument was that 'nothing can become intelligible unless seen against a background, a horizon, a surrounding field, a periphery.'[80] Merleau-Ponty's principle of 'figure and ground' invokes a sense of context forged in response to the subject and their world. This approach to globalisation would contend that our understandings of it are directly influenced by our particular backgrounds and experiences.

Digital art's technical and ontological qualities such as: immersion, interactivity, and critical responsiveness, render it a unique medium for the articulation of globalisation. It is borne of its *oeuvre,* and in spatial and temporal terms can simulatethe phenomenon's affects, from senses of space as fragmented, connected, or dispersed; perceptions of time as continuous, disjunctive or irrelevant; feelings of space as compacted, dispersed, or expansive; and experiences of speed as rapid, liberating, and excessive. Digital art's spatial, temporal and kinetic movements gen-

---

[77] Mark B.N. Hansen, *New Philosophy for New Media,* p. 3.

[78] Mark B.N. Hansen, *New Philosophy for New Media,* p. 3.

[79] Laurie Schneider Adams, *The Methodologies of Art,* p. 142.

[80] James Elkins, *On Pictures and the Words That Fail Them,* Cambridge, Cambridge University Press, 1998, p. 87.

erate eclectic responses, and emulate the construction of globalisation as a nexus of shifting flows.

While critics like Jean Baudrillard vocalise a fear, expressed by Tim Lenoir, that

> technological developments associated with computer technology, artificial intelligence, robotics, and more recently nanotechnology will succeed in displacing humanity through an evolutionary process leading first to a cyborg/human assemblage and ultimately to the extinction and replacement of the human altogether[81]

To the contrary, digital art can be highly connective. Interactive interfaces encourage human interaction, touch, reflection and bodily response. In spatial, temporal and kinetic terms, digital art can critically engage with affect. Digital artworks can invite users into their space: shifting time sequences, directing narratives and influencing kinetic flows. Further, responsive and interactive works of digital art contest the formal severance of artist and audience. They oppose the ambitions, as Pierre Borudieu observes, of the

> producer who aims to be autonomous, that is, entirely the master of his product, who tends to reject not only the 'programmes' imposed a priori by scholars and scribes, but also—following the old hierarchy of doing and saying—the interpretations superimposed a posteriori on his work.[82]

Qualities of immersion, interaction, and real-time response directly engage with the individual, transforming the corporeally-detached art spectator into a physically-involved user. Digital art's technical and discursive tools are uniquely equipped to both articulate and simulate, globalisation's bodily and perceptual impacts: interchanges of memory; the flux of reverie; the cognition of global space; reactions to digital speed; conceptualisations of the past; responses to the present; and the imagination of the future. Perhaps most critically, digital art can facilitate the contextualisation of self in relation to these torrents. As an interactive and generative medium that directly engages with individual bodies, digital art can promote a new affective consciousness of globalisation.

In his text, Hansen connects 'the aesthetics of new media with a strong theory of embodiment.'[83] In reflecting upon contemporary works of digital art, he critiques Gilles Deleuze's reading of the affect and the image, by re-introducing Bergson's theory of embodiment.[84] In his Foreword to *New Philosophy for New Media*, Tim Lenoir posits that

---

[81] Tim Lenoir, 'Foreword', in Mark B.N. Hansen, *New Philosophy for New Media,* Cambridge Mass., MIT Press, 2004, p. xiv.

[82] Pierre Bourdieu, *Distinction: A Social Critique of the Judgement of Taste,* (Trans. R. Nice), Cambridge Mass., Harvard, University Press, 1984, p. 4.

[83] Mark B.N. Hansen, *New Philosophy for New Media,* p. 3.

[84] For Deleuze's discussions on affect and the image, see: Gilles Deleuze, *Cinema 1: The Movement Image,* (Trans. B. Habberjam and H. Tomlinson), London, Athlone Press, 1986 and Gilles Deleuze, *Cinema 2: The Time Image,* (Trans. R. Galeta and H. Tomlinson), London, Athlone Press, 1989.

[r]ather than erasing an active role of the sentient body in the production of media effects as Friedrich Kittler's interpretation of digital media would have it, Hansen argues that media convergence under digitality actually increases the centrality of the body as framer.[85]

Meaning, that when art is virtualised the user becomes the processor or 'framer' of information.[86]

As an experiential construct centred upon touch, bodily involvement, interpretation and perceptual response, digital art challenges senses of self in relation to space, time and surrounding phenomena. The Bergsonian concept of the body as a 'center of indetermination', acting as a filter creatively selecting facets of images from the universal flux according to its 'own capacities'[87] provides new ways of thinking about globalisation as the sum of its subjective affects. In this construction, the individual becomes 'a source of action on the world of images, subtracting among external influences those that are relevant to its own interests. Bergson calls such isolated image components "perceptions"'.[88]

Throughout this book, digital art works are presented as the 'subtracted images' of artists and users. As Darren Tofts writes, 'indeterminacy is the nature of distributed aesthetics'[89] meaning, 'not everyone will experience the same thing'.[90] In making this claim, he contends that the interpretation of digital art is contingent upon different backgrounds and perspectives. This idea will be explored with reference to different works, ranging from ®™ark's corporate campaigns to iCinema's digital installations and Joanna Berzowska's haptic clothing.

Conclusion

Many of the most original examples of digital art remediate the traditional art binary of form and content, or the media versus the message. While digital technology may be historically unique, much of the content of digital art resonates with earlier dialogues and forms, ranging from Modern cinema to Frankfurt School criticism, Situationist art, 1980s electronic movements and 1990s net.art. The word 'art' in the term 'digital art' is important: it debunks the complete novelty of 'new media art', and the rejection of 'new media' from the field of artistic endeavour.

In a review of Dan Harries' *The New Media Book*, Richard Edwards suggests strong grounds for an historical approach to digital art, particularly if one maintains '[m]ost new media have been developed in dialogue with existing "old" and estab-

---

[85] Tim Lenoir, 'Foreword', p. xxii.

[86] Tim Lenoir, 'Foreword', p. xxii.

[87] Tim Lenoir, 'Foreword', p. xx.

[88] Tim Lenoir, 'Foreword', p. xx.

[89] Darren Tofts, 'Forward and Beyond: Anticipating Distributed Aesthetics', *Fibreculture*, <http://www.journal.fibreculture.org/issue7/issue_7tofts.html>, 2005, (accessed 23 March 2007). This link is no longer active.

[90] Darren Tofts, 'Forward and Beyond', <http://www.journal.fibreculture.org/issue7/issue_7tofts.html>.

lished media formations such as cinema and television.'[91] Edwards reflects upon the use of "historical context and previous models of technological change to blunt any facile notion of "newness".[92] Similarly, Manuel De Landa posits that digital works 'should be thought of as one more element added to a complex mix, fully coexisting with older components (energetic and material), not all of which have been left in the past.'[93] Arguably, the term 'digital art' is the most useful term for it locates digital works as 'art', and places them on a critical and historical continuum.

This chapter has argued for a flexible language in the articulation of digital art. In doing so, it seeks to counter rigid frameworks that often produce two equally problematic positions. As Mark Hansen elaborates,

> [for] almost every claim advanced in support of the "newness" of new media, it seems that an exception can readily be found, some earlier cultural or artistic practice that already displays the specific characteristic under issue. This situation has tended to polarize the discourse on new media art between two (in my opinion) equally problematic positions: those who feel that new media have changed everything and those who remain sceptical that there is anything at all about new media that is, in the end, truly new.[94]

Manuel De Landa's claim that '[t]he digital revolution should be thought of as one more element added to a complex mix, fully coexisting with older components (energetic and material), not all of which have been left in the past'[95] In challenging traditional approaches to art and artistry, this chapter has suggested that digital art can provide means of expressing inaccessible phenomena. To this end, this chapter informs the following discussions on globalisation and crises of articulation.

---

[91] Richard L. Richards, 'Review of Dan Harries (Ed.), The New Media Book', http://muse.jhu.edu/journals/the_moving_image/v004/4.1edwards.html,2004, (accessed 28 April 2006)

[92] Richard L. Richards, 'Review of Dan Harries', http://muse.jhu.edu/journals/the_moving_image/v004/4.1edwards.html

[93] Manuel De Landa, *A Thousand Years of Nonlinear History,* New York, Swerve Editions, 1997, p. 98.

[94] Mark B.N. Hansen, *New Philosophy for New Media,* p. 21.

[95] Manuel De Landa, *A Thousand Years of Nonlinear History,* p. 98.

Chapter 3
Globalisation and Digital Art

Introduction

This chapter establishes grounds for viewing globalisation through the lenses of digital art. It engages with theories of Formalism, Structuralism and Semiotics, and posits that while these frameworks may be useful in providing broad conceptualisations, the affective realms of human experience and encounter require discursive flexibility. Ethnographic, deconstructive and affective dialogues are also introduced (Fig. 3.1).

This chapter shows how open and dynamic approaches make room for the iterations and contradictions of human response. To this end, it advances particular rather than universal approaches to globalisation and art, as human phenomena. This chapter contends that digital art can offer affective articulations of globalisation, centred upon individual experience, bodily encounter and perceptive response. Through centralising human subjects, digital art can provide new ways of understanding external phenomena.

Structuralist Approaches

Popular constructions of globalisation tend to be focused upon large-scale political economic effects, underscored by the idea expressed by Walden Bello, that 'unending growth is the centerpiece of globalization, the mainspring of its legitimacy'.[1] Yet, this approach often overlooks other dynamics, such as the movements of people, media, technology and ideology. There are also strong grounds for using flexible discourses in the approach of art. In order to appreciate the need for affective

---

[1] Walden Bello, 'Globalization in Retreat', *Foreign Policy in Focus*, <http://www.fpif.org/fpiftxt/3826>, 2006, (accessed 11 December 2007). Link is no longer active.

M. Langdon, *The Work of Art in a Digital Age: Art, Technology and Globalisation*,
DOI 10.1007/978-1-4939-1270-4_3, © Springer Science+Business Media New York 2014

Fig. 3.1 Wolfgang Ammer, *Globalization 2*, 2002. (*Michigan State University*, https://www.msu.edu/user/hillrr/Louisville%20talk_files/image002.jpg)

approaches to art and globalisation, we must first understand the methods that they counter.

In commenting upon the Structuralist discourses of Lévi-Strauss, Edith Kurzweil claimed that *Tristes Tropiques* (1955) foregrounded his seminal work *Structural Anthropology* (1958), which was underscored by what she termed

> the systemic attempt to uncover deep universal mental structures as these manifest themselves in kinship and larger social structures, in literature, philosophy and mathematics, and in the unconscious psychological patterns that motivate human behaviour.[2]

Kurzweil reveals an approach premised upon systemic similarities rather than particular differences. As Lance Taylor observes, Structuralist discourses often rely upon the deduction 'of macro behavioural functions'.[3] Through building upon

---

[2] Edith Kurzweil, *The Age of Structuralism*, New York, Columbia University Press, 1980, p. 1.

[3] Lance Taylor (Ed.), *Socially Relevant Policy Analysis: Structuralist Computable General Equilibrium Models for the Developing World*, Cambridge Mass., The MIT Press, 1990, p. 4.

methods derived from psychology and the social sciences, Structuralist analyses tend to minimise the role of the individual, in the search for universal meanings.

Semiotic discourses reflect key tenets of Structuralism, in focussing upon structures, signifiers and signs. As Laurie Schneider Adams expresses, Semiotics assumes 'that cultures and cultural expressions such as language, art, music, and film are composed of signs, and that each sign has a meaning beyond, and only beyond, it's literal self'.[4] In creating links between production, consumption, 'and the forms and codes of representation in which they reproduce ideology',[5] T.J. Clark and Raymond Williams sought to identify the social 'signifiers' that made creative works understandable as art. Influenced by Structuralist and Semiotic theories, Formalist art approaches are underscored by the notion that art has an essential 'truth' or aura, which in Laurie Schneider Adams' terms, can 'be understood independently of context'.[6] Clement Greenberg was a leading proponent of Formalism. In privileging form over content, his criticism was shaped by the writings of Immanuel Kant and Roger Fry.

Yet, the reduction of phenomena to signs, systems or values is problematic, for it universalises and reduces human experience. Umberto Eco, however, offers a more flexible take on Structuralist discourses. He views art and cultural phenomena are 'simultaneously semiotic and non-semiotic, at once prone and immune to systematic linguistic and structural descriptions'.[7] In stating that '[n]o graphic mark is merely a sign, but none is a "technical", "meaningless" gesture made only in the service of some higher significance',[8] he claims that while Structuralist discourses can provide context, they should be flexibly applied. As Mark Gottdiener elaborates, 'there is always a contextual basis to "Truth" claims',[9] or in other words, 'all utterances and actions have contexts and consequences'.[10] While both writers advance systemic approaches, they also make room for individual contexts and interpretations.

James Elkins similarly claims that '[w]henever the description of a picture could do without the picture, I am suspicious'.[11] Art theorist Janet Wolff also problematises schematic approaches to art and cultural phenomena. She claims that they tend to emerge from mainstream Western doctrines, which often fail to be 'disturbed by the sociological critique of aesthetics itself as a historically specific development, and of all aesthetic judgements as class-based, gender-linked and in general ideo-

---

[4] Laurie Schneider Adams, *The Methodologies of Art*, p. 133.

[5] Janet Wolff, *Aesthetics and the Sociology of Art*, 2nd Ed., Michigan, University of Michigan Press, 1999, p. 22.

[6] Laurie Schneider Adams, *The Methodologies of Art*, p. 32.

[7] James Elkins, *On Pictures and the Words That Fail Them*, p. 78.

[8] James Elkins, *On Pictures and the Words That Fail Them*, p. 78.

[9] Mark Gottdiener, *Postmodern Semiotics: Material Culture and the Forms of Postmodern Life*, Oxford, Blackwell, 1995, p. 23.

[10] Mark Gottdiener, *Postmodern Semiotics*, p. 23.

[11] James Elkins, *On Pictures and the Words That Fail Them*, p. xviii.

logically produced.'[12] Structuralist accounts offer reductive understandings of art and globalisation. Structuralist and formalist theories are arguably more apposite to the identification of fixed formulas and principles, than the understanding of globalisation and art. The value of these approaches may be in their simplification of complex constructs into identifiable structures or systems. Yet, the application of universalism to human experience can have dangerous outcomes, such as the invalidation of divergent encounters.

The Universal and the Particular

There is a tendency for globalisation and art to be described in universal and intangible ways. Political economic analyses of globalisation, for example, are often preoccupied with the need to schematise its impacts, or agree on a definition. As published on the World Bank website, one policy group lamented that '[a]mazingly for so widely used a term, there does not appear to be any Indeed, the breadth of meanings attached to it seems to be increasing rather than narrowing over time'.[13]

Alarmist accounts of globalisation can also be reductive, in focussing upon binary senses of restriction versus freedom, as the title of Naomi Klein's text *Fences and Windows* expresses.[14] In this particualr text, Klein posits that '[m]ass privatization and deregulation have bred armies of locked-out people, whose services are no longer needed, whose lifestyles are written off as "backward", whose basic needs go unmet'.[15] While this may be true for some, the implication that these impacts are universal is problematic. Is everyone left feeling 'locked out' and 'powerless'? Responses to globalisation cannot be categorised in simple positive or negative terms. Human experiences of the phenomenon can fluctuate in contradictory ways.

Inda and Rosaldo write that Cultural Imperialist approaches present globalisation 'primarily as a process of cultural imposition and dominance—of the imposition and dominance of Western (predominantly American) culture over the remainder of the globe'.[16] This understanding is underscored by the idea advanced by Klein, that globalisation is leading to the standardisation of culture. Yet, this construction of globalisation limits the raneg of possible experiences and responses. In focusing

---

[12] Janet Wolff, *Aesthetics and the Sociology of Art*, p. 27.

[13] PREM Economic Policy Group and Development Economics Group, 'What is Globalization', *The World Bank*, <http://www1.worldbank.org/economicpolicy/globalization/ag01.html>, 2000, (accessed 1 October 2007). This link is no longer active.

[14] Naomi Klein, *Fences and Windows: Dispatches From the Front Lines of the Globalization Debate*, New Delhi, Leftword, 2002.

[15] Naomi Klein, 'No Logo', *No Logo Website*, <http://www.nologo.org/>, n. d., (accessed 23 October 2006). This link is no longer active.

[16] Jonathon Xavier Inda and Renato Rosaldo, (Eds.), *The Anthropology of Globalization*, p. 13.

upon either-or impacts, alarmist accounts negate the subtle inter-changes and contradictions of human response.

As explored in Chap. 7, artists like Justine Cooper show how globalisation can
generate contrary experiences. Her installation *Transformers* presents human, information and technological flows as simultaneously positive and negative. Cooper
engages with our ability to experience positive impacts in one context, and negative
affects in another thereby challenging the implication that all members of developing countries are 'fenced in', while those living in Western countries are afforded
'windows' of freedom. In creating a parallel conversations on globalisation, digitisation and art, this text suggest that systemic and binary approaches to phenomena
limit the possibilities of experience.

Deconstructive Discourses

Deconstructive approaches can provide greater flexibility in the exploration of globalisation and digital art. Roland Barthes is often identified as instigating a critical shift between Structuralist and Post-Structuralist thought. Barthes went from a
theory that debunked 'the old humanist superstition that artistic creation cannot be
"reduced" to a system',[17] to one where systemic approaches were discouraged. He
rejected the deification of the artist, and the 'untouchability' of Academy approved
fine arts, as advanced by the Formalism. Through a focus upon particularisation
over universalisation, Barthes' new approach was a return to Humanism.[18]

Through its close associations with the theorists Martin Heidegger, and Jacques
Derrida, Deconstruction developed as a challenge to Structuralism and Semiotics
and the premise of objectively identifiable systems and signs.[19] Contrary to Structuralist methods, deconstructive approaches show how tensions between art and its
contexts of production can actually be productive. To this end, deconstruction might
be seen as a philosophy of consciousness, through the location of created objects in
terms of cultural phenomena and encounters with them.

In contesting the notion of 'totalising reason', deconstructive discourses oppose
singular accounts, in prompting what Jacques Derrida terms as 'resistance to single
explanations, a respect for difference and a celebration of the regional, local and
particular'.[20] While Structuralists may seek to identify the universal truths underlining cultural phenomena—such as globalisation and art—Post-structuralist theorists
seek to deconstruct them. In a critique of Semiotics, Derrida rebuffs Saussure's
search for systems and signs, by arguing that meanings are not rigid or universal,

---

[17] Laurie Schneider Adams, *The Methodologies of Art*, p. 154.

[18] Laurie Schneider Adams, *The Methodologies of Art*, p. 154.

[19] Laurie Schneider Adams, *The Methodologies of Art*, p. 17.

[20] Jacques Derrida, 'Deconstruction and the Other', in R. Kearney, *States of Mind: Dialogues with Contemporary Thinkers*, Washington, New York University Press, 1995, p. 157.

but 'vary according to contexts, which themselves are continually in flux'.[21] As a philosophy of consciousness, Deconstruction opposes teleological accounts of history and culture.

Digital theorist Manuel De Landa also problematises Structuralist approaches to cultural phenomena. He argues that from

> the perspective of a bottom-up methodology, it is incorrect to characterise contemporary societies as "disciplinary", or as "capitalist", or, for that matter, "patriarchal" (or any other label that reduces a complex mixture of processes to a single factor), unless one can give the details of a structure-generating process that results in a society wide system.[22]

In advancing 'bottom-up' analyses, De Landa makes room for the movements and contradictions of individual experiences. Deconstructive approaches to globalisation and art, might show how our interpretations are influenced by particular, dynamic and localised experiences. These discourses can make room for the contradictions of individual experiences, through challenging the fixity of and creating new spaces in between.

Ethnographic Approaches

Globalisation is often popularly construed as a threat to the 'groundedness' of community: altering senses of cultural cohesion, collective history, shared purposes and traditions. In times of cultural change and diaspora, efforts to preservation local values and traditions are used as ways to address real and perceived dangers. As Akhil Gupta and James Ferguson observe, sometimes 'displaced peoples cluster around remembered or imagined homelands, places, or communities in a world that seems increasingly to deny such firm territorialised anchors in their actuality'.[23] Yet, claims founded upon uniform memories and experiences can be problematic, particularly when they are founded upon heritage myths, or a misguided remembrance of how things were (Fig. 3.2).

Arjun Appadurai writes that a 'central paradox of ethnic politics in today's world', is that through processes of preservation, local 'primordia (whether of language or skin color or neighbourhood or kinship) are often globalised'.[24] The 'universalisation' of local customs, invokes Jameson's ironic 'particularisation of the universal and the universalisation of the particular'.[25] As particularised senses of kinship, homeland, belonging and continuity are challenged by universal social,

---

[21] Laurie Schneider Adams, *The Methodologies of Art*, p. 162.

[22] Manuel De Landa, *A Thousand Years of Nonlinear History*, p. 271.

[23] Akhil Gupta and James Ferguson 'Beyond 'Culture': Space, Identity and the Politics of Difference', in Xavier Inda and Renato Rosaldo (Eds.), *The Anthropology of Globalization: A Reader*, Malden, Blackwell Publishing, 2002, p. 69.

[24] Arjun Appadurai, 'Disjuncture and Difference in a Global Cultural Economy', p. 57.

[25] Fredric Jameson, and Masao Miyoshi (Eds.), *The Cultures of Globalisation*, p. xi.

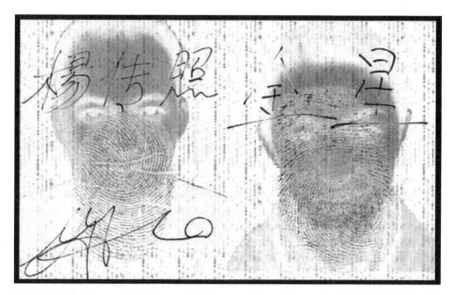

Fig. 3.2 Justine Cooper, *Transformers*, 2002. (http://justinecooper.com/transformers.html)

political and economic processes, 'generalised condition(s) of homelessness'[26] can ensue. These feelings may be impelled by actual events—the disbanding of nations, the shifting of borders, threats to security, the diaspora of people—but can also provoked by intangible, perceptual re-territorialisations, such as the sense that time has 'sped up', the world is becoming closer, or cultural values and tastes are being standardised. Yet, these affects can be difficult to pin-point, creating crises of articulation. To be aware that the world is changing—but to not know how to express it—only adds to mass senses of fear, alarm and powerlessness.

Underlining this apprehension may be the assumption that real impacts can be grasped, located and resisted. This perception, which often underscores popular protests to globalisation, is however problematic. Appadurai's vision of the phenomenon as a series of flows, challenges such rigid approaches. In resisting the tendency to assume an isomorphism between place and culture,[27] Xavier Inda and Renato Rosaldo highlight the fallacy of backlashes centred upon the 'groundedness' of culture and tradition. Instead, they show how ethnographic approaches can provide understandings of how individuals are responding in culturally specific ways.[28]

Saskia Sassen's paper 'Globalisation and the Formation of Claims'[29] also challenges singular accounts of globalisation. In demonstrating how the phenomenon

---

[26] Akhil Gupta and James Ferguson, 'Beyond 'Culture' ', p. 68.

[27] Jonathon Xavier Inda and Renato Rosaldo, (Eds.), *The Anthropology of Globalization*, p. 11.

[28] Jonathon Xavier Inda and Renato Rosaldo, (Eds.), *The Anthropology of Globalization*, p. 5.

[29] Saskia Sassen, 'Globalization and the Formation of Claims', in Joan Copjec and Michael Sorkin (Eds.) *Giving Ground: The Politics of Propinquity*, London, Verso, 1999.

generates more than one kind of affect, she employs an ethnographic approach to show how it can facilitate forms of free expression. In line with Fredric Jameson's claim,[30] Sassen suggests that as the nation state as 'the former container of social process and power'[31] breaks down, 'a new geography of politics linking subnational spaces takes shape'.[32] Globalisation, she suggests, can provides new opportunities to explore and experiment with identity, free from the constraints of national borders. As Inda and Rosaldo contend, 'the uprooting of culture is only half the story of globalization. The other half is that the deterritorialization of culture is invariably the occasion for the reinsertion of culture in new time-space contexts.[33] The diminished influence of the nation state can enable new kinds of expression to emerge. This may be particularly for those citizens that never culturally or politically identified with it, for example social minorities, immigrants, refugees and indigenous people. In this way, Sassen's ethnographic approach to globalisation makes room for the micro articulations of those at various times termed 'the other'.

Ethnographic approaches emphasise the richness and variability of particular encounters and interpretations. These methods lend themselves to particularised and affective analyses because as Inda and Rosaldo argue, they are 'interested in the individual imagination, in its perceptual negotiation with collective images and as social connection'.[34] Their discourse is primarily concerned with globalisation's contexts and conjunctures. To this end, they advance frameworks that emphasise divergence, contingency and gradation. In re-centring discourses around cultures and people, ethnographic methods can help us locate globalisation in terms of its local impacts.

Global Flows

Several writers articulate globalisation in terms of its dynamic impacts or 'flows'. In his essay 'Disjuncture and Difference in a Global Cultural Economy',[35] Arjun Appadurai describes increased movements of people, finance, media, technology and ideology around the world, using the terms 'ethnoscapes', 'financescapes', 'mediascapes', 'technoscapes' and 'ideoscapes'.[36] This fluid conceptualisation is sympathetic toManuel De Landa's notion of concomitant and organic processes. In *A Thousand Years of Nonlinear History,* De Landa writes that the 'resulting emer-

---

[30] Fredric Jameson and Masao Miyoshi (Eds.), *The Cultures of Globalization*, p. xiii.

[31] Saskia Sassen, 'Globalization and the Formation of Claims', p. 87.

[32] Saskia Sassen, 'Globalization and the Formation of Claims', p. 87.

[33] Jonathon Xavier Inda and Renato Rosaldo (Eds.), *The Anthropology of Globalization*, p. 11.

[34] Jonathon Xavier Inda and Renato Rosaldo (Eds.), *The Anthropology of Globalization*, p. 10.

[35] Arjun Appadurai, 'Disjuncture and Difference in a Global Cultural Economy', 2002.

[36] Arjun Appadurai, 'Disjuncture and Difference in a Global Cultural Economy'.

gent structures simply add themselves to the mix of previously existing ones, interacting with them, but never leaving them behind as a prior stage of development'.[37]

It is clear that globalisation is having significant human and cultural impacts,
altering the ways in which people relate to the world and each other. A rise in global
communication and travel has led to new flows of people and cultural values, or
what Appadurai terms 'ethnoscapes'. As a key manifestation of globalisation, the
Internet has heightened the sharing of cultural information and ideas, enabling individuals to communicate and connect in greater ways than ever before. Images,
videos and stories posted by travellers on websites, blogs, forums and social media
sites, are providing new levels of visual access to diverse world locations, raising
cultural awareness and inspiring others to visit. The Internet enables trips to be easily booked online, facilitating unprecedented levels of global traffic.

Global conflicts are creating different kind of human exchanges. As evidenced
by the post-2001 'War on Terror' and 2011 'Arab Spring', the sharing of information online is enabling allies, protestors and activists to forge global allegiances.
Global warfare is also leading to the uprooting of people, As nations are disband-
ed and homelands ravaged, people are becoming displaced and seeking refuge, in
numbers that have never been seen before. This flow of people can lead to the hy-
bridization of culture, where new values are welcomed or rejected, as race riots in
Europe, North America and Australia have shown.

As discussed in the previous section, viewing globalisation through a human or
ethnic lens can lead to new understandings, in privileging an approach that as Inda
and Rosaldo's explain,

> is preoccupied not just with mapping the shape taken by the particular flows of capital,
> people, goods, images, and ideologies that crisscross the globe, but also with the experi-
> ences of people living in specific localities when more and more of their everyday lives are
> contingent on globally extensive processes.[38]

By focussing upon globalisation's human and cultural flows, we can begin to trace
its impacts upon senses of identity, tradition, history, continuity, community and
culture. Ethnographic approaches counter the popular tendency to talk about globalisation in terms of economic flows. The word 'globalisation' is often mistakenly
interchanged with 'global capitalism', 'global markets' or 'Americanisation', terms
that may only tell part of the story.

In his discussion of these large-scale impacts, Appadurai adapts Marx's commodity principles of product and consumer fetishism.[39] He reflects upon the role
that corporations and the mass media play in driving global patterns of consumption. Appadurai also suggests that the deregulation of finance limits the ability of
states to impose sanctions upon corporations, which in turn leads to their global
influence. This corporatism is seen to lead to the standardisation of culture, and
patterns of consumption.

---

[37] Manuel De Landa, *A Thousand Years of Nonlinear History*, p. 271.

[38] Jonathon Xavier Inda and Renato Rosaldo, (Eds.), *The Anthropology of Globalization*, p. 5.

[39] Arjun Appadurai, 'Disjuncture and Difference in a Global Cultural Economy'.

Appadurai examines globalisation's financial flows through the prism of ideology, or what he describes as Western Capitalism's 'ideoscapes'.[40] In his exploration of what he terms 'mechanical art'[41]—a reference to the title of Walter Benjamin's seminal essay—Appadurai examines how ideology infiltrates through global advertising and the mass media, and in turn impacts upon local cultures and tastes. Ulf Hannerz's text *Modernism/Postmodernism* also shows how globalisation facilitates the advancement of Western ideologies. He claims that '[w]hen the center speaks, the periphery listens, and on the whole does not talk back'.[42] This one-sidedness, he suggests, is a result of the West's control and influence over media and communications. Hannerz connects globalisation to earlier Western Imperialist projects, such as the colonisation of Africa, Algeria, India and Oceania.[43]

Post-colonial analyses of globalisation show how Western idioms are deeply entrenched within social, political and economic processes. Frantz Fanon contends that Western ideologies are embedded in the very structures, institutions, images and cultural expressions.[44] This perspective is echoed in other dialogues, which have emerged in response to what Peter Brooker terms the

> blunt facts of economic, political and military power that have confirmed America and the West's controlling cultural influence—including the magnetism of its mythologies and the control Western intellectuals exercise over communication systems and regimes of truth.[45]

These impacts are seen to produce a kind of rampant consumerism, which affects the ways that we interact and think about the world.

In her *No Logo*,[46] Naomi Klein claims that globalisation's financial and ideological flows contribute to the corporatism of life. In her 2001 text, Klein refers to the banal infiltration of commercial value, taste and ideology. Klein's analysis reflects Baudrillard's concern that where 'old distinctions and orientations are abolished: objects no longer relate at all to their processes of human production, there is a loss of emotional content and of "objective" or critical distance'.[47] By examining the mass media's imposition of idioms, she popularised the alarmist sense that globalisation was adversely affecting local cultures, identities and traditions.

Klein's 2002 text *Fences/Windows*[48] continues the dialogue established in *No Logo*. Within the book, she places globalisation in continuation with processes of

---

[40] Arjun Appadurai, 'Disjuncture and Difference in a Global Cultural Economy'.

[41] See: Arjun Appadurai, 'Disjuncture and Difference in a Global Cultural Economy', p. 58 for the re-arrangement of the title to Benjamin's essay 'The Work of Art in the Age of Mechanical Reproduction'.

[42] Ulf Hannerz, 'Notes on the Global Ecumene', in Xavier Inda and Renato Rosaldo (Eds.), *The Anthropology of Globalisation: A Reader*, Malden, Blackwell Publishing, 2002, p. 38.

[43] Ulf Hannerz, 'Notes on the Global Ecumene'.

[44] For a discussion of contemporary forms of colonisation see: Frantz Fanon, *The Wretched of the Earth*, New York, Grove Press, 1968.

[45] Peter Brooker, (Ed.), *Modernism/Postmodernism*, London, Longman, 1992, p. 24.

[46] Naomi Klein, *No Logo: No Space, No Choice, No Jobs*, New York, Picador, 2002.

[47] Peter Brooker, (Ed.), *Modernism/Postmodernism*, p. 22.

[48] Naomi Klein, *Fences and Windows*, 2002.

Capitalism and Western Imperialism. Her post-colonial account is sympathetic to Jonathon Xavier Inda and Renato Rosaldo's thesis that globalisation is a 'continuation of a long historical process Western 'imperialist' expansion—embracing the colonial expansions of the sixteenth to the nineteenth centuries'.[49] By examining globalisation in terms of earlier histories and impacts, Klein suggests that the values of supply and demand continue to create unequal levels of advantage, entrenching cultures of inequity and divide. Yet, while the connections between globalisation and capitalism may be valid, Klein's analysis arguably focuses too heavily upon systemic effects, to the detriment of cultural and social responses.

Klein's arguments reflect the perception that the global mass media has 'sped up' the propagation of Western consumerism and ideology. Yet, her claims reveal high levels of alarmism in the suggestion that globalisation's affects are universally detrimental. Klein's analysis reduces globalisation to a series of binary impacts: advantage and exploitation. By drawing upon alarmist approaches to globalisation, she re-articulates a popular response to the phenomenon. Klein's discourse converses with Appadurai's concern that globalisation's idioms and economies might create 'distortions of a world of merchandising so subtle that the consumer is consistently helped to believe that he or she is an actor, where in fact he or she is at best a chooser'.[50] Yet, in focussing upon globalisation's negative impacts, this account leaves little space for positive or mixed responses. Ironically, alarmist frameworks reflect elements of the Imperialism that they oppose, in speaking on behalf of others and making assumptions about their experiences.

A rise in digital technologies and global connectivity is also characteristic of the global *oeuvre*. The transformation of data into numerical code has had a significant impact upon the ways in which we communicate and disseminate information. On the one hand, it has made data far more transferable, and information immediate than with analogue formats. The mass infiltration of responsive and interactive media like MP3 players, mobile phones, flash drives, and personal devices, has also led to an increased awareness of digital technology—shifting perceptions of the world, and ourselves in relation to it. The growth of the Internet in particular, has facilitated unparalleled levels of global information exchange.

The popularisation of complementary devices such as web-cams, voice over Internet protocol (VoIP) and instant messaging, and their facilitation of websites and mobile apps such as 'Facebook',[51] 'Skype',[52] and 'YouTube',[53] has contributed to conflicting senses of immediacy, involvement, nearness, distance and divide. These may involve senses of space, speed, and time as regulated, constant, linear, disjunctive, ephemeral and/or arbitrary. These different ideas influence many of the artworks explored in this book. From the global production and realisation of iCinema's *T_Visionarium II*, to Ross Mawdsley's presentation of global exploita-

---

[49] Jonathon Xavier Inda and Renato Rosaldo, (Eds.), *The Anthropology of Globalization*, p. 14.

[50] Arjun Appadurai, 'Disjuncture and Difference in a Global Cultural Economy', p. 57.

[51] *Facebook*, <http://www.facebook.com>, (accessed 6 July 2014).

[52] *Skype*, <http://www.skype.com>, (accessed 6 July 2014).

[53] *YouTube*, <http://www.youtube.com>, (accessed 6 July 2014).

tion and cultural division in his *Simian* series, digital artists are engaging with the possibilities and limitations, of globalisation technologies.

One of the consequences of globalisation's 'technoscapes', is the creation of digital divides between the 'haves' and 'have-nots'; with levels of access, digital literacy and bandwidth affecting user experiences. By way of example, interactive digital artworks, require reasonable levels of technical knowledge and ability for the navigation of hyperlinks, audio cues and graphical user interfaces (GUIs). The seemingly simple act of 'surfing the web' requires technical language command, computer education, computer software, hardware, and associated infrastructure. Peter Brooker, for highlights the limitations of the technoscape, arguing that '[a]s an historical condition, digital inequity is connected to the blunt facts of economic, political and military power, that have confirmed the West's cultural, political and economic hegemony'.[54]

Levels of imbalance clearly shade digitisation's 'democratic' ideals. While digital technology may liberate users from the restrictions of sequential time and Euclidean space, problems of access, literacy and usability confirm that its affects are experienced differently. Hansen writes that '[f]rom the very beginning of critical engagement with computer technology, concern has been voiced about the potential, feared by many, celebrated by some, of the end of humanity.'[55]

Online surveillance and regulation also threaten senses of the Internet as an open, democratic and inclusive space. Equally, closed networks such as intranets and secure sites suggest that digital information does not always flow freely. While innumerable sites offer universal access, there are perhaps just as many that require membership and/or login information. Just as there are grounds for seeing the Internet as a fluid domain, there are grounds for describing it as a highly structured and regulated environment. While technological determinists tend to view the Internet as open and non-heirarchical, cultural theorist Mark Tribe claims that he 'cannot help but view the Internet as a communal apartment of the Stalin era: no privacy, everybody spies on everybody else, always present are lines for common areas such as the toilet or the kitchen.'[56] In suggesting that everyone can be surveilled and controlled, Tribe's contests the binary of the 'West and the rest'.

In the face of criticism by writers like Baudrillard, Timothy Allen Jackson encourages us to see digital technology's diverse potentialities: 'to envision the transformative potential of cyberspace, as well as its implicit limitations'.[57] Jackson argues that by broadening our understanding of globalisation's technological impacts, we might articulate perceptions of 'rootlessness, alienation, and psychological distance between individuals and groups on the one hand, and fantasies (or nightmares) or electronic propinquity on the other.'[58] By viewing these affects as

---

[54] Peter Brooker, (Ed.), *Modernism/Postmodernism*, p. 24.

[55] Tim Lenoir, 'Foreword', pp. ix–x.

[56] Mark Tribe, 'Foreword' in *The Language of New Media*, p. xi.

[57] Timothy Allen Jackson, 'Towards a New Media Aesthetic', p. 349.

[58] Arjun Appadurai, 'Disjuncture and Difference in a Global Cultural Economy', p. 47.

differential and non-uniform, we might review universal assumptions about digitisation and globalisation's affects. The perception of globalisation's 'technoscapes' as spatially, temporally, and kinetically dynamic might provide a way for thinking about globalisation and digital art in complementary terms: as temporally organic evolving phenomena.

Affective Readings

Globalisation is often described in binary terms: either causing of fragmentation and disintegration, and simulation,[59] or heightening our consciousness of the world as a connected place. In their text *The Global Village: Transformations in World Life and Media in the 21st Century,* Marshall McLuhan and Bruce R. Powers describe new senses of human connectedness and the rise of the 'global village'.[60] Yet, these analyses construct a binary of fragmentation-connection that arguably overlooks the polymorphic iterations of experience. Human encounters are often inter-changeable, contradictory, or simultaneously love-hate; thereby blurring the boundaries of 'either-or' (Fig. 3.3).

The issue is particularly pertinent, if interpretation is seen to be variable, unpredictable, and contigent upon context. On an Internet chat forum, for example, a user may enjoy strong senses of emotional connection, yet detest the lack of physical proximity. In a different way, the global media coverage of September 11, 2001 instilled in many shifting waves of feelings: from shock to de-sensitisation followed by a desire to connect. What these examples suggest, is that affects are not static: they are often fleeting, contingent and contradictory.

Highly structured articulations often fail to express the movements and iterations of these impacts. They also fall short in the articulation of affect. Like globalisation, affective response is fluid, formed of surges in and between the real and the imaginary; the virtual and the physical; the rational and the abstract; the actual and surreal. Theories drawn from universal constants can tend to negate the flux of bodily awareness and individual sentience. While these theories may be useful in describing fixed structures and systems, affective approaches can facilitate more human-centric understandings of phenomena.

However, to perceive globalisation as a conglomerate of its affects may reveal how in variant contexts, individuals experience phenomena differently. For example, an individualrespond differently to its impacts: from expressing resistance to technological change; to an appreciation of expanded financial markets; alarm at

---

[59] For a discussion of simulation in relation to the rise of digital communications and the global mass media see: Jean Baudrillard, "From 'Simulcra and Simulations" in Peter Brooker (Ed.), *Modernism/Postmodernism*, London, Longman, 1992.

[60] Marshall McLuhan and Bruce R. Powers, *The Global Village: Transformations in World Life and Media in the Twenty-first Century*, New York, Oxford University Press, 1989.

Fig. 3.3 Lara Baladi, *Alone, Together…In Media Res*, 2012. (3 channel video installation, 42 min, Image courtesy of the artist, 2012)

the rise of global terror networks; an embrace of global communications and knowledge sharing; or apprehension in response to the growth of travel and diaspora. The broad range of globalisation's impacts—and the complexity of responses to them—seem to call for more personal means of articulation. Without such means of expression individuals may be left feeling that globalisation is impossible to express in personal terms, and therefore beyond their grasp or level of influence.

The 'open' and fluid methods of Arjun Appadurai and Arturo Escobar—centred upon subjectivity and difference—might facilitate a broader range of articulations. As Escobar, Sonia Alvarez, and Evelina Dagnino contend:

> [t]he forms of subjectivity that we inhabit play a crucial part in determining whether we accept or contest existing power relations. Moreover, for marginalised and oppressed groups, the construction of new and resistant identities is a key dimension of a wider political struggle to transform society.[61]

The writers' focus upon subjective interpretation returns the autonomy of experience to the individual. In reviewing these ideas, this chapter proposes that globalisation generates multiple impacts, which can be contradictory and fluctuating. In one context, for example, an individual might experience globalisation's technological divides. In another, however, they might reap the financial rewards of global markets and new economic flows. In generating contradictory perceptions of globalisation, these paradoxes point to the value of an affective, human-centric approach.

This text conceptualises affect as an an apprehension or bodily response: a sensory or affective process involving individual intuition, interpretation, memory, and bodily reaction. In his discussion of affect, Marc Augé writes that any generalised claim 'is plainly reckless'[62] because it reduces the complexity and specificity of human difference and response. In ascribing a kind of 'crude empathy',[63] Jill Bennett argues that general claims are premised upon 'a very reductive form of observation

---

[61] Sonia Alvarez et al., 'The Cultural and Political in Latin American Social Movement' in *Cultures of Politics and Politics of Culture: The Cultural and the Political in Latin American Social Movements*, Boulder, Westview Press, 1998, p. 5.

[62] Marc Augé, *The War of Dreams*, (Trans. L. Heron), London, Pluto Press, 1999, p. 7.

[63] Jill Bennett, 'Face-to-Face Encounters: Testimonial Imagery and the South African Truth and Reconciliation Commission', *Australian and New Zealand Journal of Art*, Vols. 2–3, 2001–2002, p. 41.

based not upon any thorough or sustained engagement or understanding but on a spurious identification with select features of another's experience'.[64]

In his exploration of affect, Mark Hansen invokes French philosopher Henri Bergson's theories of perception and affect. Bergson's texts describe the individual body 'as a kind of filter that selects, from among the universe of images circulating around it and according to its own embodied capacities, precisely those that are relevant to it'.[65] The body in Bergson's account becomes the 'glue' that binds interpretation and response.[66] Hansen posits that through 'placing the embodied viewer-participant into a circuit with information'[67] digital artworks might operate as 'laboratories for the conversion of information into corporeally apprehensible images'.[68] By facilitating this 'conversion', digital artworks might offer means for transforming experiences of globalisation into perceptually and 'corporeally apprehensible images'.[69]

Conclusion

As explored further in the previous chapter, art is an experiential construct, which can facilitate alternative perspectives, and generate affective ways of 'seeing' and experiencing the external world. Its technical and discursive tools can facilitate new articulations of globalisation's shifts, and contribute a new critical voice. Through making room for micro encounters in the articulation of art and globalisation, digital art might return the autonomy of experience to the individual.

The next chapter launches a discussion on a style of digital art that is uniquely engaged with its moment of production. It suggests that the radical art of Ross Mawdsley, ®™ark, and The Yes Men is borne of a particular moment in time, sharing a unique history with globalisation and digitisation. The chapter 'Digital Art and Political Revolt', connects net.art and hactivism to wider political protests to globalisation. Finally, it shows how digital art offers diverse means for conceptualising the external world, as well as fresh ways of thinking about globalisation as a cultural phenomenon.

---

[64] Jill Bennett, 'Face-to-Face Encounters', p. 41.

[65] Mark B.N. Hansen, *New Philosophy for New Media*, p. 3.

[66] Tim Lenoir, 'Foreword', p. xxiv.

[67] Mark B.N. Hansen, *New Philosophy for New Media*, p. 11.

[68] Mark B.N. Hansen, *New Philosophy for New Media*, p. 11.

[69] Mark B.N. Hansen, *New Philosophy for New Media*, p. 11.

Chapter 4
Digital Art and Political Revolt

Introduction

Building upon the discourses on digital art explored in previous chapters, this chapter engages with art works that explore the idea of political revolt. These radical expressions show how digital art can both perpetuate—and break free from—earlier discourses and practices in art. This chapter focusses on the tactical art of Ross Mawdsley, ®™ark, and The Yes Men. It shows how resistance can be innovative, creative and essentially artistic. Their works are contextualised in terms of backlashes to globalisation and expressions of political revolt. This chapter suggests that while the form may be different, digital art messages often continue dialogues established by earlier works of art (Fig. 4.1).

Enactments of Global Revolt

Ross Mawdsley is one of the United Kingdom's earliest digital artists, and a strong critic of globalisation. His opposition is manifested in a series of online volumes published in 2000 as part of the anthology *Simian*.[1] The term 'simian' reveals something of his take: that globalisation is diminishing cultural difference, and turning individuals into ape-like replicas of each other. Mawdsley's art aligns globalisation to earlier projects of imperialism. In the volume *Revolt,* this connection becomes clear. The artwork slowly unfolds to reveal a man wielding a rifle. The image of an Asian gun-man, evokes the possibility of 'other' actors rising up against Western cultural and political regimes. The graphic is overlaid with the text:

> The world is a dangerous and unstable place at the moment. Riots, civil disorder, urban unrest and war are rife right across the globe. People are rising up and making a stand.

---

[1] Ross Mawdsley, *Simian*, <http://www.simian.nu>, 2000, (accessed 6 February 2001). This link is no longer active.

M. Langdon, *The Work of Art in a Digital Age: Art, Technology and Globalisation,*
DOI 10.1007/978-1-4939-1270-4_4, © Springer Science+Business Media New York 2014

Fig. 4.1 ®™ark, *Promotional Still*, 2000. (http://www.rtmark.com/images/bitygraphgs.jpg 2007)

> This day has been coming a long time. The revolution will not be televised. The day of the simian is upon us.[2]

Mawdsley's appropriation of Public Enemy's slogan: 'the revolution will not be televised',[3] links his art to popular expressions of revolt.

Ross Mawdsley expresses a concern about the demise of individuality, through the repetition of simian clones in *Revolt* and *Journey Into Darkness*. To 'enter' *Journey Into Darkness* is to be struck by emotive images of chemical warfare, suicide, terrorism, ethnic exploitation, and prostitution. Each is articulated in terms of globalisation's political-economic impacts. Mawdsley strongly attributes the rise of global corporate culture and ideology, to the decay of individualism. This theme

---

[2] Ross Mawdsley, *'Revolt', Simian*, <http://www.simian.nu>, 1993, (accessed 6 February 2001). This link is no longer active.

[3] The phrase was used by Public Enemy on their album: *It Takes a Nation of Millions to Hold us Back*, New York, Def Jam/Columbia Records, 1988.

Fig. 4.2 Ross Mawdsley, *Journey Into Darkness*, 2000. (http://www.simian .nu).

is expressed through the emblazoning of UK pharmaceutical brand Boots™ on a razor blade, and contradictory brandishing of tribal or 'particular', insignia upon the disembodied black form. The slow, fatalistic crawl of the insect across the blade portrays a sense of hopeless imminence to the global 'take-over' of culture and individuality, while the disembodied male torso suggests a lack of resistance, and an absence of critical mind. The objectification of the black form, suggests that non-Western actors have little say or opportunity for resistance, against the idioms inflicted upon them by Western corporations (Fig. 4.2).

Within the work *Revolt* the ironic portrayal of simians wearing Che Guevara berets in *Melbourne* and references to 'The Revolution' engage with Frankfurt School uses of imagery in the formation of Marxist critique. Set to the sounds of a sombre aural refrain, *Melbourne* presents an ominous account of globalisation. As population dots move across a globe, the cities of Tokyo, Croatia, Norway, Havana, Liverpool, and Melbourne are identified. Moments later, six video screens appear, with the option of user selection made evident. Although each represents a different location, they all depict the same images of rioting and affray. The similarity in footage suggests parallel enactments of revolt and dissidence across the world.

In the *Simian* series, Mawdsley uses interactive technology to generate individual responses to globalisation. In the volume *Tokyo Love Hotel Mistake,* the user is invited inside a Tokyo brothel. An Asian prostitute greets us in broken English. She attempts to gain our custom with the cliché: 'well baby, me so horny: me love you long time'.[4] Within seconds of this dialogue, a JVC branded video camera appears, with the 'play' button lit up. Pressing 'play' changes the blank screen to a video clip of a Western client engaging in her services. As the action plays out, dollar signs scroll down the page along with the slogan: '[w]hat can I have for $ 400?'.[5] followed by the client's defence: 'it was only one night'.[6] Set to rhythmic beats, *Tokyo Love Hotel Mistake* portrays the Asian sex-trade as a form of global discrimination. Mawdsley's *Tokyo Love Hotel Mistake* offers a bleak insight into the Asian sex-trade and its abuse by Western nationals. It suggests that global consumption has

---

[4] Ross Mawdsley, *'Tokyo Love Hotel Mistake', Simian* <http://www.simian.nu>, 2000, (accessed 6 February 2001). This link is no longer active.

[5] Ross Mawdsley, *'Tokyo Love Hotel Mistake'*, <http://www.simian.nu>.

[6] Ross Mawdsley, *'Tokyo Love Hotel Mistake'*, <http://www.simian.nu>.

Fig. 4.3 Ross Mawdsley, *Tokyo Love Hotel* Mistake, 2000. (http://www.simian.nu)

influenced the strategic marketing of this exploitative 'product'. *Tokyo Love Hotel Mistake* shows how globalisation has facilitated a rise in international travel and 'tours' such as these. As such, Mawdsley's art connects globalisation to forms of Western imperialism, exploitation of local cultures, and flow of goods and capital across borders.

In *Tokyo Love Hotel Mistake,* Mawdsley presents the user with distinct choices. One option is to press 'play' on a video camera and watch an illicit prostitution scene. This action might be seen to make the user a witting consumer and voyeur, echoing Manovich's claim that 'making a choice involves a moral responsibility'.[7] This claim is more applicable to didactic works, where users are required to make moral decisions in order for the narrative to progress. Lawrence Grossberg, however, argues that the very complexity of art's situation within globalisation indicates that 'such artistic practices, even if they situate the audience as consumer, may also situate them in other contradictory subject-positions',[8] including bringing to light illuminate our ethical dilemmas. Mawdsley's critique of globalisation, however, is compromised by the use of didactic imagery, which simplify complex issues. The generalised portrayal of a Thai prostitute, Asian gunman and disembodied black torso, encourage crude and reductive understandings of others' traumas and experiences. Ross Mawdsley's backlash to globalisation in *Tokyo Love Hotel Mistake* is underscored by the sense that global consumption leads to the standardisation of culture (Fig. 4.3).

---

[7] Lev Manovich, *The Language of New Media*, p. 44.

[8] Lawrence Grossberg, *Dancing in Spite of Myself: Essays on Popular Culture*, Durham, Duke University Press, 1997, p. 155.

Fig. 4.4 ®™ark, *Promotional Still*, 2000. (http://rtmark.com/ads.html)

®™ark

As a radical alliance of digital artists, programmers and activists, ®™ark (pronounced 'art mark') use digital art to address a perceived lack of critical press on globalisation. Within their works, they raise questions about corporate hegemony and political legitimacy. Through documenting and parodying the actions of corporate power brokers, the artists attempt to repossess global media. ®™ark's actions have included political interventions and depositions. Using a combination of hacking and activism termed 'hactivism', ®™ark have targeted perceived perpetuators of global exploitation, ranging from The George W. Bush administration to the World Trade Organization, World Health Organization and World Bank. Their use of interventionist tactics such as hacking, floodnetting, phishing, digital sabotage and hijack connect their art earlier political art styles, including Pop Art, 1908s Electronica, and Situatist, Dadaist and Frankfurt School works (Fig. 4.4).

One of ®™ark's earliest interventions was a campaign against online toy distributor eToys™.[9] The case began as a clash over domain names, with ®™ark arguing that it lodged the domain 'www.Etoy.com'[10] before the toy company's eToys domain.[11] Yet, the similarity in names led to the company's concern at being mistaken with the art organisation. In late 1999, eToys made an offer of US$ 500,000 in cash and stocks to ®™ark for their domain name rights. ®™ark declined the offer, which led to a legal suit against the artists. eToys succeeded in gaining an injunction that prevented ®™ark from operating their similarly named site. Although ®™ark's site was lodged first and eToys had never been cited on the site, it was ruled that the similarity in names, and the nature of ®™ark's activities—seen to include 'pornography and calls to violence'[12]—were damaging to the toy company's business. ®™ark however, vehemently opposed the claims that their site was

---

[9] See: eToys, <http://www.etoys.com>, (accessed 6 July 2014).

[10] See: *Etoy,*<http://www.etoy.com>, (accessed 6 July 2014).

[11] See: *®™ark*, <http://www.rtmark.com/legacy/etoymain.html>, (accessed 26 April 2007). Link no longer active.

[12] *®™ark*, <http://www.rtmark.com>.

violent and/or pornographic, arguing that 'only a primitive conception of art could lead one to see pornography or violence on its pages'.[13]

In 1999, ®™ark launched its counter-attack on eToys, in the form of a satirical multi-player game featuring Lego® men in military uniforms.[14] The objective was to force the crash of eToys' website, thereby affecting customer access and the company's market share. The game's mission statement read: '[o]n your team, thousands of players. Your opponents: eToys and its shareholders—as long as they still own shares. The stakes: art, free expression and life on the Internet'.[15] A key tactic used in the campaign was 'floodnetting', a program specifically designed for ®™ark's campaign. Floodnetting was centred upon an applet called 'Flood-Net' developed by Electronic Disturbance Theater—a radical group that used art to instigate forms of civil disobedience. As Coco Fusco writes, the FloodNet applet produced 'a command that retools the usual "refresh" or "reload" button on a web server'.[16]

In December 1999, the applet was offered to users from around the globe to simultaneously login and crash the eToys site. ®™ark's 'web-jamming' had detrimental consequences for the company's trade. The tactic, coupled with the hacking of search engines so that 'Etoy' came up first, revealed the extent of ®™ark's revolt. The collaboration defended its use of invasive tactics, arguing that 'eToys says etoy.com is hurting sales by disturbing those who stumble upon it',[17] but the company is also

> disturbing people who want to see great Internet art but stumble upon eToys instead, and so why not say eToys shouldn't exist? Why should financial might make right? If they want to play by barbaric rules, we will too.[18]

The case of ®™ark versus eToys suggested an ongoing antagonism between radical artists and global corporations, as well as world leaders and NGOs seen to support globalisation's market economy.

In constructing itself as a 'corporation' of artists, ®™ark blurs the boundaries between art and commerce. The collective seems to confirm Frith and Home's sense, as expressed by Lawrence Grossberg, that 'texts cannot be separated from their market effects'.[19] On ®™ark's website they state that they are 'indeed just a corporation'.[20] In their use of global media to extend operations, the group ironically replicates the actions of the companies it protests. The artists' name invokes

---

[13] ®™ark, <http://www.rtmark.com>.

[14] ®™ark was later forced to remove all Lego® images from their campaigns.

[15] ®™ark, <http://www.rtmark.com>.

[16] Coco Fusco, 'The Unbearable Weightness of Beings: Art in Mexico after NAFTA', *The Bodies that Were Not Ours: And Other Writings,* London, Routledge, 2001, p. 70.

[17] ®™ark, <http://www.rtmark.com>.

[18] ®™ark, <http://www.rtmark.com>.

[19] Lawrence Grossberg, *Dancing in Spite of Myself,* p. 154.

[20] ®™ark, <http://www.rtmark.com>.

corporate trademarks, while their 'dot.com' domain is evocative of commercial websites. The group's advertisement of projects with financial rewards strengthens this link.[21] Yet, while ®™ark is constructed like a corporation—benefitting from corporate protections and shareholder investment—its artists contend that unlike its opponents, its 'bottom line' 'is to improve culture, rather than its own pocketbook; it seeks *cultural* profit, not financial'.[22] They claim that just as:

> ordinary corporations are solely and entirely machines to increase their shareholders' wealth (often to the detriment of culture and life) so ®™ark is a machine to improve its shareholders' culture and life (sometimes to the detriment of corporate wealth).[23]

®™ark insist that their members 'will never promote a project that is likely to result in physical harm to humans. That is ®™ark's only ethical compunction'.[24] Through an internal system of communications exclusively available to its 'share holders', the collective maintains its members' anonymity. The provision of an external 'face' via a website 'advertising' its activities and goals, simulates the organisation of a global corporation. On this public site, ®™ark encourages new members to 'invest' in its campaigns.

The Yes Men

The campaigns of radical art collective The Yes Men are strongly sympathetic to ®™ark's protests to globalisation. They describe themselves as honest people impersonating 'big-time criminals' in order to humiliate them.[25] As they declare on their website:

> The Yes Men agree their way into the fortified compounds of commerce, ask questions, and then smuggle out the stories of their hijinks to provide a public glimpse at the behind-the-scenes world of business. In other words, the Yes Men are team players... but they play for the opposing team.[26]

The Yes Men have besieged some of the world's most prominent corporations through their physical and virtual attacks. Through 'hijacking' websites, staging 'sit-ins' at press conferences, releasing a documentary film and conducting 'spoof' television interviews, they have drawn wide public attention to their activities. Each intervention or 'hijink' is proudly listed on The Yes Men site.[27]

The artists use the principle of 'identity correction' to justify their form of hactivism. Central to their campaign is the program Reamweaver™, a piece of software

---

[21] *®™ark*, <http://www.rtmark.com>.

[22] *®™ark*, <http://www.rtmark.com>.

[23] *®™ark*, <http://www.rtmark.com>.

[24] *®™ark*, <http://www.rtmark.com>.

[25] *The Yes Men*, <http://www.theyesmen.org>.

[26] *The Yes Men*, <http://www.theyesmen.org>.

[27] *The Yes Men*, <http://www.theyesmen.org>.

that gains website templates allowing the artists to 'spoof' or replicate opponents' sites. The point of spoofing, argue the collaborators, is to create a moment where users question what they are looking at. Like their ®™ark counterparts, The Yes Men show a sophisticated use of art, complementing their virtual and physical protests. Their virtual presence on the Internet—and physical calls for street action in cities like Salzburg and Melbourne—enables their forms of political art to reach wide audiences.

In 1999, The Yes Men registered the web domain GWBush.com. Through their 'spoof' site, the artists sought to attract genuine users who intended to access the legitimate GeorgeWBush.com site. Using software to grab the graphics and layout form the original site, the artists created a spoof site in near replica. In following the principle of *détournement,* The Yes Men's intention was to catch users unaware and, upon having their attention, explain what they saw to be the 'real' motives of George W. Bush: 'to help the rich at the expense of the poor and the environment'.[28]

Like their protests to the Bush administration, The Yes Men's backlash to the World Trade Organization (WTO) have attracted global controversy. Their key objective in this campaign was to cast light onto the human effects of the WTO's economic policies. The Yes Men claimed:

> the facts are that in the last 25 years the poor of the world have gotten even poorer…while the rich have gotten astronomically richer. And all that during the implementation of policies that the WTO claim will help the poor.[29]

Using the domain name http://www.gatt.org, reminiscent of the acronym 'GATT' for the 1999 WTO Global Agreement on Tariffs and Trade, The Yes Men set up a rival site with content appropriated from their opponents' web pages. The timing was strategic, coinciding with the World Trade Organization's Seattle Ministerial held in November 1999. The WTO's reaction to the spoof site was immediate: on November 23rd 1999, a press release was given condemning The Yes Men's spoof site. Relishing the publicity, the collaboration responded with further tactical campaigns.

On May 2000, The Yes Men gate crashed the International Legal Studies Conference in Salzburg. Posing as members of the WTO, they presented a paper making outlandish calls for economic productivity at any cost. They suggested, for example, that Spain be forced to eradicate its tradition of 'siesta' because of its detrimental effects upon market efficiency. They argued further that market principles should be extended into the political realm, with votes legally bought and sold on election 'share markets'. Ironically, much of the audience was said to blindly support the claims made. In their own words:

> [s]ome audience members are intrigued, and ask interesting questions; some, however, are dismayed by the insults to Italians, and Andy must explain that he is simply being more frank than the WTO usually is, and is presenting its message more clearly than normal. No one objects to Dr. Bichlbauer's scheme for American voting; perhaps they are just being polite?[30]

---

[28] ®™*ark*, <http://www.rtmark.org>.

[29] *The Yes Men,* <http://www.theyesmen.org>.

[30] *The Yes Men,* <http://www.theyesmen.org>.

Fig. 4.5 The Yes Men, *CNBC, Market Wrap*, 2000. (http://www.theyesmen.org/en/node/112)

On the 6th July 2001, The Yes Men received an email from the CNBC television program Market *Wrap Europe*. The station had located the 'GATT' domain and, confusing it with the legitimate WTO site, were seeking an expert to discuss the 'Group of Eight' (G8) protests in Genoa.[31] 'Andy', a member of The Yes Men, happily obliged. Disguised as a WTO representative in a business suit, Andy joined the live forum which was televised from CNBC's Paris studio. Seated alongside high profile lobbyist, Barry Coates, Andy assumed the identity of Granwyth Hulatberi. The host Nigel Roberts, proceeded to introduce the prominent World Development Movement anti-globalisation activist Barry Coates and Vernon Ellis, the International Chairman of Andersen Consulting. Ellis opened with the statement: 'I *do* believe that multinational corporations *can* be good for business'.[32] 'Granwyth' agreed, in extolling the virtues of free enterprise, capitalism and the global economy (Fig. 4.5).

Granwyth proceeded to inform his opponent Barry Coates that the privatisation of education would hail in a new era of thought, so that the next generation would think differently about global commerce. Granwyth argued that youths would reap the rewards of free trade and revert to the philosophies of Friedman and Darwin, as they embraced the dictum: 'the rich are right because they have power, and the poor are wrong because they don't'.[33] After the interview, the station was apparently none the wiser and sent a copy of the proceedings to The Yes Men.

The Yes Men's hijinks engage with backlashes to globalisation, and as Inda and Rosaldo express, the perceived installation worldwide of western versions of basic social-cultural reality: the West's epistemological and ontological theories, its values, ethical systems, approaches to rationality, technical-scientific worldview,

---

[31] The 'Group of Eight' refers to the eight global economic powers: Canada, France, Germany, Italy, Russia, the United Kingdom, and the United States.

[32] *The Yes Men,* <http://www.theyesmen.org>.

[33] *The Yes Men,* <http://www.theyesmen.org>.

political culture, and so on.[34] Central to the ensemble's campaigns is the question of how economic globalisation affects non-western actors. In arguing that behind the WTO's actions 'there is a bizarre logic that supported colonialism,[35] The Yes Men offer an account of globalisation centred upon the West's political, economic and ideological infiltration of other cultures.

Globalisation and Political Protest

In protesting against the WTO, The Yes Men suggest that Western nations have used their political and economic might to take advantage of weaker states. Those actions include making its currency the international reserve and exploiting cheap service and production opportunities within Asia and the Third World. This presentation is echoed in Ross Mawdsley's depiction of the Asian trade and its abuse by Western nationals in *Tokyo Love Hotel Mistake*. These outcomes, argues cultural theorist Pierre Bourdieu, ensure that powerful Western nations not only influences, but decide 'the rules of the game'.[36] This can lead to one-way economic flows that entrench the binary of advantage and disadvantage. As the power of non-Western nations diminishes, so too their cultural and political visibility is lessened or overshadowed, by more powerful economic nations. What transpires, is a predicament in which the oppressed can never re-gain control.

By challenging the political-economic platforms of the WTO, The Yes Men vocalise a fear that local cultures will be subsumed into a global cultural centrifuge. Their account

> attributes the increasing synchronization of world culture to the ability of transnational capital, most often seen as US-dominated and mass-mediated, to distribute cultural goods around the globe.[37]

This 'synchronisation' or standardisation of culture and political economy is to many critics, one of the most alarming facets of globalisation. As Kenneth Frampton and Paul Ricoeur express, this can lead to 'a mediocre civilisation',[38] whereby suddenly 'throughout the world, one finds the same bad movie, the same slot machines, the same plastic or aluminium atrocities, the same twisting of language by propaganda'.[39]

---

[34] Jonathon Xavier Inda and Renato Rosaldo, (Eds.), *The Anthropology of Globalization*, p. 14.

[35] The Yes Men, 'CNBC Market Wrap Still', <http://www.theyesmen.org/en/node/112>. Link is no longer active.

[36] Pierre Bourdieu, 'The Myth of 'Globalisation' and the European Welfare State' in *Acts of Resistance: Against the New Myths of Our Time,* Cambridge, Polity Press, 2001, p. 38.

[37] Jonathon Xavier Inda and Renato Rosaldo, (Eds.), *The Anthropology of Globalization*, p. 13.

[38] Kenneth Frampton and Paul Ricoeur, 'Towards a Critical Regionalism: Six Points for an Architecture of Resistance', in Hal Foster (Ed.) *The Anti-Aesthetic: Essays on Postmodern Culture,* Seattle, Bay Press, 1983, p. 16.

[39] Kenneth Frampton and Paul Ricoeur 'Towards a Critical Regionalism', p. 16.

Yet, alarmist accounts of globalisation—like those of digitisation—can be simplistic and reductive, in failing to acknowledge the diverse impacts phenomena, which are often both positive and negative. To this end, works by artists such as Ross Mawdsley, ®™ark and The Yes Men tell only part of the tale. As Inda and Rosaldo note, there can be positive impacts as well, for the 'deterritorialisation of culture is invariably the occasion for the reinsertion of culture in new time-space contexts'.[40]

Cultural Imperialism

The artistic critiques of Ross Mawdsley, ®™ark and The Yes Men locate globalisation alongside Imperialism: the expansion of the British Raj, the colonisation of 'new' lands, and the exploitation of indigenous people. Post-colonial critiques of globalisation might perceive it as the generator of a certain power dynamic, with political-economic hegemony flowing primarily in one direction: from the West to 'the rest'. The artists' expressions construct binaries between centres and peripheries; with the periphery cultures of the developing world, located well outside of the realm of political-economic influence.

In exploiting the Internet's ability to generate global publicity, Ross Mawdsley, ®™ark, and The Yes Men emulate the corporations that they protest. Through attempting to gain control of mass communications systems, ®™ark, and The Yes Men recognise the power of the global media. George Landow claims that '[i]n tracing our way through such intricate works…we should not forget their place within the strongly hierarchical, well sign-posted and ordered space of the Net'.[41] Equally, while the art of Ross Mawdsley, ®™ark and The Yes Men's seeks to represent the politically marginalised, the politics of the 'digital divide' means that this audience would likely have limited access to the Internet. Poor infrastructure, inferior speed, inadequate bandwidth and digital illiteracy means that the people that these artists speak about, are probably unable to enter the conversation. There is a clear danger in speaking on behalf of others, for as previously discussed in relation to *Tokyo Love Hotel Mistake*, it can generalise and reduce others' experiences.

Ideological Revolt

The expressions of Ross Mawdsley, ®™ark and The Yes Men resonate with Marxist discourses and Situationist interventions. Their practices are defined by content appropriation, or 'cutting and pasting' without reference. The collaborators' encouragement of peer-to-peer (P2P) file sharing and collaborative production, presents

---

[40] Jonathon Xavier Inda and Renato Rosaldo, (Eds.), *The Anthropology of Globalization*, p. 11.

[41] *The Yes Men*, <http://www.theyesmen.org>.

a vision of art as open and democratic. Through encouraging their work to be appropriated and reproduced, Ross Mawdsley, ®™ark and The Yes Men challenge principles of artistic autonomy.

In opposing the ideal of 'art for art's sake', Karl Marx held that art did not belong in an ivory tower but on the streets of society.[42] Through their global collaborations and enactments of revolt, ®™ark and The Yes Men challenge the limits of art production and the formal principles of originality, authenticity, aura and authorship. While cooperation has long existed in the arts, digitisation enables artistic alliance to take place on a global scale. A digital artwork can be streamed from the Internet in 'real-time' or globally saved as data on CDs, thumb drives, and disks. It is in conversation with these discourses, that Ross Mawdsley, ®™ark, and The Yes Men's political protests push the boundaries of analogue art.

By connecting economic outcomes with cultural and political affects, Ross Mawdsley, ®™ark, and The Yes Men offer Marxist critiques of capital, art and politics. Laurie Schneider claims that 'Marx believed that the production of art necessarily depended on its immediate context',[43] or in this case, globalisation. In his 1935–1939 *Notebooks,* the Marxist and Social Realist Bertolt Brecht, argued that art, 'if it is truthful, must also reflect decay'.[44] Brecht, writes Schenider Adams, believed that 'unless it wants to break faith with its social function, art must show the world as changeable. And help to change it'.[45] According to this account, art functions as something more than a sublime construct: it becomes a means for inciting social and political change. As revealed in Chap. 2, throughout the 1930s and 1940s, the tensions between art and production were drawn tight by the Marxist 'revisionists' of the Frankfurt School: Theodor Adorno, Walter Benjamin, Max Horkheimer, Leo Lowenthal, and Herbert Marcuse. Through acting as self-appointed social 'watchdogs', artists like Mawdsley, ®™ark and The Yes Men take on some of the responsibilities formerly attributed to nation states.

Although some fear that globalisation will lead to art becoming a commodity that alienates artists from their works,[46] ®™ark, and The Yes Men have embraced this commercialisation. By establishing themselves as 'corporations' and advertising projects for 'sponsorship', they control the political-economy of their art. ®™ark and The Yes Men claim that in emulating the structure of global corporations, their organisations are 'perfectly capable of acting in concert, of long-term forward planning, and of systematic destruction of their opponents'.[47] Corporate principles influence the political strategies of both artistic groups, with ®™ark claiming that their 'bottom line' is to improve culture:

---

[42] Laurie Schneider Adams, *The Methodologies of Art,* p. 59.

[43] *The Yes Men,* <http://www.theyesmen.org>.

[44] Laurie Schneider Adams, *The Methodologies of Art,* p. 63.

[45] Laurie Schneider Adams, *The Methodologies of Art,* p. 62.

[46] For a discussion of this idea see: Alan Bradshaw, 'The Alienated Artist and the Political Economy of Organised Art', *Consumption Markets&Culture,* Vol.9 , Issue 2, June 2006, pp. 111–117.

[47] Julian Stallabrass, *Internet Art,* p. 95.

[j]ust as ordinary corporations are solely and entirely machines to increase their shareholders' wealth, so ®™ark is a machine to improve its shareholders' culture and life (sometimes
to the detriment of corporate wealth.[48]

®™ark has a clear understanding of how corporate structures can be used to generate creative 'wealth' and global output. The Yes Men also play with corporate
principles. Their 2009 documentary *The Yes Men Fix The World* centred upon two
political activists posing as corporate executives that managed to con big businesses
(Fig. 4.6).[49]

In their critique of the global mass media, Ross Mawdsley and ®™ark, The Yes
Men present a Baudrillardian critique of digital culture's 'representations of representations'.[50] Mawdsley's depiction of simian clones in *Revolt*, for example, engages with Baudrillard's description of 'Disney-like simulacra [entering] into every
facet of cultural life, emptying active content by exploiting images'.[51] The notion
of 'simulacra' is central to Baudrillard's claim that in a digital world, simulation
replaces reality, leading to a 'hyperreal' existence. As Darley elaborates, according
to this account contemporary culture 'exists and grows entirely through self-refer-
ence, definitively uncoupled from traditional notions of representation (which en-
tails such concepts as "the referent", "innovation", "authenticity" and "the new").'[52]

Net.Art Style

As the art of Ross Mawdsley, ®™ark, and The Yes Men demonstrates, the Internet
can operate as a critical space for the articulation of globalisation and digitisation's
spatial, temporal and kinetic affects. Their art shows a deliberate use of digital technology, from their exploitation of 'free' spaces online, to manipulation of technical
glitches and incorporation of 'spoofing', 'hacking', and 'floodnetting' techniques
in their works. Geert Lovink claims that 'many struggles appear to have left the
street and the factory floor and migrated into an ideological space of representation,
constructed by and through the media'.[53] Yet, contrary to democratic or idealistic
constructions of the Internet, Lovink asserts that it

has not freed artists and activists from the necessity or perils of having to deal with institu-
tional politics. There is no Internet without power, cable policy, money and access rights.
Don't believe the hype of a disembodied, pure and unspoiled Virtual Organisation.[54]

---

[48] ®™*ark*, <http://www.rtmark.com>.

[49] The Yes Men, 'Still from *The Yes Men Fix the World'*, *The Yes Men,* <http://theyesmenfix-
theworld.com/>, 2009, (accessed 17 December 2010).

[50] Michael Heim, *Virtual Realism*, p. 3.

[51] Michael Heim, *Virtual Realism*, p. 3.

[52] Andrew Darley, 'The Digital Image in the Age of the Signifier', p. 127.

[53] Geert Lovink, *Dark Fiber,* p. 263.

[54] Geert Lovink, *Dark Fiber,* p. 263.

Fig. 4.6 The Yes Men, *The Yes Men Fix the World*, 2009. (http://www.theyesmen.org)

Revealing their understanding of these issues, ®™ark and The Yes Men use the Internet to generate critical masses to fight these struggles. Their mass virtual and physical protests reflect the awareness that to have any kind of impact, artists and activists must collaborate on global campaigns.

®™ark and The Yes Men augment online and offline campaigns, as well as digital art with political activism. They reflect a hybrid approach to revolt, in taking to the streets, targeting military bases, orchestrating simultaneous online action, constructing 'spoof' campaigns and holding guerrilla film screenings. Their strategies engage with one of the most striking characteristics of hactivist art: the augmentation of physical and virtual action. As Internet Theorist Geert Lovink writes, an effective campaign 'constantly mediates between the real and the virtual, switches back and forth, unwilling to choose sides for the local or the global'.[55] In these ways, their works converse with what Stallabrass describes as 'the actions of street protestors attached to the new anti-capitalist politics, who have found ways of uniting actions comparable to performance, environmental and installation art with practical ends of subversion.[56]

®™ark and The Yes Men's hacking of search engines, staging of political sit-ins, and crashing of opponents' sites may be seen as 'guerrilla' tactics. Yet, in seeking to preserve the democracy of the Internet through giving voice to expressions of revolt, they thwart and, at times, destroy users' rights of access. The alliances do not apologise for these affects. The radical artists ®™ark and The Yes Men claim to 'attempt a redefinition of sabotage as social practice, but not in the usual destructive sense, rather in a constructive, innovative and creative way'.[57] That intent may be questionable to users who stumble upon their sites by mistake. ®™ark and The Yes Men's use of pop-ups, hyperlinks and construction of replica 'spoof' sites, deliberately disorient users searching for legitimate sites. Although their techniques may be innovative in terms of art, the confusion and frustration caused can detract from the message. Lovink notes that in some of these expressions there 'is the faint hope that if a campaign generates enough velocity and resonates with enough people, it might just take on some of the qualities of a movement'.[58] Yet, as Stallabrass contends, some of these expressions to the contrary, have 'an air of desperation to them, a panicked rush to occupy a new and important territory'[59].

In a scathing attack of early the net.artist Heath Bunting, critics Pit Schultz and Timothy Druckrey scorn the 'vanguard, innovatory, artist-on-the-edge'[60] image, which they argue is 'not so far from the capitalist fantasy of Net pioneers exploring the new frontier'.[61] In an attack on the so-called 'net intellegentsia', Schultz denounces artists like Bunting, and probably Mawdsley, who 'believe themselves to be the leading edge of the coming "Netzvolk", updated modernist supermen riskily performing at the boundary of commercialisation and institutionalisation'.[62] Yet, as Julian Stallabrass argues, '[t]here is a danger that the lack of context that enables this effect also limits the work, since mere confusion, rather than a radical undermining of expectations, could be the result'.[63] As Stallabrass argues '[t]he making

---

[55] Geert Lovink, *Dark Fiber,* p. 262.

[56] Julian Stallabrass, *Internet Art,* p. 95.

[57] Geert Lovink, *Dark Fiber,* p. 271.

[58] Geert Lovink, *Dark Fiber,* p. 257.

[59] Julian Stallabrass, *Internet Art,* p. 90.

[60] Julian Stallabrass, *Internet Art,* p. 89.

[61] Julian Stallabrass, *Internet Art,* p. 89.

[62] Julian Stallabrass, *Internet Art,* p. 89.

[63] Julian Stallabrass, *Internet Art,* p. 94.

of such complex structures, using blind links which leave the user disoriented, is so regularly employed as to have become a cliché of internet art'.[64] The cultivation of critical context can be difficult for digital artists because of the range of online and offline spaces in which their art is displayed. Their audiences are also so diverse, from radical users actively engaging with their art, to children looking to buy toys and accidentally happening upon ®™ark's *Etoy* site.

There is a clear cohesion in the politics of Ross Mawdsley, ®™ark and The Yes Men. While their campaigns reflect cultural-imperialist understandings of globalisation, they tend to focus upon generic effects: Americanisation, political exploitation, cultural homogenisation, and capitalist forces of consumption. On ®™ark's website the artists write:

> [f]or those people caught in the vague uncharted territory outside of business—politics, art, dissent, community, or terror—there are clearly other standards. Is culture for everyone? It turns out that the gap between the "haves" and "have-nots" is just as great whether we're talking about economic capital, or "cultural" capital.[65]

While ®™ark, Ross Mawdsley, and The Yes Men vocalise concern for globalisation's impacts upon culture and capital, their approach is generally one-dimensional. From ®™ark's punishment of eToys™—to The Yes Men's limited explanation of what 'Americanisation' and George W. Bush's mean in the context of globalisation—the commentaries are at times reductive. As Akhil Gupta and James Ferguson observe, the culture should be considered in flexible rather than discrete ways.[66]

As previously explored, cultural theorists Augé, Enwezor and Appadurai approach globalisation as a series of movements, advancing an approach that is equally dynamic in accounting for the intricate flows of people, ideas, information, ideologies and technologies across the globe. These dialogues counter the alarmist tendency to reduce the phenomenon to either-or outcomes. Yet, in their examination of globalisation's human impacts and affects, Ross Mawdsley, ®™ark, and The Yes Men fail to offer that level of critical nuance. Marc Augé, for example, challenges the inter-changeable use of terms 'globalisation' and 'Americanisation'. While he acknowledges the popular fear of 'being colonised',[67] he does claim 'we don't exactly know who by; the enemy is not easily identifiable, and one can venture to suggest that this feeling now exists all over the world, even in the United States'.[68] In arguing that this sense of foray exists 'even in the United States',[69] Augé suggests that globalisation has no single 'colonist', with North Americans being just as affected by globalisation's shifts.

To base an analysis of globalisation on a 'North America versus the rest of the world' dichotomy is problematic in the assumption that North America—or any other nation—exhibits cultural uniformity. Augé denounces '[e]very generalised prophecy that is based on a single sector of the social'.[70] He argues that categorical

---

[64] Julian Stallabrass, *Internet Art,* p. 59.

[65] *®™ark,*<http://www.rtmark.com/rtcom/protester>.

[66] Akhil Gupta and James Ferguson, *Beyond Culture,* p. 6.

[67] Marc Augé, *The War on Dreams,* p. 6.

[68] Marc Augé, *The War on Dreams,* p. 6.

[69] Marc Augé, *The War on Dreams,* p. 6.

[70] Marc Augé, *The War on Dreams,* p. 7.

assumptions are 'reckless'[71] in their denial of the difference and 'complexity of innovation within a global totality which is still broadly diversified'.[72] Augé claims:

> [i]t may very well be the case that culture is being dislodged from one locality and placed in
> another, thus generally weakening the ties of culture to particular sites. But this says nothing
> about the sort of culture that is being disembedded or about its origins and destinations.[73]

General and isomorphic accounts of politics and economy negate the 'particular'
divergences of encounter and bodily affect. While Ross Mawdsley's art generates
some user response, his deterministic engagement with digital media often compromises the effectiveness of his message. One might claim that '[w]ithout the ability to reflect, the viewer's perception is continuously structured by the totalizing
environment'.[74] Under these conditions, Scott Weiland contends, 'memory is read-
only'[75] that is, limited in its capacity to respond.®™ark and The Yes Men's expressions however, show little engagement with individual experience and subjective
response. This issue recurs in much of the early digital art, defined by an excitement
for the technology rather than a critical awareness of how it might be used with
subtlety. To this end, digital artists might re-negotiate the boundaries of medium and
message—or politics and affect—in their address of globalisation.

Political Critique

The expressions of Ross Mawdsley, ®™ark and The Yes Men reveal a particular
style of critique; their art is understandable in terms of radical protests to globalisation. The tactical art of Ross Mawdsley, ®™ark and The Yes Men is an irreverent
style that opposes formal systems and structures of control. The digital expressions
of Ross Mawdsley, ®™ark, and The Yes Men also reflects strong postmodern tendencies, in their critique of hegemonic structures and re-situation of media and
contexts. The use of tactics such as pop-ups, hyperlinks, stickiness and hacking
bombard and disorient users, forcibly raising awareness of cultural, political and
economic issues.

The radical art of Ross Mawdsley, ®™ark and The Yes Men's offers Marxist
analyses of capitalism and consumption. ®™ark and The Yes Men's construction
of spoof campaigns against authoritative bodies such the G.W. Bush administration and World Trade Organisation, also engages with Frankfurt School ideals.
Their shocking and subversive styles rely upon current contexts, which inform
their opposition to globalisation and its cultural, political and economic cultures
of production. The themes of Mawdsley's art in particular, demonstrate concern

---

[71] Marc Augé, *The War on Dreams*, p. 7.

[72] Marc Augé, *The War on Dreams*, p. 7.

[73] Jonathon Xavier Inda and Renato Rosaldo, (Eds.), *The Anthropology of Globalization*, p. 13.

[74] Scott Weiland, 'Sense, Memory and Media', <http://www.digitalartsource.com/content/featur/
feat17/feat17p1.html>.

[75] Scott Weiland, 'Sense, Memory and Media', <http://www.digitalartsource.com/content/featur/
feat17/feat17p1.html>.

over globalisation's alleged standardisation of social values through modern mass communications technology and advertising'. His work *Journey into Darkness*, for example, features a razor blade with a corporate logo. Yet, the extent to which Ross Mawdsley and for that matter ®™ark and The Yes Men, actively fulfil the ideal that 'art, if it is truthful, must also reflect decay. And unless it wants to break faith with its social function, art must show the world as changeable. And help to change it',[76] is questionable.

The works of Ross Mawdsley, ®™ark, and The Yes Men strongly oppose formalist notions of art through raising questions about ownership, production and intellectual property, that are paralleled in the debates that they raise through forums on the Internet. Central to their art, is the assumption that images should be freely accessed and manipulated, with the ability to cut and paste text and media and change their meanings. The freedom to appropriate text and imagery is central to ®™ark and The Yes Men's own creative practice. To enforce ownership over their content would contravene their own actions. These ideas reflect their understandings of art as open and collaborative, and their sense of global technology such as the Internet as a liberal and democratic space. A concern for divergent expressions underscores the art of Ross Mawdsley, ®™ark and The Yes Men.

In their criticism of global economics and the affects of capitalism upon developing nations, the artists ®™ark and The Yes Men set up rival 'commercial' websites in order to express their opposition. These artists attempt 'a redefinition of sabotage as social practice, but not in the usual destructive sense, rather in a constructive, innovative and creative way',[77] with the intention of generating 'a movement without organs or organisations, with a variety of perspectives'.[78] Their art sparks dialogues on the structures and hegemonies of the Internet, as a global construct. While expressions of net.artists such as ®™ark and The Yes Men heighten awareness of issues such as economic exploitation and subjugation, the level to which they contribute to the resolution of these issues is questionable. Some of their gestures appear token and cursory, with Mawdsley's depiction of prostitutes and black torsos appearing as somewhat generalised and didactic constructions of the 'other'.

The Centre and the Periphery

The art of Ross Mawdsley, ®™ark, and The Yes Men also converse with postcolonial discourses underpinned by senses of 'centre' and 'periphery'. It reveals an understanding of globalisation as intrinsically inequitable: generating unequal levels of access to the core mechanisms of cultural and economic production: governments, corporations, trade organisations and the mass media. According to this reading, the 'centre' is much more likely to exploit the 'periphery'. As Hannerz elaborates, '[w]hen the center speaks, the periphery listens, and on the whole does

---

[76] Laurie Schneider Adams, *The Methodologies of Art*, p. 62.
[77] Geert Lovink, 'An Insider's Guide to Tactical Media', p. 271.
[78] Geert Lovink, 'An Insider's Guide to Tactical Media', p. 271.

not talk back'[79]. Ross Mawdsley, ®™ark, and The Yes Men's incorporation of post-colonial discourse, connects globalisation's cultural de-territorialisations to earlier colonisations. In the work *Modernism/Postmodernism,* Peter Brooker explores this construction of globalisation, and argues that it is

> intimately connected to the blunt facts of economic, political and military power, that has confirmed America and the West's controlling cultural influence—including the magnetism of its mythologies and the control Western intellectuals exercise over communication systems and regimes of truth.[80]

Brooker presents globalisation as perpetuating the same Western 'mythologies' used to justify earlier projects of imperialism. Yet, the focus upon the West's 'controlling cultural influence' creates a binary between Western cultures and 'the other', implying that globalisation's affects are universally either-or. As Inda and Rosaldo discuss, discourses led by cultural imperialism tend to present dichotomous accounts of globalisation.[81] Central to this understanding, is the role of North American culture and ideology in 'leading to the cultural homogenisation of the world'.[82]

In Chap. 2, alarmism was explored in relation to Naomi Klein's texts, and showed how this approach tends to systemise globalisation according to binary impacts. Yet, as Inda and Rosaldo elaborate, cultural imperialist understandings of globalisation largely reduce the phenomenon to two central affects: the first focusing upon 'the ability of transnational capital, most often seen as American-dominated and mass-mediated, to distribute cultural goods around the globe',[83] and the second, attributing the perceived 'synchronisation of the world to the spread of Western culture more generally'.[84]

The simplification of affect and vocalisation of others' experiences reduces the understanding of the complexity and variability of experiences. In their art, Ross Mawdsley, ®™ark and The Yes Men voice concerns on behalf of culturally, economically and sexually subjugated others, without actively letting them speak. Their approach to globalisation is at times didactic and culturally imperialistic. Their expressions, while aesthetically captivating, show a limited understanding of affect. As Geert Lovink contends, in many early works, active criticism was often replaced with 'the faint hope that if a campaign generates enough velocity and resonates with enough people, it might just take on some of the qualities of a movement'.[85] The art of Ross Mawdsley, ®™ark, and The Yes Men arguably lacks the levels of nuance required to offer an analytical account of globalisation, relying too heavily upon shock tactics and striking aesthetics. Lovink claims that this style is inconsistent with the methods of traditional activists for whom 'the equation is simple: discourse plus art

---

[79] Ulf Hannerz, 'Notes on the Global Ecumene', p. 38.

[80] Peter Brooker, (Ed.), *Modernism/Postmodernism,* p. 24.

[81] Jonathon Xavier Inda and Renato Rosaldo, (Eds.), *The Anthropology of Globalization,* p. 13.

[82] Jonathon Xavier Inda and Renato Rosaldo, (Eds.), *The Anthropology of Globalization,* p. 13.

[83] Jonathon Xavier Inda and Renato Rosaldo, (Eds.), *The Anthropology of Globalization,* p. 13.

[84] Jonathon Xavier Inda and Renato Rosaldo, (Eds.), *The Anthropology of Globalization,* p. 14.

[85] Geert Lovink, *Dark Fiber: Tracking Critical Internet Culture,* Cambridge, Mass., MIT Press, 2002, p. 257.

equals a spectacle'.[86] He observes however, that in more critical forms of art activism, artists 'insist on a distinction between real action and the merely symbolic'.[87]

Arjun Appadurai claims that globalisation is not simply a battleground between 'centre' and 'periphery', nor is it just another term for cultural homogenisation. Through arguing that discourses must not be reduced to 'simple models of push and pull (in terms of migration theory) or of surpluses and deficits (as in traditional models of balance and trade)',[88] Appadurai challenges the tendency to regard 'the dominant' and 'the subjugated', or 'the West' and 'the rest' as discrete concepts. Pierre Bourdieu also offers a far more active position, by contesting the assumption that 'the other' is powerless in critiquing change or that 'economic forces cannot be resisted'.[89] Like Appadurai, Bourdieu contests singular assumptions about globalisation that produce simplistic understandings of affect and the experiences of the 'other'.

Conclusion

Ross Mawdsley, ®™ark and The Yes Men show how digital art is uniquely placed to converse with globalisation—as a phenomenon that has enabled its development and distribution. Their works show the marks of both globalisation and digitisation, and test the relationship between the two phenomena. From engaging with advertising on the Internet, to globally sourcing funds to make their works, crowd-sourcing content and seeking global collaborators, these artists also rely upon globalisation's flows of finance, people, media, information, ideas and technology to make their art and communicate their revolt. They do not, however, critically reflect upon this tension in their works. Equally, the at times didactic reduction of globalisation and digitisation may be partly attributed to their moments of production: the early to mid-1990s. The era was characterised by alarmist accounts of globalisation and the deterministic embrace of digital technology as 'new media'.

As Geert Lovink's argues, 'the current political and social conflicts are way too fluid to be dealt with in such one-dimensional models like propaganda, 'publicity', or 'edutainment'.[90] In other words, a complex topic such as globalisation requires a polymorphic understanding of the different influences at play. As explored in the following chapter, by the late 1990s many artists were beginning to see that globalisation's affects were far too complex to be addressed in uncritical ways. As discussed in relation to iCinema's installation *T_Visionarium II* and Marnix de Nijs' *Beijing Accelerator,* digital artists sought to generate more complex user responses to globalisation, through interactive, haptic and responsive technologies emulated its spatial, temporal and kinetic impacts.

---

[86] Geert Lovink, *Dark Fiber,* p. 257.

[87] Geert Lovink, *Dark Fiber,* p. 257.

[88] Ulf Hannerz, 'Notes on the Global Ecumene', p. 40.

[89] Pierre Bourdieu, 'The Myth of Globalization', p. 31.

[90] Geert Lovink, *Dark Fiber,* p. 261.

Chapter 5
Global Space, Time and Speed: *T_Visionarium II* and *Beijing Accelerator*

Introduction

Following on from the previous chapter that explored radical 1990s art works, this chapter considers two digital installations from the new millennium: *iCinema's T_Visionarium II* and *Marnix de Nijs' Beijing Accelerator*. Both works use dynamic technologies to offer more particular understandings of globalisation's spatial, temporal and kinetic affects. The roles that interactive, haptic and responsive technologies can play in triggering personal and affective responses are examined (Fig. 5.1).

The Construction of *T_Visionarium II*

T_Visionarium II is a live digital environment set within a 9 × 12 m inflatable dome. The 2008 installation features a Graphical User Interface (GUI), composed of a touch screen, headset, projector, and surround audiovisual system. Users enter keywords such as 'environment', 'media' or 'warfare' into a keypad, generating montages of live and archived news footage from around the world. A motorised tilt/pan mechanism enables the projector to beam the imagery across the surface of the dome. The installation integrates old footage with new, blurring senses of present and past, local and global, and the real and hyperreal. The news stories are sourced from diverse channels including the politically conservative North American news station CNN to the more liberal Arabic network Al-Jazeera. As a responsive work, *T_Visionarium II* reacts to bodily movements and lines of gaze. If a user looks at a segment for a length of time, the image increases in size until it dominates the dome. The sound levels also rise, which intensifies the affects. *T_Visionarium II* challenges the binary of 'the West and the rest' present in earlier works, by enabling local and global stories to collide and intersect.

T_Visionarium II was developed in 2001, the same year that the iCinema Centre for Interactive Cinema Research was launched. Based at The University of New South Wales, the research centre was collaboratively formed between the School of

M. Langdon, *The Work of Art in a Digital Age: Art, Technology and Globalisation*,
DOI 10.1007/978-1-4939-1270-4_5, © Springer Science+Business Media New York 2014

Fig. 5.1 Neil Brown, Dennis
Del Favero, Jeffrey Shaw and
Peter Weibel, *T_Visionarium
II,* 2008. (Sara Kolster, '*T_
Visionarium II*', http://sarako.
net/work/tvisionarium-cen-
tury-of-the-city/)

Computer Science and Engineering and the College of Fine Arts. With a council of artists and academics including Jeffrey Shaw, Neil Brown, Dennis Del Favero, and Peter Weibel, iCinema reflects a critical approach to digital art, which locates practice in terms of discourses. The centre's early projects and research interests shaped the development of *T_Visionarium II*. In 2000, for example, Jeffrey Shaw worked with Bernd Lintermann and Volker Kuchelmeister to create *Placeworld*, an adaptable multiple user installation that enabled individuals to interact across space. The use of a dynamic video projection system or 'panoramic navigator' (PN), locates *Placeworld* as a precursor to *T_Visionarium II*.

In making this installation, the artists saw that

> [w]hile the past implementation of the PN used the real environment as its frame of reference for interactive information delivery, this technology could also be an ideal interface to explore and interact with wholly virtual environments.[1]

In making *Placeworld,* the artists wanted to create a PN that would intersect with the touch screen.[2] As *T_Visionarium II* demonstrates, their solution was to 'connect a video projector to the PN, and install a circular projection screen'.[3]

As a product of academic research, *T_Visionarium II* reflects a different approach to some of the other artworks discussed in this text. It converses with theories of distributed aesthetics, digital media and affect, following on from studies conducted at the iCinema Centre for Interactive Cinema Research, The University of New South Wales (UNSW), Australia, ZKM Institute for Visual Media (ZKM), Karlsruhe Germany and EPIDEMIC in Paris. A fibre-optic communications link enabled international participants to collaborate on this globally produced work,

---

[1] Neil Brown, Dennis Del Favero, Jeffrey Shaw and Peter Weibel, 'Placeworld', *iCinema*, <http://www.icinema.unsw.edu.au/projects/prj_placeworld.html>, 2007, (accessed 17 December 2007). This link is no longer active.

[2] Neil Brown et. al, 'Placeworld', <http://www.icinema.unsw.edu.au/projects/prj_placeworld.html>.

[3] Neil Brown et. al, 'Placeworld', <http://www.icinema.unsw.edu.au/projects/prj_placeworld.html>.

defying the traditional art ideals of originality, authenticity and individual author-ship that traditionally defined art. This project would not have been possible with-out digital communications. As iCinema's use of the technology iC_Link reveals, digital programs and networks are facilitating unprecedented levels of global col-laboration. By employing artists, programmers, developers, and theoreticians in the project, the work also unites the fields of art and science, traditionally separated into subjective/objective and rational/abstract dichotomies. The group's engagement with critical discourse is also reminiscent of Frankfurt School works, which sought to unite theory and practice. As a globally produced work, iCinema might force a reconsideration of what art might be in an age of digitisation.

The User Turned Artist

In his text *The Language of New Media*[4] Manovich downplays convergences be-tween past and present, old media and new. Equally, his relegation of message and media to separate fields is not only structurally reductive, but limiting as an account of digitisation's possibilities. If governed by its 'message', a digital work simply be-comes discourse. If perceived purely as a technological object, it is simply 'media'. Yet, one of the elements what makes *T_Visionarium II* 'understandable' as a work of art is its original re-orientation of medium and message. Equally, its critical engage-ment with its moment of production resonates with Frankfurt School expressions. By engaging with earlier practices such as Modern montage and cinema, *T_Vision-arium II* raises critical questions about the nature of art production in a digital age.

Pierre Bourdieu observes how new forms of art often converse with precedent styles. He posits that

> [w]hen a new literary or artistic group makes its presence felt in the field of literary or artistic production, the whole problem is transformed, since its coming into being, i.e. into difference, modifies and displaces the universe of possible options.[5]

However, what is novel about *T_Visionarium II* as a digital work is that it does not 'displace' cinema. While Technological Deterministic expressions may render earlier formats and expression as outmoded, iCinema embraces modern cinema's visual and narrative elements, integrating them into their digital work in a continu-ous rather than disjunctive way.

In terming their collective iCinema, the group recognises and forges links be-tween analogue and digitally interactive cinematic forms. Their use of projection, surround sound, montage and cinematic editing is distinctly cinematic. *T_Vision-arium II's* non-linear narrative resonates with the films of Dali, Lang, Antonioni

---

[4] Lev Manovich, *The Language of New Media*.

[5] Pierre Bourdieu, 'The Field of Cultural Production', in Anthony Giddens (Ed.) *The Polity Reader in Cultural Theory*, Cambridge, Polity Press, 1994, p. 53.

and Lynch's films, which challenge the formal principles of narrative order. Within these works, chaotic and disjunctive narratives make meaning contingent upon individual viewers' senses of space, time and context. In dialogue with Deleuze, iCinema collaborator Dennis Del Favero argues that 'even in conventional cinema the beholder's direct awareness of unfolding events is complicit in bringing narrative to closure'.[6] To this end, the user may be construed as an artistic collaborator—a notion that challenges the dichotomy between artist and spectator.

While *T_Visionarium II* features cinematic elements, its interactive and responsive technologies enable it to go beyond. iCinema's provision of a multi-temporal, 'recombinatory' narrative provides heightened opportunities for user interaction and engagement. The experience of *T_Visionarium II* also differs from that of going to the cinema or theatre. The VR headset physically connects the user to the work, while the GUI directly response to user interactions. Unlike conventional cinema—which is directed at mass audiences—*T_Visionarium II* engages with individual users at the bodily level. The user's literal connection to the art defies the limits of physically detached spectatorship. In making *T_Visionarium II*, iCinema engaged with a principle of transcriptive narrative, sympathetic to the Duchampian idea that 'the artist begins the artwork and the witness completes it'.[7] When understood in this way, *T_Visionarium II* might become what Gene Youngblood terms 'an extension of the cinematic enterprise',[8] enabling users to determine narrative outcomes, 'as they branch through a relatively open-ended cinematic space in ways made possible, but not directly determined, by the author of that space.'[9]

iCinema disrupts the modern principle of 'spectatorship' through transforming the physically detached observer into a corporeally active user. Interactive, multisensory and responsive technologies—such as the PN and search engine—enable users to influence the direction of the artwork's narrative, resolving iCinema's question of 'how to conceptualize and develop Internet interfaces which maximize the seamless integration of interface design and user input.'[10] iCinema argues that such a level of responsiveness would be particularly useful in exploring the realm of digital affect. While writers like Jay Bolter observe that the 'mouse and the pen-based interface allow the user the immediacy of touching, dragging, and manipulating visually attractive ideograms',[11] with those interactions rendering the 'computer interface 'natural' rather than arbitrary',[12] these claims can be contested. By involving users in the artwork's audiovisual evolution, *T_Visionarium II* defies the formal severance of artist and spectator.

---

[6] Dennis Del Favero, 'Digitally Expanded Forms of Cinematic Narration', p. 3.

[7] Gene Youngblood, 'A Medium Matures: Video and Cinematic Enterprise', p. 47.

[8] Gene Youngblood, 'A Medium Matures: Video and Cinematic Enterprise', p. 47.

[9] Gene Youngblood, 'A Medium Matures: Video and Cinematic Enterprise', p. 47.

[10] Neil Brown et al., 'Interactive Narrative as a Multi-Temporal Agency', *Future Cinema*, Cambridge Mass., MIT Press, p. 312.

[11] Jay David Bolter and Richard Grusin, 'Immediacy, Hypermediacy and Remediation', p. 23.

[12] Jay David Bolter and Richard Grusin, 'Immediacy, Hypermediacy and Remediation', p. 23.

Del Favero states that much has been written about the 'death' of cinematic narrative, however 'limited attention has been given to its powerful persistence, albeit in new and emergent forms'.[13] While interactive digital art may draw upon cinematic conventions, principles of immersion and real-time responsiveness enable it to go beyond. As Blais and Ippolito contend,

> [f]ar from the traditional epicentres of artistic production and distribution, creative people sitting at computer keyboards are tearing apart and rebuilding society's vision of itself. Though they may call themselves scientists, activists, or entrepreneurs rather than poets or artists, many of these visionaries are playing the roles of Dante or da Vinci.[14]

iCinema's creative enterprise seems to reflect Youngblood's claim that digital art can resonate with Post-structuralist cinema, as a practice negotiating

> two traditions previously regarded as incompatible—first, the cinematic tradition (including surrealist and mythopoetic traditions of avant-garde personal cinema, whether actor/dialog based or purely formalistic) with its emphasis on illusion, spectacle, and external reference through metaphoric or allegorical narrative; and secondly, the post-modernist tradition in the fine arts, characterized by minimalism, self-reference, and a rigorous, didactic investigation of the structures and materials of the medium. [15]

The installation's integration and investigation of these traditions, connects with Foucault's idea of a 'field of strategic possibilities'[16] or disjunctions, which define the work of art. While Anna Munster questions digital artists need to 'avow the necessity of this historical gesture, the basis of which amounts to a requirement of thinking new media in relation to old media',[17] the severance of art and digital media from historical discourses and forms creates a problematic distance, which not only distances digital expressions from the realm of art, but implies there is nothing about 'new media' that resonates with the old.

In conceiving T_Visionarium II, iCinema felt that '[o]nly within the technical possibilities afforded by digital technology can the beholder, retaining their role as beholder, assert autonomy over the temporal direction of the narrative.'[18] While many aspects of the installation are user directed, iCinema still directs key elements. In recording participants' 'private' encounters, for example, the artists' retain some level of control over their experience. iCinema's choice of archival footage and subscription to certain news channels also means that they have some influence over the searchable content. There is also an expectation about how the user will behave within the installation. It is assumed that they will walk into the dome, don the VR headset and interact with the GUI. If the subject simply entered the space, stood still and watched the narrative unfold, they would thwart iCinema's intentions by becoming a physically detached spectator instead of an active user. The artists

---

[13] Dennis Del Favero, 'Expanded Cinematic Forms of Narration, p. 1.

[14] Joline Blais and Jon Ippolito, At the Edge of Art, p. 7.

[15] Gene Youngblood, 'A Medium Matures', p. 48.

[16] Pierre Bourdieu, 'The Field of Cultural Production', p. 53.

[17] Anna Munster, 'New Media as Old Media', p. 22.

[18] Dennis Del Favero, 'Expanded Cinematic Forms of Narration', p. 3.

also assume that the user will have some digital literacy and proficiency, to enable them to conduct meaningful searches and physically respond to the interface.

Spatial, Temporal and Kinetic Flow

Jeffrey Shaw—one of the founders of iCinema—writes that one of iCinema's key objectives was to create a spatially distributed and multi-temporal environment that not only generated but also captured the affects on film. As discussed in their essay 'Interactive Narrative as a Multi-Temporal Agency', the collaboration wanted to address what they saw to be the limited understandings of multi-modal time systems.[19] By creating seamless spatial and temporal flows, Neil Brown claims that iCinema's recombinatory software provides 'multiple entry and exit points to the information'.[20]

The concept of organism shapes the narrative of *T_Visionarium II*. The work's recombinatory narratives montages and search functions emulate non-linear streams of memory, information processing and conceptualisation. According to iCinema, the installation provides an 'aesthetic transcription',[21] which challenges traditional principles of cinematic duration, authorship and creative control. Manuel An understanding of organism informs the construction of *T_Visionarium II*, as a work that physically embeds the user within the work. By connecting the individual to the dome's multi-sensory environment, the artists converse with De Landa's theory that 'structures as different as rock, animal species, and social classes may be viewed as historical products of the same structure-generating process',[22] for they share moments in time and influence each other. This notion can be applied to digitisation and globalisation, as historically entwined phenomena. De Landa's integration of human and non-human structures can be used to contextualise iCinema's use of 'hard' technologies to facilitate 'soft' and affective experiences. *T_Visionarium II* shows how digital art can generate sensory, intimate and particular encounters of otherwise inaccessible and universal subjects such like globalisation.

The dissolution of borders manifests in the artists' presentation of globalisation as a fluid and 'felt' phenomenon that is simultaneously public and private, local and global, past and present, simulated and real. This fraying of borders converses with Andreas Huyssen's notion of art underscored by an 'evolving dissolution, of aesthetic entropy, a reciprocal emptying out of traditions, a loss of form and truth content'.[23] Flexible dialogues on globalisation parallel new approaches to digital media, which oppose the idea that digital technology only produces positive (or negative) affects. In their rejection of Technological Determinism and the reductive approaches of earlier digital artists discussed in the previous chapter, iCinema cre-

---

[19] Neil Brown et al., 'Interactive Narrative as a Multi-Temporal Agency', p. 4.
[20] Neil Brown et al., 'Interactive Narrative as a Multi-Temporal Agency', p. 312.
[21] Neil Brown et al., 'Interactive Narrative as a Multi-Temporal Agency', p. 1.
[22] Manuel De Landa, *A Thousand Years of Nonlinear History*, p. 271.
[23] Andreas Huyssen, 'Back to the Future', p. 149.

ate spaces 'in between' binaries, opposing accounts that render digital technology as either: controlled or democratic, ordered or manoeuvrable, hostile or tactile, static or transcendent. The artists suggest that Structuralist discourses derived from linguistics and sociology, might limit the range of experiences that digital works like *T_Visionarium II* generate.

T_Visionarium II's contradictory fragmentations and integrations invoke Theodor Adorno's concept of 'Verfransung der Kunste',[24] discussed in Chapter Two. Adorno's 'fraying of borders' manifests in the projection of thematically similar and different images from both near and far contexts. Dynamic constructions of globalisation and digitisation are also evident in the writings of Arjun Appadurai and Gilles Deleuze, as previously discussed. While *T_Visionarium II*'s content might seem chaotic, it also displays strong structural elements as exemplified by the artists' deliberate selection of footage, choice of news stations, and the technical architecture of the work. To this end, the artists explore iterations between flux and astaticism, autonomy and loss of control, physicality and virtuality.

iCinema's installation questions what is real and simulated, through challenging the rootedness of place, regulation of time, calculation of speed and coordination of space. It disrupts users' senses of space and time through the fusion of archived and real-time news images with local and international footage. The installation's 'recombination' of content provides new way of thinking about globalisation as simultaneously local and global, rather than one construct or the other. The saturation of sound and imagery within *T_Visionarium II* emulates the constant flow of information in a global-digital age, and the idea that time is perpetual and space boundary-less. In this way, the work mimics the experience of trawling the Internet or traversing the globe: in an age where global flows of transport, communications, media and ideas have sped up. The kaleidoscope of images drags the user through social, historical and geographical contexts, rupturing our senses of place and reality.

The projection of television images across the surface of the dome also points to the ubiquitous presence of the mass media in a global age. *T_Visionarium II*'s hardware enables the user to search 'through every shot in the last 24 hours to find just those that had fast camera movement, loud noises or both and then having the capacity to combine them in fresh ways.'[25] According to Keir Smith, this kind of art offers 'an alternative, active and potentially creative engagement with a familiar data set, one which may lead to new, unexpected and, often unintended synchroneities.'[26] The user might contemplate their responses to news stories, and

---

[24] Andreas Huyssen, 'Back to the Future', p. 150.

[25] Keir Smith, 'Rewarding the Viuser: A Human-Televisual Data Interface Application', *iCinema*, <http://72.14.253.104/search?q=cache:s3oXhII19jUJ:www.icinema.unsw.edu.au/pdf/rewarding_viuser.pdf+Keir+Smith+'Rewarding+the+Viuser:+A+Human-Televisual+Data+Interface+Application'&hl=en&ct=clnk&cd=1&gl=au>, 2003, (accessed 01 January 2005). This link is no longer active.

[26] Keir Smith, 'Rewarding the Viuser', <http://72.14.253.104/search?q=cache:s3oXhII19jUJ:www.icinema.unsw.edu.au/pdf/rewarding_viuser.pdf+Keir+Smith+'Rewarding+the+Viuser:+A+Human-Televisual+Data+Interface+Application'&hl=en&ct=clnk&cd=1&gl=au>.

consider whether knowing their geographical contexts impact upon their affective responses.

Globalisation and Affective Experience

Through responsive and recombinatory technology, *T_Visionarium II* presents globalisation as a series of individually felt affects. The sequences emulate individual 'recombinations' of current events or the news with 'archived' memories and encounters. The movements and iterations of the user's cognitive processes add unchartered elements to the mix. *T_Visionarium II's* narrative, in that sense, might be viewed as an iterative construct that oscillates between the artists' intention and the audience's response. The process of selecting information from the global media—and subjectively responding to—may be seen to mimic this process.

Through locating the user at the centre of its 'globe', iCinema presents the relationship between the individual and these phenomena as one of mutual affect. While agency may be circumscribed, the individual always retains the power of choice. In the case of this installation, this may be to disengage with, thwart or exit the work. The installation's juxtapositions articulate globalisation as a dynamic, contradictory, and relative phenomenon. To view it as the sum of their affects is to privilege a relational approach centred upon the changeability of contexts, the indeterminacy of human cognition, and variances of subjective response. iCinema's negotiation of objectivity and subjectivity in relation to global news, imagery and ideology, suggests the fallacy of empirical accounts centred upon what globalisation is or is not.

T_Visionarium II creates a dialogue between globalisation and digitisation as contemporaneous phenomena. In contrast to some of the alarmist accounts of globalisation and digitisation that pervaded 1990s art, iCinema shows both phenomena to be complex, often generating contradictory spatial, temporal and kinetic impacts. *T_Visionarium II* shows how digital art can disrupt the binaries of local and global, universal and particular, objective and subjective, and artist and spectator. In challenging reductive accounts, it shows human experience to be unclassifiable—a dynamic construct and the product of iterations between memory, interpretation and affect.

Beijing Accelerator

In a similar way to iCinema's T_Visionarium II, Marnix de Nijs' uses responsive and cinematic media to explore individual responses to globalisation in his 2006 installation *Beijing Accelerator*. Based in the Netherlands, de Nijs' art encourages contemplation of the relationships between bodies and digital technology. He has exhibited his works at festivals and exhibitions around the world. De Nijs' *Beijing Accelerator* explores notions of freedom and alienation, diaspora and dislocation. The installation shows how digital art can function as a unique mode of expression, through physically emulating some of globalisation's spatial, temporal and kinetic impacts. The work directly engages with the individual, transforming them from a physically detached spectator into a corporeally engaged user (Fig. 5.2).

Beijing Accelerator facilitates micro responses to globalisation's macro changes. It converses with Marc Hansen's notion that through 'placing the embodied viewer-participant into a circuit with information, the installations and environments they create function as laboratories for the conversion of information into corporeally apprehensible images.'[27] To this end, what an interactive and responsive work like *Beijing Accelerator* generates 'is less a framed object than an embodied, subjective experience that can only be felt.'[28] This affective account of globalisation counters impersonal and systemic analyses, centred upon political or economic impacts. In this way, it connects with iCinema's T_Visionarium II.

Beijing Accelerator tests the limits of physical endurance and survival, in a world of high-speed technology and media saturation. In reflecting upon this reality, de Nijs claims that '[t]echnology must literally merge, become absorbed into the body so that it becomes a co-determiner of perception.'[29] The installation features a racing car chair, which is fixed to a motorised frame.[30] The frame is controlled by a joystick and spins at different speeds in clockwise and anti-clockwise directions. A 160×120 cm screen is fixed to the frame. The user's objective is to align a square icon on the screen with a magnified image. This is a difficult task given the chair's momentum. It can, however, be achieved if the speed of the chair and flow of images are brought into line. However, a new panorama is soon displayed, which moves at a more rapid speed. There are 6 levels for the user to complete.

In commenting upon *Beijing Accelerator*, Marian Van Mourik claims that it 'clearly belongs to the recreation ground.'[31] Like his installation Run Motherfucker Run (2004) discussed in Chapter Seven, *Beijing Accelerator* has game-like elements. Both installations engage with the body: they draw subjects in and test their physical limits. The sensory experiences generated are reminiscent of early VR arcade games, featuring surround sound and evolving narratives that relied upon movement and interaction. Yet, within both works, it is difficult for the user to gain control over the narrative and 'win'. Their rapid movements can make users feel nauseated or disoriented, forcing their resignation.

Beijing Accelerator builds upon senses of urban tempo and technological change, evident in *Run Motherfucker Run.* The latter installation presented a dark and threatening cityscape. The images changed in size and saturation in response to the user's interaction with the treadmill. Like *Run Motherfucker Run, Beijing Accelerator* presents an ominous urban landscape. The installation was created after the artist's visit to Beijing and 'realization of how quickly the dynamics of a city could

---

[27] Mark B.N. Hansen, *New Philosophy for New Media*, p. 11.

[28] Mark B.N. Hansen, *New Philosophy for New Media*, p. 14.

[29] Marnix De Nijs, *Marnix De Nijs Website*, <http://www.marnixdenijs.nl/>, (accessed 30 September 2010).

[30] Marnix De Nijs, *Marnix De Nijs Website*, <http://www.marnixdenijs.nl/>.

[31] Marian Van Mourik, 'Beijing Accelerator', *Rhizome*, 27 June 2006, <http://rhizome.org/editorial/archive/2006/jun/?page=18>, 2006, (accessed 4 April 2013). This link is no longer active.

Fig. 5.2 Marnix de Nijs,
Beijing Accelerator, 2006.
(Image courtesy of the artist).

transform into such apparent modernism'.[32] De Nijs observed key changes, such as the spread of advertising media and dizzying tempo of life (Fig. 5.3).

After visiting Beijing, de Nijs noted that globalisation's temporal and kinetic flows were influencing human behaviours, by leading to 'such things as *speed dating* (for our love lives), *power naps* (for our health and exercise), *quality time* (for being with the family) and *fast food* (for staving off hunger).'[33] The artist claimed that 'this desire to control and optimise every aspect of our lives is matched by a nagging feeling that we never have enough time.'[34]In reflecting upon these changes, he notes that '[o]ne of the characteristics of a technological culture is that change is constant. Everyone who wants to keep pace is continually required to adjust; which does not happen automatically and can, in time lead to cultural-pathological anomalies.'[35] Like iCinema, the artist locates technological change in historical terms, noting that 'travellers had to get used to the first trains and aeroplanes. The introduction of such travel technology initially led to disorientation and required a new outlook.'[36]

Beijing Accelerator was featured in Strozzina Gallery's exhibition *As Soon as Possible: Acceleration in Contemporary Society* (Florence, 14 May—18 July 2010). The exhibition explored the influences of high-speed media and connective technologies upon urban lives.[37] Some of the artworks showed how professional demands had become so great, that workers were left feeling physically unable to keep up. As the curators observed, the perceived intensification of time and speed were leading to 'widespread anxiety and depression which are frequent indicators

---

[32] Marnix De Nijs, *Marnix De Nijs Website*, <http://www.marnixdenijs.nl/>.

[33] No author, *Strozzina Gallery Website*, <www.strozzina.org/asap/e_index.php>, (accessed 30 September 2010).

[34] No author, *Strozzina Gallery Website*, <www.strozzina.org/asap/e_index.php>.

[35] Marnix De Nijs, *Marnix De Nijs Website*, <http://www.marnixdenijs.nl/>.

[36] Marnix De Nijs, *Marnix De Nijs Website*, <http://www.marnixdenijs.nl/>.

[37] No author, *Strozzina Gallery Website*, <www.strozzina.org/asap/e_index.php>.

Fig. 5.3 Marnix de Nijs,
Beijing Accelerator, 2006.
(Image courtesy of the artist).

of the malaise of people living on the edge of their own potential in a high-speed world.'[38] This is a strong theme within de Nijs' art.

In his astatements, de Nijs' has also expressed concern about our degraded environment, which is unable to meet human demands. Through its physical simulation of lives 'sped up' *Beijing Accelerator* encourages the critique of a perceived new speed of existence. It shows how globalisation's spatial, temporal and kinetic changes are negatively impacting upon urban life, in leading to feelings of cultural dislocation, social alienation, or even physically illness if the user's body succumbs to the work's dizzying effects. *Beijing Accelerator* shows how increased flows of finance, information and technology are heightening urban tempos and generating time-poor 'wage slaves'.

This sense connects with Paul Virilio's observations about the negative impacts of global media and technology upon urban life. As interpreted by Rob Bartram, 'Virilio has long argued that dromology, time compression and visualizing technology are closely linked concepts that together have created a new ocular reality'.[39] Bartram builds upon Virilio's thesis by positing 'that a new ocular centrism has emerged in the last ten years that has reconfigured the way in which we view [the] world and dramatically changed the way in which we participate in it'.[40] There is a strong sense of 'dromocracy' or as Virilio terms, 'the dictatorship of speed governed by the principle that "if time is money, speed is power"'.[41] These tensions are strongly evident in de Nijs' art.

Beijing Accelerator raises concerns about globalisation's spatial, temporal and technological impacts of upon bodies and consciousnesses. It converses with alarmist critiques globalisation, centred upon senses of alienation and disconnection.

---

[38] No author, *Strozzina Gallery Website*, <www.strozzina.org/asap/e_index.php>.

[39] Rob Bartram, 'Visuality, Dromology and Time Compression: Paul Virilio's New Ocularcentrism, *Time & Society*, September 2004 vol. 13, no. 2–3, pp. 286.

[40] Rob Bartram, 'Visuality, Dromology and Time Compression'.

[41] No author, *Strozzina Gallery Website*, <www.strozzina.org/asap/e_index.php>.

While in many ways this is reductive, *Beijing Accelerator* does show individual perception pertains not only to how 'not external stimuli are interpreted by the five senses, but also the feelings that come from within the body itself, the information that is derived from one's own muscles and nerves (the technical term being proprioception).'[42] De Nijs' work encourages instinctual responses, in generating primordial feelings such as apprehension, alarm and fear. *Beijing Accelerator* provides understanding of the global city, as a familiar yet radically accelerated space.

While many elements of the installation are artist directed, its 'recombinatory' narrative framework—to borrow the term from iCinema—encourages unique encounters of globalisation. The user as 'beholder' directs the narrative revelation through their physical movements and choices. In promoting particular and affective experiences, *Beijing Accelerator* emphasises the arbitrariness of affect and the overlapping of binary constructs such as the real and the simulated, the physical and virtual. However, it does not go as far as *T_Visionarium II,* which challenges either-or accounts of globalisation through emphasising the fluid interchanges of memory and encounter, as well differential human response. iCinema's art also blurs the constructs of past and present, local and global, cultural nearness and distance. By creating new spaces 'in between', it points to the fallacy of alarmist accounts such as de Nijs', which seem to assume that all experiences of globalisation are negative or potentially injurious.

Conclusion

As with all art, it is possible that users of *T_Visionarium II* and *Beijing Accelerator* will not respond as the artists intended. Both works feature game-like interfaces, and incorporate cinematic principles of projection, surround sound and immersion. It seems that the artists' intentions are for individuals to experience emulations of globalisation, including the 'speeding' up of time, compression of space and saturation of images. Yet, these messages could be lost if users chose to only experience the works' playful elements. As the blogger 'Nova' writes, *Beijing Accelerator* is '[g] iddy, disorienting and fun, it's tempting to ignore what the artist intends and just spin as fast as possible while trying not to fall off.'[43] As argued in Chapter Two, this points to the importance of form and function in the understanding of digital art. With these understandings in mind, the next chapter considers how global cities can provide new ways of thinking about globalisation, with reference to the exhibition *Metropolis.*

---

[42] Marnix De *Nijs, Marnix De Nijs Website,* <http://www.marnixdenijs.nl/>.

[43] Nova, 'Sona8', *TagR.tv,* <http://tagr.tv/tag/beijing-accelerator/>, 2008, (accessed 4 April 2013).

Chapter 6
Metropolis: Imagining The Global City

Introduction

This chapter explores the exhibition *Metropolis* held at the National Gallery of Victoria's (NGV) in 2004. It focuses on how interactive and immersive digital media can re-imagine human life within the global city. The predominantly North American cinematic works range from animation to documentary. All are connected by the central question of what is the nature of existence within the global city? They show lives punctuated by the need to connect, questions of cultural identity, global economies, terrorism and the remembrance of home. Each artwork presents a different vision of the global city, shaped by heightened flows of people, media, finance, ideas and technologies.

The nine works discussed are: Shoba's *Blowing Zen* (2003), Nicholas Golebiewski's *This is Where I Live* (2003), Tom Otterness' *Nine Eleven* (2003), Cristian Alexa's *10-Second Couples* (2000), Abbey Williams' *YES* (2002), Andy Diaz Hope *Financial District Infiltration: Everybody is Somebody's Terrorist* (2004), PHAT's *Harlem: The Ghetto Fabulous* (2004), Beat Streuli's *Pallasades 05-01-01* (2001) and Brian Alfred's *Overload* (2004). Each artwork presents a different vision of the global city, shaped by heightened flows of people, media, finance, ideas and technologies (Fig. 6.1).

The films selected by curators Anonda Bell and Kelly Gellatly use different techniques to present individual articulations of life in the global city. Many of the works challenge formal constructions of art, conversing with Walter Benjamin's sense that

> [a]s it became more feasible to reproduce works of art (by mechanical means) and to arrange for exhibits (through improved communication and more efficient travel), art lost its ritual aura and became a political commodity.[1]

In as much as they are cinematic works, the *Metropolis* films are performance pieces, literary narratives, soundscapes and memoirs, which share social and political messages about life in a global era. As these expressions reveal, digital art can provide a unique platforms for the intimate contemplation of globalisation's impacts.

---

[1] Laurie Schneider Adams, *The Methodologies of Art*, p. 63.

M. Langdon, *The Work of Art in a Digital Age: Art, Technology and Globalisation*,
DOI 10.1007/978-1-4939-1270-4_6, © Springer Science+Business Media New York 2014

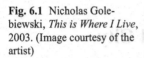

Fig. 6.1 Nicholas Golebiewski, *This is Where I Live*, 2003. (Image courtesy of the artist)

The Metropolis artists use digital technology to emulate and articulate urban shifts. Some of the artworks—like Nicholas Golebiewski's *This is Where I Live*—suggest that globalisation creates new spaces 'in between'. With the rise of 'glocalisation', city dwellers can feel simultaneously globalised and localised. This contradiction is evident in Andy Diaz Hope's, *Financial District Infiltration: Everybody is Somebody's Terrorist*, which creates inter-spaces in its negotiation of the local/global, past/present, and real/simulated. In this way, some of the *Metropolis* works mirror iCinema's more flexible approaches to globalisation, as explored in the previous chapter.

Constructing the City

The *Metropolis* films engage with the concept of the global city as a space fundamentally defined by heightened flows of technology, people, finance, information, and ideas. An awareness of globalisation's social, political and technological impacts is evident in many of the works. While similar urban affects have been documented in earlier periods of time, the scale of influence is unprecedented. As explored in Chap. 2, Modern industrialization also altered popular senses of urban space and time. The advent of Modernism shifted perceptions of the metropolis and the role of citizens. The notion of the *flânerie* centred on the idea of the citizen observing the city's altered landscape. This awareness inspired new thoughts about urban life in art and literature.

As Lewis Mumford observed, the city was 'the seat of the temple, the market, the hall of justice, the academy of learning'.[2] Within its streets, 'human experience is transformed into viable signs, symbols, patterns of conduct, systems of order'.[3] This

---

[2] Lewis Mumford, *The Culture of Cities,* New York, Harcourt Brace and Co., 1938, p. 4.

[3] Lewis Mumford, *The Culture of Cities,* p. 4.

articulation resonates with Stuart Hall's construction of global cities, as cultural, political and economic hubs operating as

> centres of political power, both national and international, and of the organizations related to government; centres of national and international trade...centres of banking, insurance, and related financial services; centres of advanced professional activity of all kinds...centres of information gathering and diffusion, through publishing and the mass media; centres of conspicuous consumption, both of luxury goods for the minority and of mass-produced goods for the multitude; and centres of arts, culture, and entertainment.[4]

The films discussed in this chapter engage with earlier notions of the city, as well as present and future possibilities.

As explored in relation to the exhibition *Metropolis,* analyses centred upon the dynamics of global cities, provide means for understanding globalisation as a series of local events and particular affects. This method also offers a different approach to the systemic construction of globalisation in terms of the broad political responses or financial manoeuvres of nation states. An approach centred upon the global city, also avoids the simplicity of 'backlash accounts', which focus exclusively on the actions of corporations or nations states. These understandings can downplay the autonomy of local services and industries—such as small-scale factories and financial markets within the city—which are also part of globalisation's tale. In her text *Cities in a World Economy, Sociology for a New Century,* Saskia Sassen argues that analyses of globalisation centred upon the global city, can add a micro or 'human' element to understanding.[5]

Using the global city as a site of reference, Sassen shifts the emphasis away from universal to particular contexts. In *Cities in a World Economy*, she contends that the inclusion of the city to analyses of globalisation adds three important elements.[6] Firstly, it provides more intimate and particular contexts for analysis. Secondly, it shifts the focus away from top-down examinations centred upon governments, corporations and other political-economic power brokers. Lastly, it allows for the exploration of the human 'microgeographies' existing within local spaces.[7] Through her analysis of cities, Sassen contests positivist accounts centred upon universal assumptions. The *Metropolis* films engage with the cultural flows of global cities. Nicholas Golebiewski's film *This is Where I Live,* for example, explores the layering of traditions and cultural practices in New York. As cultural microcosms of globalisation, global cities can offer new ways of accessing this macro phenomenon.

The global city shares many of the same qualities of the classical metropolis. In classical antiquity, the city was at the helm of social, political and economic exchange. While ancient ideas of the metropolis remained, the rise of industrialism

---

[4] Stuart Hall 'Globalization and the World Cities', in F-C Lo and Y-M Yeung (Eds.), *Globalisation and the World of Large Cities,* Tokyo, United Nations University Press, 1998, p. 17.

[5] Saskia Sassen, *Cities in a World Economy, Sociology for a New Century,* Second Ed., Thousand Oaks, Pine Forge Press, 2000.

[6] Saskia Sassen, *Cities in a World Economy*.

[7] Saskia Sassen, 'Globalization and the Formation of Claims'.

in the late nineteenth century transformed the city through increasing human flows, and strengthening systems of finance, politics, transport and communications. Modernity brought an eclecticism of class, ethnicity, and political perspective to the city's space. As Lewis Mumford discusses, this shift in social landscape inspired new ideas about humanity, and its potential within the urban realm.[8] The creation of the modern metropolis occurred in historical synchrony with the rise of capitalism as a form of economic exchange.[9] The rise of capitalism arguably transformed the city site, centralising production and creating a hierarchy of production and exchange.

While the global city reflects many of the same functions and features of the classical metropolis, digitisation heightens many of these flows and contributes to intensified experiences of globalisation's impacts. However, globalisation's impacts can be contradictory. It can lead to new forms of connection—online for example—enabling individuals to come together in defiance of geographical borders. Yet at the same time, globalisation can also heighten senses of alienation, as Nebojš a Šerić Shoba (Shoba)'s film *Blowing Zen* explores.

Shoba: *Blowing Zen*

Shoba moved to New York from Sarajevo in 2002. In *Blowing Zen*, he offers a post-apocalyptic vision of New York, which is both recognisable and obscure. Released in 2003, the film presents Times Square as a metaphor for Western cultures of consumption. Instead of being packed with consumers, the iconic space has been emptied of human and vehicular traffic. The only movement within the square is the flicker of advertising imagery, and continuous cycle of traffic lights moving from green to red. The sounds of urban hustle are replaced with the Zen-like sounds of an Oriental flute. With the frenetic flows of space, time and speed diminished, Time Square might be seen as a contemplative space. Shoba's re-arrangement is reminiscent of Situationist art styles, which used irony to generate emotive responses from audiences (Fig. 6.2).

Blowing Zen presents New York as a city that privileges materialism over humanism. The empty streets are overlooked by advertising images and corporate logos. In the wake of its citizens, billboards for global brands such as TDK, Panasonic and Swatch blink in vain. By removing the consumers that contextualise them, the advertisements become meaningless images. There is nothing in this urban space that is culturally defining or unique. The city appears like any other. Its billboards advertise the same products found everywhere, making New York materially indistinguishable from global cities such as Sydney or Tokyo. With New York emptied of consumers, *Blowing Zen* might leave its audience to question: to what extent does

---

[8] For an historical exploration of the city see: Lewis Mumford's *The City in History*.

[9] Lewis Mumford, *The City in History*.

Fig. 6.2 Shoba, *Blowing Zen*, 2003. (http://www.ngv.vic. gov.au/metropolis/resources/ rb_metropolis.pdf)

consumerism overshadow cultural imperatives? And, what are the elements that make cities culturally rich and generative spaces?

In *Blowing Zen*, scrolling stock prices and neon news headlines confirm Jean Baudrillard's fear that in a digital age, simulation will come to replace human reality.[10] Shoba's art engages with his concern that in an era of digitisation,

> old distinctions and orientations are abolished: objects no longer relate at all to their processes of human production, there is a loss of emotional content and of 'objective' or critical distance.[11]

The transmission of imagery from 11 September 2001 was extremely rapid—facilitated by global news networks and online sharing. Straight after that tragedy, neon depictions of the U.S. flag and the slogan 'God Bless America' flooded advertising billboards, raising questions about the boundaries between cultural and commercial space. *Blowing Zen* conveys the powerful message that despite the influence of global advertising, finance, technology and media, the city is nothing without its citizens.

In *Blowing Zen*, the billboard avatars seem to replace life itself, while the reflections of the U.S. flag in the mirrored glass of a skyscraper act serve as haunting reminders of a culture left behind. With the city devoid of its people, the Modern notion of *flânerie* is given currency in *Blowing Zen*. The early Twentieth century notion of the *flâneur* was centred upon the idea of urban spectatorship. Within the film, the concept is reversed with the city left to 'look back'. The concern that virtual simulation is negatively impacting upon humanity is a key theme. Shoba's art raises the question what happens to a city when it is emptied of its people? This

---

[10] See Baudrillard's theories of digital simulation in: Jean Baudrillard, 'From 'Simulcra and Simulations'.

[11] Jean Baudrillard, From 'Simulcra and Simulations', p. 22.

question was raised in the wake of 11 September 2001. It is said that an eerie hush befell New York, as it was evacuated.

Arguably, *Blowing Zen* functions as something more than just 'art for art's sake'. It encourages the viewer to question the impacts of globalisation upon the city. In contemplating Times Square, Shoba described 'thousands of people are stepping over your feet, pushing you around. Noise is unbearable, smell of burned meat from nearby food stands, hundreds of advertising panels decorated by millions of flashing lights, outbursts of shopping hysteria'.[12] In this way, *Blowing Zen* connects with Ernst Fischer's notion introduced in Chap. 2, that art is not just about beautiful aesthetics—if it's truthful 'it must also reflect decay'.[13]

Nicholas Golebiewski: *This is Where I Live*

In contrast to *Blowing Zen*, Nicholas Golebiewski's 2003 film *This is Where I Live* explores some of the private spaces where globalisation manifests. A high level of intimacy is achieved through first person narration and handheld camera work, which invite us into the filmmaker's world. While we never see the narrator, he directly addresses us as he takes us on a tour of his Brooklyn apartment. A nostalgic feel is achieved through black and white film, a 1950s voice over style, and depictions of old photographs, souvenirs and artefacts. The narrator's instructive tone is reminiscent of early television and radio broadcasts. In this way, Golebiewski emphasises the roles of individual memories, interpretations and encounters in articulations of globalisation (Fig. 6.3).

As explored in Chap. 2, globalisation can elicit different responses, ranging from senses of spatial nearness to distance, temporal stillness and speed, feelings of global connection and alienation, or the feeling that the world as known has changed. These affects can alter our perceptions of cultural constructs such as individuality, reality, history, culture, community and homeland. The concept of home features strongly in Golebiewski's work. Contrary to alarmist accounts by writers like Naomi Klein, who perceives globalisation as de-territorialising, *This is Where I Live* shows how it can humanise and encourage human connections, through highlighting the powerful persistence of local rituals, unique traditions, private memories and subjective interpretations. While Shoba's work presents alienation and the triumph of commerce over cultural generation, Golebiewski's offers an account of globalisation centred upon personal, localised and culturally divergent responses.

This is Where I Live shows how the global city can provide heightened opportunities for cultural exchange. The narrator discusses his own eclectic background, with reference to personal photographs and effects. As curator Anonda Bell suggests, Golebiewski's art raises questions about cultural identity in a global age, and

---

[12] Anonda Bell, '*Metropolis* Exhibition Brochure', <http://www.ngv.vic.gov.au/metropolis/resources/rb_metropolis.pdf>, (accessed 10 December 2006). This link is no longer active.

[13] Laurie Schneider Adams, *The Methodologies of Art*, p. 62.

Fig. 6.3 Nicholas Golebiewski, *This is Where I Live*, 2003. (http://www.ngv.vic.gov.au/metropolis/resources/rb_metropolis.pdf)

seems to ask: '[a]t which point or in what generation does an individual have the right to feel they belong to a place with all the responsibility, pressures and pleasures that this entitlement may entail?'[14] The film asks what it might mean to be a New Yorker—versus a North American—and creates space for divergent responses.

The existence of cultural precincts—such as Little Italy and Chinatown—highlights the complexity of cultural identities in a global age, which are often shaped by competing influences. *This is Where I Live* challenges the binary of local/global through providing a more iterative construction of cultural identity in a time of globalisation. Through raising issues of ethnic versus national identity, the film suggests that the global city creates new possibilities for us to 'narrate' our own cultural realities.

As previously discussed in this text, Inda and Rosaldo observe that globalisation's 'deterritorialization of culture is invariably the occasion for the reinsertion of culture in new time-space contexts'.[15] Golebiewski 're-inserts' the individual in the global landscape through revealing its capacity to generate highly personal and intimate 'time-space contexts'. Through this process, he counters reductive accounts of globalisation, focused upon universal outcomes and affects. While top-down analyses may offer macro explanations of globalisation, their grand claims leave little room for the contrary iterations of individual response. As a more private expression, *This is Where I Live* offers a different account of globalisation.

---

[14] Anonda Bell, '*Metropolis* Exhibition Brochure', <http://www.ngv.vic.gov.au/metropolis/resources/rb_metropolis.pdf>.

[15] Jonathon Xavier Inda and Renato Rosaldo, (Eds.) *The Anthropology of Globalization,* p. 11.

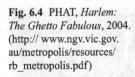

Fig. 6.4 PHAT, *Harlem: The Ghetto Fabulous*, 2004. (http:// www.ngv.vic.gov. au/metropolis/resources/ rb_metropolis.pdf)

In conversing with globalisation and its urban impacts, Golebiewski creates contrasts between public and private realms. Point of view camera gives the impression that the narrator is peering down at the street, concealed from view. We share this vision, and observe the bustling flow of metropolitan life. Within the global city, the narrator suggests the need for introspective escape, at one point joking that 'the only place to go for privacy is an uninteresting art exhibition'.[16] The contrasts between interior and exterior space encourage us to consider internal and intuitive responses to globalisation.

Montage sequences emulate the layering of the past, present and imagined. Like iCinema's *T_Visionarium II, This is Where I Live* prompts contemplation of how globalisation can affect constructions of cultures and ourselves. The film provides an intensely personal expression of life within the frantic city of New York. Like *Blowing Zen,* Golebiewski's presentation of urban calm contrasts with images of chaos and commotion. Yet, while Shoba offers a de-humanised vision, Golebiewski's New York is personally and culturally generative.

PHAT: *Harlem: The Ghetto Fabulous*

PHAT offer a different vision of New York in their 2004 film *Harlem: The Ghetto Fabulous*. The collective, formed of David Mesfin, Nathaniel Belcher, Adam Wheeler and Stephen Slaughter, explore Harlem's evolution. The film documents the neighbourhood's transition from a ghetto to gentrified precinct. Within the work, Harlem is presented as a site of great cultural significance: a place where innovations in art and music have emerged alongside the revolutionary ideas of political leaders like Martin Luther King and Malcolm X (Fig. 6.4).

The film's narrator describes how Harlem was once a border town, 'watched over' by its wealthier cousin Manhattan. It was the seat of The Black Rebellion of the 1960s, characterised by backlashes to racial intolerance and the government's

---

[16] Anonda Bell, '*Metropolis* Exhibition Brochure', <http://www.ngv.vic.gov.au/metropolis/resources/rb_metropolis.pdf>.

failure to address social, political and economic inequities. Through tracing the 'gentrification' of Harlem, PHAT suggests that this traditionally Black American locale is now becoming culturally standardised. The conclusion of the film shows an altered landscape: a gentrified city where glamorous penthouse apartments are built on former project sites. Provoking thoughts of cultural territorialisation, PHAT's art connects with the expressions of Ross Mawdsley, ®™ark and The Yes Men examined in Chap. 4.

PHAT uses music to signal a historical progression in the city's development, and to point to its changing social identity. 1920s jazz is replaced by rap and more recent hip-hop. *Harlem: The Ghetto Fabulous* shows the city's transformation from a poor and disenfranchised black American heartland, to an increasingly prosperous and sanitised white neighbourhood. It suggests that consumerist values have had a negative impact upon Harlem's local culture. The film shows how Harlem—once a radical Black American site—is becoming a culturally standardised space.

Harlem: The Ghetto Fabulous challenges the motives of urban developers, provoking thoughts of cultural appropriation, de-territorialisation and imperialism. To this end, the film presents a somewhat alarmist account of globalisation, whereby local cultures are threatened by Capitalist imperatives. In exploring the phenomenon's impacts upon urban spaces, the film engages with Inda and Rosaldo's question: 'is there a power geometry to globalisation and what might it be?'[17] PHAT's presentation of Harlem suggests that cultural influence has traditionally flowed in one direction—from the majority to minority.

Within the film, there is an ironic power shift. The final scene presents affluent Black Americans living the 'American Dream'. It shows how globalisation has created a new power divide: between rich and poor city dwellers. This points to a new kind of cultural imperialism—one that is internally rather than externally applied. While contemporary Harlem is presented as a city empowered by its 'ghetto status', the glamour ascribed is simplistic. PHAT shows Harlem to be a kind of post *fin de siècle* Paris enjoying its *belleépoque*. In showing how 'gangster culture' has infiltrated music and art, PHAT shows Harlem to have a profane vibrancy. As the title affirms, there is an assumption that the city was 'fabulous' just the way it was. As the final sequence demonstrates, global economic values have created new urban imbalances, not just between Black and White, but Black and Black. However, the complex dynamics of affluence versus poverty, and agency versus powerlessness, are given only a cursory address within the film.

Beat Streuli: *Pallasades 05-01-01*, 2001

In 2001, Swiss artist Beat Streuli created his cinematic work *Pallasades 05-01-01*. Set within the city of Birmingham, the piece depicts the incessant flows of people moving through a shopping centre. Commissioned by the gallery Ikon, the film shows the great diversity of people sharing the same city space. Women in hijabs

---

[17] Jonathon Xavier Inda and Renato Rosaldo (Eds.), *The Anthropology of Globalization*, p. 12.

Fig. 6.5 Beat Streuli, *Pallasades 05-01-01*, 2001. (http://www.beatstreuli.com/beatstreuli/instal-lations_data/2006krakow04.jpg)

walk alongside men of African descent, while Indian women in saris cross paths with Western teenagers on their mobile phones. As Golebiewski's film *This is Where I Live* similarly explores, global cities are defined by cultural dynamism (Fig. 6.5).

Pallasades 05-01-01 engages with the human momentum of the global city. It supports an ethnographic approach to globalisation, confirming Saskia Sassen's no-tion that as nations break down, and no longer act as the sole definers of cultural identity, 'a new geography of politics linking subnational spaces takes shape'.[18] Globalisation, Sassen suggests, can give us new opportunities for us to combine cultural practices and to consider ourselves as citizens of the world. This idea reso-nates with Inda and Rosaldo's sense that while globalisation can be de-territorialis-ing, it can also provide opportunities for new forms of cultural remix.[19]

In focussing upon individuals, Streuli offers a more localised and particular ac-count of globalisation. In many of Streuli's works, photographic and cinematic me-dia are used to explore life in the city. His art depicts how 'a wide reservoir of pos-sibilities is best and most easily encountered in the centre, the meeting point of the city'.[20] *Pallasades 05-01-01* captures the banal realities of everyday people. Every-one walks with purpose, seemingly caught in the human current. Seemingly oblivi-ous to the camera, the film shows urban dwellers going about their usual business: conversing with friends or chatting on their mobile phones. Although their actions are banal and unspectacular, human curiosity draws us. The camera offers close-ups on the faces of individuals, caught in the throng of the urban crowd. As the masses of faces approach the camera lens, there is the potential to feel overwhelmed. Yet, the use of silence and slow motion effect softens the impact of the onslaught.

---

[18] Saskia Sassen, 'Globalization and the Formation of Claims', p. 87.

[19] Jonathon Xavier Inda and Renato Rosaldo (Eds.), *The Anthropology of Globalization*, p. 10.

[20] Beat Streuli, '*The Pallasades 05-01-01*', *National Gallery of Victoria*, <http://www.ngv.vic. gov.au/metropolis/resources/rb_metropolis.pdf>, 2004, (accessed 19 April 2013). This link is no longer active.

Fig. 6.6 Tom Otterness, *Nine Eleven*, 2003. (Image courtesy of the artist)

Pallasades 05-01-01 was publicly screened close to the shopping centre that it depicts. One BBC reviewer noted how '[w]hen you move closer, you don't want to watch it for too long while everyone else is rushing past you in a number of different directions'.[21] To this end, the use of silence and slow motion ironically emphasises the speed and sheer force of people moving through the space. A telephoto lens allows Streuli to achieve a strong, and almost overbearing sense of proximity. It also enables the artist to capture people unaware, and offer a more natural eye-witness account of life in a time of globalisation.

Tom Otterness: *Nine Eleven*

In his 2003 animated film *Nine Eleven*, Tom Otterness claims that New York is still 'the great predictor'[22] of Western trends. Like Shoba's *Blowing Zen*, the global city is presented as a cultural icon. Many felt that New York was targeted on 11 September 2001 because it symbolised North American and the Western values. As Otterness' film suggests, the crumbling of the World Trade Centre's twin towers led some artists to question the city's resilience and indestructibility (Fig. 6.6).

Nine Eleven has a fairy tale quality about it: it is in some ways reminiscent of *Gulliver's Travels*.[23] It also has strong resonances with the Biblical story of the

---

[21] 'Spinky', 'Beat Streuli—The Pallasades 05-01-01 2001', *BBC The Collective,* March 2004, <http://www.bbc.co.uk/dna/collective/A2373103>, 2004, (accessed 19 April 2013).

[22] Anonda Bell, '*Metropolis* Exhibition Brochure', <http://www.ngv.vic.gov.au/metropolis/resources/rb_metropolis.pdf>.

[23] Jonathon Swift, *Gulliver's Travels,* World's Classics, New York, Oxford University Press, 1998.

tower of Babel—the tower that watched over the city and came crashing down. The affect is to make the audience question the lines between fact and fiction, the real, and the simulated. In reflecting upon his art, Otterness notes that 'there's a dark edge underneath a lot of the work. You can never predict what is going to happen day-to-day, so this work is all kind of disjointed vignettes, like small chunks of meaning'.[24]

The use of animation in *Nine Eleven* has a disquieting affect, given the horror and brutality of the terrorism attacks. The film features simple, coloured figures that leap from buildings with clasped hands. The animated characters seem to make the events of 11 September 2001 all the more sinister. By using animation—an innocent format designed for children—Otterness generates shocking affects, reminiscent of Situationist art. In watching the film, there are moments where the audience might question what they are seeing, forcing them to construct new contexts of understanding. That confusion mirrors the disbelief that many viewers would have experienced as they watched live footage of the attacks on their television and computer screens. The imagery of 11 September 2001 spread quickly across the world, via global news networks and Internet sites.[25] The rapid dissemination of content confirmed Appadurai's contention that in an age of globalisation, media, ideas and information move rapidly.

In the past, Tom Otterness' art has taken on a number of forms. It has appeared in galleries as well as informal spaces like New York subways, challenging traditional expectations senses of art and exhibition. In *Nine Eleven* animation generates a new kind of shock, which encourages the viewer to question the appropriateness of the global televising of traumatic events. To this end, the film affirms Jameson's claim discussed in Chap. 2 that 'there is very little in either the form or the content of contemporary art that contemporary society finds intolerable and scandalous'.[26] Whether Otterness' presentation of 11 September 2001 is appropriate, however, is up to the viewer to judge.

Andy Diaz Hope: *Financial District Infiltration: Everybody is Somebody's Terrorist*

Andy Diaz Hope also engages with the 11 September 2001 attacks in *Financial District Infiltration: Everybody is Somebody's Terrorist*. His 2004 film deals with the social repercussions after the event, and the suspicion that pervaded the West

---

[24] Anonda Bell, '*Metropolis* Exhibition Brochure', <http://www.ngv.vic.gov.au/metropolis/resources/rb_metropolis.pdf>.

[25] For images of September 11 as captured by news sites see: <http://www.september11news.com/AttackImages.htm>, *September 11 News,* (accessed 16 December 2007).

[26] Fredric Jameson 'PostModernism and Consumer Society', p. 124.

Fig. 6.7 Andy Diaz Hope,
Financial District Infiltra-
tion: Everybody is Some-
body's Terrorist, 2004.
(Image courtesy of the artist)

that 'anyone could be a terrorist'.[27] This fear took hold at the level of the State, with Western governments issuing warnings to citizens to report seemingly 'suspicious' behaviours of neighbours, shopkeepers and colleagues. As the curator Anonda Bell states, '[f]or many people those events of 2001 continue to evoke a sense of utter sadness and anger, and a suspicion of those we do not directly know'.[28] In the wake of the tragedy, Bell notes how 'the social perception of threat has a power almost equivalent to that of the threat itself'.[29] Within the film, a masked man in a business suit casually walks the city's streets. Suspicion turns to comical disbelief as pedestrians encounter this 'everyday' terrorist (Fig. 6.7).

The film's title points to a key theme within the work: the influence of global economic flows within the city. The balaclava worn by the businessman is symbolic not just of terrorism, but the perceived 'facelessness' of corporate culture. As Bell

---

[27] Anonda Bell, '*Metropolis* Exhibition Brochure', <http://www.ngv.vic.gov.au/metropolis/resources/rb_metropolis.pdf>.

[28] Anonda Bell, '*Metropolis* Exhibition Brochure', <http://www.ngv.vic.gov.au/metropolis/resources/rb_metropolis.pdf>.

[29] Anonda Bell, '*Metropolis* Exhibition Brochure', <http://www.ngv.vic.gov.au/metropolis/resources/rb_metropolis.pdf>.

observes the mask highlights the generic or 'bland nature of the suited brigade of corporate workers who frequent city spaces',[30] with the same anonymity as terrorists. The subject's corporate 'uniform' makes him indistinguishable from the other financial district workers. If not for his mask, he would probably go unnoticed.

A camera traces the suspected terrorist's banal movements. He casually checks his watch, reads the newspaper, completes an ATM transaction and crosses the road, unaware of the attention he is attracting. What makes the piece comical is the normality with which he pursues his daily activities. As he moves through the streets of San Francisco, the camera records the mixed reactions of passers-by—from shock to apathy. Shot at close range, the camera captures the suspect's every move. The jarring hand-held camera work creates the sense that the viewer is the pursuer, while over-the-shoulder shots give a sense of surveillance.

The camera tracking, which record's the subject's every movement, simulates closed circuit television (CCTV) cameras that are increasingly common in urban sites The ATM acts as another point for surveillance: a prominent sign states 'you may be video recorded during this transaction'.[31] The theme of video surveillance connects with dialogues regarding online monitoring and privacy, in an age where information can be shared globally via the Internet. Yet, while online identities can be easily concealed, it is more difficult to do so in the physical world—unless we all don balaclavas. *Financial District Infiltration: Everybody is Somebody's Terrorist* makes us question our initial judgements of others. As the work's title suggests, no one is exempt from this judgement, for anyone can be someone else's suspected terrorist.

In creating the film, Diaz Hope was influenced by popular concerns about terrorism post 11 September 2001. He notes that 'events of recent years have taught us that the key strength of terrorists is the unexpected nature of their activities—the traditional boundaries of warfare have dissolved and a seemingly mild-mannered office worker may have ulterior motives'.[32] However, our surveillance of the suspect within the film fails to produce any incriminating evidence. Apart his different dress, there is nothing about his behaviour that is different or unusual. When the film ends, we may be left with a sense of disappointment or shame, as we contemplate our false suspicion. As Diaz Hope observes, 'we are left feeling deflated, amused, and slightly guilty for having been so paranoid without due cause'.[33] To this end, *Financial District Infiltration: Everybody is Somebody's Terrorist* encourages us to think about the bases for our judgements and vilifications of others—be they neighbours, peers or simply those from different cultures.

---

[30] Anonda Bell, '*Metropolis* Exhibition Brochure', <http://www.ngv.vic.gov.au/metropolis/resources/rb_metropolis.pdf>.

[31] Anonda Bell, '*Metropolis* Exhibition Brochure', <http://www.ngv.vic.gov.au/metropolis/resources/rb_metropolis.pdf>.

[32] Anonda Bell, '*Metropolis* Exhibition Brochure', <http://www.ngv.vic.gov.au/metropolis/resources/rb_metropolis.pdf>.

[33] Anonda Bell, '*Metropolis* Exhibition Brochure', <http://www.ngv.vic.gov.au/metropolis/resources/rb_metropolis.pdf>.

With global cities such as San Francisco experiencing heightened flows of refuges, immigrants and visitors, almost everyone is a stranger to someone else. As captured by local media and often exploited by politicians, there is some popular fear that these unknown people will threaten our jobs, children, safety, or way of life. After 11 September, the US government posted the slogan '[i]f you see something, say something'[34] inside New York subways. Similar campaigns were run in Australia, with fridge magnets sent to citizens to remind them to be on the lookout. This points to the frightening banality of terrorist policing, with everyday people encouraged to identify and turn in 'suspects'.

As Diaz Hope's art powerfully captures, the events of 11 September 2001 significantly affected urban life, not just in North America, but also around the world. Cities like Sydney and Tokyo staged evacuation drills, and assessed their levels of attack preparedness, and implemented security measures such as CCTV. As Western governments continue their respective 'wars on terror', we are left to consider this question posed by the curators: 'who will fall under the scrutiny of the government as traditional terrorists become harder or more difficult to find?'[35] With civil liberties potentially threatened by false claims, the notion of democratic freedom in a global age comes to the fore.

Abbey Williams: *YES*

In her 2002 film *YES*, Abbey Williams further explores the notion of the stranger. Her focus, however, is not on danger but romantic potential. Williams shows how the cramped space of a New York subway train forces strangers to make contact, through minor bumps and physical collisions or crossing lines of gaze. She reflects on the awkwardness of being in such close proximity to strangers. The artist shows commuters resisting contact by down casting their eyes, and creating 'buffer zones' next to their bodies. In this way, *YES* evokes senses of human transience and forced connection in a global city space. Through camera close-ups, eye-line and point-of-view shots, Williams articulates the global city in terms of individual encounters. To this end, she offers a micro and affective account of a space, which is often defined by the macro and impersonal: colossal architecture, industrial triumphs, soaring stocks, and great cultural and political feats (Fig. 6.8).

William' film *YES* also explores the idea that friendships and relationships can be difficult to sustain, in a city where life is often too fast to catch one's breath. The train's circular route emulates the cyclical turnovers of partners, fleeting human relationships, and difficulty of making lasting connections in fast-paced and constantly shifting metropolis. As the train pauses at each station, new passengers

---

[34] Anonda Bell, '*Metropolis* Exhibition Brochure', <http://www.ngv.vic.gov.au/metropolis/resources/rb_metropolis.pdf>.

[35] Anonda Bell, '*Metropolis* Exhibition Brochure', <http://www.ngv.vic.gov.au/metropolis/resources/rb_metropolis.pdf>.

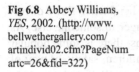
Fig 6.8 Abbey Williams, *YES*, 2002. (http://www. bellwethergallery.com/ artindivid02.cfm?PageNum_ artc=26&fid=322)

alight replacing that have disembarked. This action emulates the movement of part-ners through people's lives: each seat has been occupied and vacated, and old decla-rations have been overlaid with new graffitied expressions. The jarring movements of the hand-held camera and flickering neon lights add to these feelings of human impermanence. In sharp contradiction, the train also offers a notion of timeless con-tinuity—one that resonates with Shoba's portrayal in *Blowing Zen*. There can be conflicting senses of the global city, which points to the difficulty of categorising experiences in either-or terms.

Although no words are ever exchanged, potential lovers are identified within the film. The camera pans up and down the bodies of commuters, occasionally zooming into allow for scrutiny. A bold caption staring 'YES', 'NO' or 'MAYBE' briefly appears next to their body, reflecting the observer's superficial assessment of them as a suitable mate. From time to time, the camera lingers on a subject and the caption changes, presumably after the viewer has had a better look. This show how assessments of others can be arbitrary within the global city, confirming Diaz Hope's notion in *Financial District Infiltration: Everybody is Somebody's Terrorist*.

Handheld camera and point-of-view shots allow us to share the protagonist's perspective, and perhaps become a 'co-conspirator' in their harsh assessments of others. We might even catch ourselves ruling out others based on surface criteria as physical attributes or ethnicity. As Anonda Bell observes, in a fast-paced metropolis

[t]here is no time to be wasted on someone who is not up to par. Williams states that through her work she traces 'the line between ecstasy and the constraint of my consumption as an attempt to break down the fuzzy binarism of our yes-or-no culture.[36]

By involving the viewer, Williams encourages us to question our judgements of strangers.

---

[36] Anonda Bell, '*Metropolis* Exhibition Brochure', <http://www.ngv.vic.gov.au/metropolis/ resources/rb_metropolis.pdf>.

Fig. 6.9 Cristian Alexa,
10-Second Couples, 2000.
(Black and white video with
sound, 6'38" on a loop,
Image courtesy of the artist,
2000)

In *YES* close-ups on breasts, legs and buttocks reveals our sexualisation of others. This brutal or even predatory behaviour is mirrored online—on dating sites, for example, where assessments of others are quickly made based upon upon superficial search criteria such as 'tall', blonde' or 'athletic'. Yet, while online profiles can be heavily edited, other users can still feel that they intimately know the person that they are communicating with, quickly shifting them from the status of stranger to friend or mate. Within *YES*, an exchange of looks, a fleeting smile, or the brief meeting of hands can also alter our perceptions of others, which can be arbitraily made. In this way, Williams' film engages with the construction of would-be terrorists in Andy Diaz Hope's *Financial District Infiltration: Everybody is Somebody's Terrorist*. Williams' art shows how people can be treated like global stocks: traded, sold and ruthlessly replaced. Love it seems is simply another commodity up for grabs. In non-stop cities such as New York—where speed dating, power walks and quick meals are common—time is of the essence, and judgments need to be made quickly. The fleetingness of human encounter is explored in the following work: *10-Second Couples* by Cristian Alexa.

Cristian Alexa: *10-Second Couples*

Like Abbey Williams' *YES*, the theme of urban transience is strong within Cristian Alexa's *10-Second Couples*. Alexa's film features a woman striding down 14th Street, between 5th and 6th Avenues in New York. A hand-held camera tracks her movements from behind, providing the audience with a voyeuristic view. As the subject walks on, she casually links hands with those of passers-by. Her walking remains purposeful, as she fails to acknowledge the person by her side. This seems to show a lack of emotional connection or commitment to the exchange. After linking hands for 10 s, the woman inexplicably breaks the connection and joins hands with another. Her actions leave strangers dumbfounded, particularly when she on her way, without so much as looking back. As each new 'relationship' is formed, she shows no acknowledgement of the person by her side (Fig. 6.9).

Alexa's use of a single cinematic take dramatises the impact of the female subject's actions. In doing so, the artist questions the unwritten conventions of 'acceptable' social behaviour. As Anonda Bell elaborates, the pavement can function as an 'equalising place where people are forced to mingle, however briefly, with other occupants of the city, irrespective of gender, class, or occupation. It is a place where both predetermined and involuntary interactions occur, sometimes in stifling proximity.'[37] Notions of proximity and physical encounters connect this work to the previous case study discussed.

As the title suggests, *10-Second Couples* points to the fleetingness of human connections in a global city. Each transaction is flippant and arbitrary, with the connection typically lasting no more than a few seconds. Within the film, relationships are shown to be disposable and replaceable. This speaks to the countless 'friendships' that people have on social media sites, and the difficulty of sustaining them in meaningful ways. At times contact lists are reviewed, with names ruthlessly deleted from social media and mobile phone address books. In a similar way, Cristian Alexa presents a city shaped by rapid and insincere connections. His film echoes Joseph Nye's sense that since the 1990s, globalisation seems to have 'sped up' life in the metropolis. He notes that while it has been around for some time, 'it's been increasing in pace during the recent period…you could say that what's happened to globalization is that it's become quicker.'[38] *10-Second Couples* shows how in fast cities such as New York, there is little time to forge lasting human connections.

The film's protagonist approaches love in a clinical way. Her tunic—which is stylistically akin to a lab coat—suggests a rationalist scientific approach to the 'business' of love. The subject's lack of emotion suggests that dating in New York is just like a transaction. However, the conjugations are random and chances of success limited. The provincial score, which merrily plays in the background, ironically evokes notions of village weddings and traditional romantic ideals. A faint drumbeat however, suggests a new primordialism built upon impulsive and carnal desires. In *10-Second Couples*, the protagonist does not discriminate between partners—it does not seem to matter who she is with, just as long as she is with someone. In making the film, Alexa was intrigued by what he terms the 'contingency aspect of relationships'. His artwork is guided by three key questions 'How do people meet and drift away? What does the first moment of a chance encounter entail? How do we remember it?' These questions engage with need for human connection, stability and continuity in a time when senses of homeland, tradition and togetherness can be challenged.[39]

---

[37] Anonda Bell, '*Metropolis* Exhibition Brochure', <http://www.ngv.vic.gov.au/metropolis/resources/rb_metropolis.pdf>.

[38] Joseph Nye, 'Globalization and its Discontents', *UN*, <http://209.85.173.104/search?q=cache:Iykpey-GIkwJ:unpan1.un.org/intradoc/groups/public/documents/APCITY/UNPAN005944.pdf+sped+up+time+globalization&hl=en&ct=clnk&cd=3&gl=au>, 2001, (accessed 15 December 2007). This link is no longer active.

[39] Christian Alexa, 'Email conversation', 18 July 2013.

Fig 6.10 Brian Alfred, *Overload*, 2004. (http://www. textura.org/imagesgraphics/ brianalfred1.jpg)

Brian Alfred: *Overload*

Metropolis curator Anonda Bell writes that there are 'certain types of structures that differentiate cities from smaller towns; they include towering office blocks, commuter transit zones, large-scale sporting arenas and industrial zones'.[40] Brian Alfred's xxx animated film *Overload* explores the built environment of New York City. His work engages with what he terms 'the visual experiences we encounter in our everyday global, corporate, natural, urban and technologically enhanced environments'.[41] The American artist integrates techniques derived from painting, illustration and collage. Alfred incorporates images derived from advertising, print and the Internet. Through combining analogue and digital media, Alfred creates art that converses with the rise of technology, spread of corporatism, saturation of media, expansion of industry within the global city. To this end, his work serves as a form of cultural critique, much like a Modernist film or expression (Fig. 6.10).

Overload is constructed as a city symphony. The film begins at dawn and closes at dusk, capturing the cyclic flows of New York. Rhythmic music contributes to this sense of continuity. Yet, the artwork offers a desolate rendering of the city. Human figures are presented in black silhouette, with their individual features obscured. In an Intel office, balloons drift up to the ceiling, pointing to the remains of an office party. While human life is suggested, there is no one in sight. In one of the final scenes, a skyscraper's lights slowly switch off, pointing to the human 'ghosts' that the building. This 'facelessness' suggests a cold and hostile urban landscape, which is dominated by corporatism and industry.

Alfred is intrigued by the interplay between what he describes as 'the control and chaos…comfort and anxiety'[42] of life within the city. *Overload* depicts computers and keyboards piled high, servers left to blink, and nuclear plants on the horizon.

---

[40] Anonda Bell, '*Metropolis* Exhibition Brochure', <http://www.ngv.vic.gov.au/metropolis/ resources/rb_metropolis.pdf>.

[41] Anonda Bell, '*Metropolis* Exhibition Brochure', <http://www.ngv.vic.gov.au/metropolis/ resources/rb_metropolis.pdf>.

[42] Anonda Bell, '*Metropolis* Exhibition Brochure', <http://www.ngv.vic.gov.au/metropolis/ resources/rb_metropolis.pdf>.

The title of the work is revealing, in suggesting the detrimental impacts that industrialisation is having upon the environment, and the inability for humans to keep with technological advances. As a plane flies overhead, birds and leaves slowly scatter. Alfred shows an urban landscape that appears hostile to human life. An Exxon logo and biohazard sign are contrasted with images of a natural environment. In the final scene, skyscraper office lights spell out the word 'help'.

Overload presents a calm environment that seems to be acquiescent with its fate. Like Otterness' *Nine Eleven*, colourful animation and child-like depictions only serve to heighten the impact of the message. The flat, two-dimensional images of nuclear reactors and high voltage electrical wires suggest that there is only a surface public awareness of the impacts that industry is having upon the natural environment. Alfred's remediation of content sourced from the mainstream media, suggests that shallow reporting on environmental issues is leading to a popular apathy. Alfred portrays a futuristic, technological world, where civilisation appears on the verge of collapse.

Conclusion

Each artwork discussed in this chapter, provides a diverse account of globalisation, its affects upon the city and the individuals that inhabit its spaces. The Metropolis artists' eclectic expressions converse with Adam Kuper's claim that 'globalisation occurs as the personal experience of a great many people in networks where extremely varied meanings flow'.[43] This statement reflects the subtle iterations between the local and global, in the formation of collective meaning and individual response. This interplay is expressed as a juxtaposition of public and private space in *This is Where I Live,* and in the contrast between local and global politics evident in PHAT's *Harlem: The Ghetto Fabulous.*

As a key global city, New York figures prominently in the *Metropolis* films. In Tom Otterness' *Nine Eleven,* Abbey Williams: *YES* and Shoba's *Blowing Zen,* New York is depicted as the epitome of the global metropolis: a key generator of political, ideological, media, human and economic flows. Shoba's ironic rendering of New York in his sublime digital film *Blowing Zen* explores the 'emptying out' of the metropolis in the aftermath of 11 September 2001. Shoba's New York functions as a critical mirror, which captures the rise of the global flows of media and consumption. While *Blowing Zen* presents a transcendent and post-apocalyptic vision of the city, Tom Otterness' *Nine Eleven* directly engages with the event. Using mythology and allegory, his whimsical animations challenge the perceived indestructibility of global cities. He notes how the city 'is both growing and dying; it is subject to continuous change'.[44] This sense is sympathetic to Frank Stilwell's belief that 'cities are focal points of structural change, caught between contradictory pressures'.[45]

---

[43] Adam Kuper (Ed.), *Conceptualizing Society,* London, Routledge, 1992, pp. 146–147.

[44] Anonda Bell, '*Metropolis* Exhibition Brochure', <http://www.ngv.vic.gov.au/metropolis/resources/rb_metropolis.pdf>.

[45] Frank Stilwell, 'Going Global', p. 2.

Abbey Williams' *YES* focuses on love and the difficulties of making lasting human connections in a global city like New York. By setting her film on a New York subway train, Williams constructs metaphors for human transience and momentum. Through presenting a crowded space, she counters Shoba's de-humanised rendition of New York. The packed train symbolises the relentless human flow, the sense of people colliding

and moving apart, short-term relationships of patterns of fleeting encounter, which offer the contexts in which globalization occurs as the personal experience of a great many people in networks where extremely varied meanings flow.[46]

These three diverse artworks reveal how a single theme such as New York City in an era of globalisation, can generate three very different responses, and unique ways of framing them through digital art. Those differences highlight the danger of making macro or general claims about the experience of phenomena.

A central idea of *Metropolis* is the notion that the city is the sum of its people. From Tom Otterness' *Nine Eleven* to PHAT's *Harlem: The Ghetto fabulous,* the cultural values, practices, and aspirations of people are what shape its identity, and give it its *raison d'être.* Shoba's message in *Blowing Zen,* for example, is that a city devoid of people is a city without a soul. That claim is also evident in Nicholas Golebiewski's *This is Where I Live,* Tom Otterness' *Nine Eleven* and PHAT's *Harlem: The Ghetto Fabulous,* which provide highly personal accounts of life within global cities. These artworks resonate with the Aristotelian sense that 'we must rather regard every citizen as belonging to the city, since each is a part of the city; and the provision made for each part will naturally be adjusted to the provision made for the whole'.[47]

The *Metropolis* films suggest new readings of globalisation, as a relational and essentially 'human' phenomenon creating new spaces beyond traditional borders and constructs. The works suggest that in understanding globalisation, individual affects are just as important as macro political-economic processes. The exhibition presents contrary accounts of globalisation and the ways in which it manifests in urban spaces. Artists like PHAT and respond positively, while others such as Cristian Alexa and Abbey Williams show about its impacts upon human relationships. Golebiewski offers a more shaded response in *This is Where I Live.* The artist engages with the phenomenon's positive and negative social impacts and in doing so, disrupts the binary of alarmism/determinism that tends to dominate popular accounts. By showing how digital media can facilitate different perspectives, *Metropolis* makes room for individual experiences of the global city. The following chapter will further explore this new awareness of art and in the context of globalisation and digitisation.

---

[46] Ulf Hannerz, 'Notes on the Global Ecumene', p. 46.

[47] Aristotle, *Politics,* (Trans. E. Barker), Oxford, Oxford University Press, 1998, p. 298.

Chapter 7
In the Line of Flight: Changing Practices in Digital Art

Introduction

This chapter continues to explore digital art's ability to localise globalisation, though focussing upon the micro, affective and personal experiences of participants. Key artworks from the exhibition *In the Line of Flight* are used as examples. With a focus upon 'changing practices in digital art, this chapter will examine a global exhibition held in synchrony with an international symposium in Beijing. This exhibition also showcases contemporary practices in the curation of digital artworks. It will explore curators' understandings of digital art, and how it might offer critical perspectives on globalisation. The inclusion of this chapter and its sequencing enables a direct comparison to be made to the *Metropolis* exhibition discussed in the previous chapter. It also points to some of the diverse practices characteristic of digital art, foregrounded in Chap. 2. The exhibition featured an eclectic array of digital art formats, from video games to responsive garments and haptic installations. *In the Line of Flight* also reflects the different degrees to which artists are identifying changing practices in art, and engaging with those realities in their works will be examined. Lastly, the organisation of this exhibition was a global endeavour, involving artists and participants from around the world. The curation of exhibitions such as *In the Line of Flight* points to the new ways that art is being made and curated, in an era of globalisation (Fig. 7.1).

Through direct reference to *In the Line of Flight* this chapter will show how globalisation can gain context and meaning through affective expression. It will explore the idea that digital art can offer rich and individuated expressions of globalisation, through technologies that engage and personally respond to users. In making this claim, it will be argued that the unique interactive, haptic, and responsive 'tools' of digital art can create layered and nuanced understandings of globalisation and provide new modes of understanding it as a human and localised phenomenon. In selecting seven standout works from the exhibition, this chapter will examine the degree to which digital artists observe changing practices in the field, and engage with globalisation's influences upon production.

M. Langdon, *The Work of Art in a Digital Age: Art, Technology and Globalisation*, DOI 10.1007/978-1-4939-1270-4_7, © Springer Science+Business Media New York 2014

Fig. 7.1 *In the Line of Flight,* 2005. (http://newmediabeijing.org/md2005/exhibition.php?section=2)

The seven key works that will be discussed from the exhibition are: Leon Cmielews-ki and Josephine Starrs' *Floating Territories* (2004), Blast Theory's *Can You See Me Now?* (2001–2007), Justine Cooper's *Transformers* (2002), Marnix de Nijs' *Run Motherfucker Run* (2004), Kaho Abe and Jung Sin's *Haptic Glove* (2004), and Joanna Berzowska's *Intimate Memory Shirt* (2004), and *Feathery Dresses* (2004). Each case study has been deliberately chosen for its original use of digital media, reflection of cultural diversity and critical commentary on globalisation and its human affects.

This international digital art exhibition was held at the China Millennium Art Museum in Beijing 2005. A key theme of the exhibition concerned changes to art production and distribution in an era of globalisation. The exhibition title *In the Line of Flight* captured the cultural flux of the times. The term 'flight' suggests motion and transcendence from earlier cultural and artistic practices, while reflecting a consciousness of homeland, destination and the departed. A line of flight is also a concept expressed by Deleuze and used extensively in his work with Guattari. As translated by Brian Massumi, 'there are lines of articulation segmentarity, strata and territories; but also lines of flight, movement deterritorialisation and destratification'.[1] We might conceptualise affective digital art works—and individual responses to them—in terms of the 'multiplicities, lines, strata and segmentarities, lines of flight and intensities'[2] that they generate.

---

[1] Gilles Deleuze and Félix Guattari, *A Thousand Plateaus*, p. 3.

[2] Gilles Deleuze and Félix Guattari, *A Thousand Plateaus*, p. 4.

Global Collaboration

The exhibition and symposium that comprised *In the Line of Flight* were hosted by Tsinghua University, in conjunction with Karlsruhe's ZKM: Centre for Art and Media, and V2_Institute for Unstable Media, Rotterdam. The artistic director, Zhang Ga (China), worked in close association with curators from around the world, to include: Alex Adriaansens (The Netherlands), Sara Diamond (Canada), Antoanetta Ivanova (Former Soviet Union), Yukiko Shikata (Japan), and Peter Weibel (Australia). As such, the exhibition was the product of global endeavour—it was organised through digital communications, created through global collaboration, featured works from around the world, and was held in Beijing—a leading global city. As a collaborative project between artists, theorists and curators, *In the Line of Flight* emulates the global construction of *T_Visionarium* described in Chap. 4.

All of the works explored are examples of global art. A number of the pieces, such as Marnix de Nijs' *Run Motherfucker Run,* have been produced through worldwide collaborations between individuals and research centres. Others artworks—such as Blast Theory's *Can You See Me Now*—have been distributed over the Internet and have employed global media and modes of networking and communicating, such as GPS technology and online chat forums. These practices suggest new levels of mobility, communication and transferability in the production and display of art. To this end, global exhibitions like *In the Line of Flight* signify new trends in art collaboration, creation, distribution and display. Many of the artworks exhibited explored the symposium's themes of global cultural change, ideological flow, Westernisation, consumption, travel and de-territorialisation.

This interplays between artistic practice and discourse within the works, converse with the Modern notion of the 'creative industrialist' discussed in Chap. 2, and reflects a new style of production, evocative of iCinema's critical art. This relationship between digital art practice and discourse, confirms artistic director Zhang Ga's claim that these works wittingly use digital media in the construction of critical messages.[3] He writes that '[n]o longer sufficient are simple questions of ideology, economical determinism, the new condition demands ad hoc improvisation, rapid prototyping, instantaneous sampling'.[4] Ga points to a new kind of artistic 'alchemy that operates not only on the production of objects but also on the (re)construction of subjectivity'.[5] To this end, digital art can offer micro, personalised and affective responses to globalisation.

In seeking to creating linkages between the seven works selected, we might explore the curator's statement that the exhibition 'presents representative works of telematic art, virtual reality, net art, robotic art, interactive cinema, software art, nano art, and other new forms facilitated through media technologies. It testifies to a new aesthetic sensibility accentuated by the struggle of city dwellers, proposing

---

[3] Zhang Ga, 'Section One: New Media Art as Global Cultural Alchemy', *NewMediaBeijing.org*, <http://newmediabeijing.org/md2005/symposium.php?section=3>, 2004, (accessed 22 September 2007).

[4] Zhang Ga, 'Section One', <http://newmediabeijing.org/md2005/symposium.php?section=3>).

[5] Zhang Ga, 'Section One', <http://newmediabeijing.org/md2005/symposium.php?section=3>).

new perspectives on contemporary urban conditions from around the world'.[6] The first implication of this claim is that the artworks reveal a shift in the construction and facilitation of art. In their experimentations with mixed technologies—from digital software to robotics, and nanotechnology—they are seen as representative of the digital art genre. The second is that the exhibition explores life within the global city, and a new aesthetic realisation. If the artists indeed convey this 'sensibility', then how is it demonstrated and further, how might it contribute to our understandings of globalisation? In considering these questions, this chapter begins with an exploration of Josephine Starrs and Leon Cmielewski's *Floating Territories*.

Leon Cmielewski and Josephine Starrs: *Floating Territories*

Floating Territories is a collaborative project between Australian artists Josephine Starrs and Leon Cmielewski. Both practitioners are known for creating works that transcend the boundaries of art, in creating cross-sections between digital video and games. They use video gaming 'as a springboard for exploring contemporary issues around real and virtual territory'.[7] The artists' 2004 interactive *Floating Territories* is presented as a video game. A typical experience consists of the user entering the small, darkened space to be confronted by an interactive console, connected to a projection screen and speaker system. Five options are marked on the display: escape; defend; petition; colonise and wander. If a user selects 'defend', they are confronted with gridlines reminiscent of early computer games. An ominous grey cloud slowly passes across the screen; it can only be repelled through user response. The conquering mass is threatening, and might be seen as being symbolic of globalisation's cultural, political and economic de-territorialisations (Fig. 7.2).

If one chooses the option 'petition', a Lego™ styled figure appears within a rotating sphere. By interacting with the console, the user can direct the avatar to pick up written petitions. Manoeuvrability is however, highly limited. This may be designed to encourage the user to contemplate wider issues, such as the difficulty of gaining support for petitions against global threats. The artists ®™ark and The Yes Men explored in 'Chap. 4', similarly depict this impenetrability. To 'wander' in the art, is to create 'boundaries' that appear in response to the user's movements. Grid-lines are constructed and illuminated in vibrant paint box hues such as yellow, white, and red. Through constructing differently coloured zones, Starrs and Cmielewski's art evokes globalisation's cultural divisions and segregations of 'haves' and 'have-nots'. Klein's 'fences and windows' analogy, explored in detail in Chap. 2, might articulate this conception of globalisation.[8]

---

[6] Zhang Ga, 'Section One', <http://newmediabeijing.org/md2005/symposium.php?section=3>).

[7] Antoanetta Ivanova, *'Floating Territories', NewMediaBeijing.org*, <http://newmediabeijing.org/md2005/exhibition_display.php?section=2&link_id=8&title=Floating+Territories+%28AU%29&artist_id=8_3>, 2004, (accessed 22 September 2007).

[8] Naomi Klein, *Fences and Windows*.

Fig. 7.2 Josephine Starrs and Leon Cmielewski, *Floating Territories*, 2004. (Image courtesy of the artist)

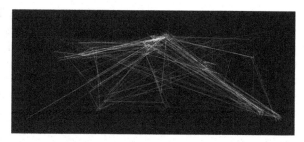

As a work of art *Floating Territories* converses with the rise of digital technology that has facilitated global communication. The graphics of *Floating Territories* are designed along Mondrian lines, revealing the artists' remediation of 'old-school' art graphics in dialogue with the latest digital art forms. If not for the provocative game titles, the installation might appear as benign as a children's game. In doing so, it engages with curator Antoanetta Ivanova's claim that 'when playing, gamers are asked to make decisions, placing them in the arbitrary position of being, for example, a defender of territory, a nomad or a wanderer'.[9] *Floating Territories* localises globalisation, through placing complex social and political choices in the hands of individuals. The use of a innocent gaming frameworks has resonances with Blast Theory's *Can You See Me Now?* The tactic accentuates the malignance of global events such as de-territorialisation, and human responses that can range from engagement to ineffectual action to ambivalence.

Cmielewski and Starrs' installation also suggests that digital art has the capacity to explore 'spaces in-between', led by critical nuance, perception, physical instinct and subjective response. To this end, their art defies the fixity of boundaries through temporal fluctuations and negotiations of real and virtual space. The artists' installation provides an affective and localised framework for articulating globalisation's movements of people and impacts such as migration, colonisation and human disapora. The artists argue that the installation 'provide(s) pathways for gamers to engage with and explore a range of issues around territory and space'.[10] The notion of individual accountability comes into play, as users are made to feel responsible for their actions. Their slowness in response, for example, can see a territory conquerered, leading to political 'game over'.

Floating Territories casts globalisation and digitisation as a series of causal processes, that involve: escape; defence; petition; colonisation; and wandering. As these categories suggest, Starrs and Cmielewski's perception of globalisation is largely pessimistic. In games such as 'petition', the joystick and interface were often difficult to manoeuvre or unresponsive, making it difficult to gain a positive outcome. Territories were invaded, regions were conquered, and it was difficult to gain the petitions required to progress. This seemed to pre-determine a negative

---

[9] Antoanetta Ivanova, '*Floating Territories*', <http://newmediabeijing.org/md2005/exhibition_display.php?section=2&link_id=8&title=Floating+Territories+%28AU%29&artist_id=8_3>.

[10] Antoanetta Ivanova, '*Floating Territories*', <http://newmediabeijing.org/md2005/exhibition_display.php?section=2&link_id=8&title=Floating+Territories+%28AU%29&artist_id=8_3>.

outcome, and accordingly, engage with only one side of globalisation's story. While Starrs and Cmielewski's articulate globalisation's movements of people across geographical borders, only one side of the story is presented. While the artists contend that *Floating Territories* produces 'a trans-local, multifaceted experience',[11] this claim might be challenged due to the predominantly pessimistic view of globalisation presented, which limits the complexity of its positive and negative human affects.

Blast Theory: *Can You See Me Now?*

Blast Theory is a UK group of artists concerned with the boundaries between reality and simulation. Using performance, video games, and mobile technologies in their art, they raise questions about surveillance, regulation and control. Modelled on the children's game *Scotland Yard™*, Blast Theory's *Can You See Me Now?* is produced as an interactive game: with a video screen, speaker system and interactive console. The live video feeds, reveal the locations of six players located on the streets of Rotterdam. The artwork uses GPS data that is fed back into the system. The game takes place over five days, and is constructed as a battle between virtual users at their computers, and the Blast Theory gamers on the streets (Fig. 7.3).

When users log in to the game, a white pawn appears as their virtual representation. The objective is for the online users to locate and corner, the orange pawns representing the members on the street. Through this dynamic, *Can You See Me Now?* stages an ironic battle between digital artists and users. The participants are able to influence the narrative direction of the art. Advanced digital communications enable virtual and physical players to communicate with each other, devise tactics and create alliances. Through communicating by digital radio transmitters, the online users can attempt to track Blast Theory members through analysis of the audio feeds.

Through blurring the binaries physicality and virtuality, object and subject, game and art, *Can You See Me Now?* blends complex digital media with everyday communication technologies. Blast Theory uses a simple game concept, adopts video game principles and incorporates GPS enabled mobile phones, satellite feeds, digital radio transmitters and Palm Pilot™ technologies. The work may be perceived as work of digital art, an interactive video game, an experiment in recombinatory technology, or a discursive construct. Through highlighting some of the more intrusive and voyeuristic aspects of global communication technologies, *Can You See Me Now?* demonstrates high levels of self-reflexivity: it uses digital media to pose questions about surveillance, simulation, and the fluidity of boundaries.

In this way, digital art such as *Can You See Me Now?* emerges from a two-way dialogue between medium and message. As examined earlier in this book, this re-

[11] Antoanetta Ivanova, '*Floating Territories*', <http://newmediabeijing.org/md2005/exhibition_display.php?section=2&link_id=8&title=Floating+Territories+%28AU%29&artist_id=8_3>.

Fig. 7.3 Blast Theory, *Can You See Me Now?* 2005. (http://www.blasttheory. co.uk/bt/work_cysmn.html)

lationship has often been weighed differently. For formal artists, the onus was upon aesthetics, and the level of artistry and 'aura' attained. Post-structuralists however, placed a greater emphasis upon the message, and the artwork's deconstruction of its media. What artworks such as *Can You See Me Now?* and *Territorism II* achieve, is a more subtle negotiation of subject and object, or message or medium. As explored further in this chapter, many of the more critical expressions in digital art have wittingly used the digital 'medium' to create critical messages about global technologies, and their impacts upon art and experience.

In conceptual terms, *Can You See Me Now?* is not dissimilar from 'old school' analogue games. Yet, the incorporation of online gaming, digital avatars, chat groups, and global surveillance, specifically connect it to this moment in time. The artwork only makes sense in terms of globalisation and digitisation, as phenomena that share the same historical space. While the makers' stance on global surveillance is not explicitly expressed, we might assume from the tensions within the game, that these issues are met with some trepidation. The capture of victims, and online archival of their 'blue prints', highlights digital technology's systems of control, and issues such as the ownership of the image, classifications of information, and restrictions of access. Self-referencing tendencies and ironic misuses of media, might locate *Can You See Me Now?* in terms of post-structuralist works, by artists like ®™ark and The Yes Men. Yet, Blast Theory arguably goes further, in exploring the limits of digital media-message dynamics. Through hybrid elements that incorporate video gaming, installation art, Internet art, online chat rooms and performance art, *Can You See Me Now?* tests the boundaries of digital art practice and discourse.

Rosemary Klich engages with N. Katherine Hayles' theories of subjective embodiment in her discussion of *Can You See Me Now?*[12] The installation, she argues, upsets the formal dichotomy of physical presence/virtual absence. The binary, Klich claims, is founded on the notion that 'live performance involves the disappearing

---

[12] Rosemary Klich, 'Performing Posthuman Perspective: *Can You See Me Now?*', <http://scan.net. au/scan/journal/display.php?journal_id=91>, *Scan Journal of Media Arts Culture*, Vol. 4, No. 1, 2007, (accessed 11 December 2007).

presence of the body, while mediated representation denies presence, presenting an *absence* of the body'.[13] As discussed in Chap. 7, the digital work *Can You See Me Now?* integrates real-time street action with virtual play. Klich states that 'the concept of presence is no longer associated with corporeality and the distinction between absence and presence becomes blurred'.[14] Through employing Hayles' 'semiotics of virtuality',[15] Klich suggests that 'the dialect of presence/absence, and by association the dialectic of live/mediated, has become limited frameworks through which to articulate the complexities of mixed-reality performance'[16] works such as *Can You See Me Now?* The installation provides new ways to interact, create, and play, using global technoscapes and media. Instead of suggesting an absence of presence, Klich argues that the installation locates the participant in three distinct but simultaneous spatialities: "[t]hey exist as a body in front of the computer, as a constructed identity in the online gaming world, and then they are also represented by the locative technology of the runners as a 'blip', a 'data-body', a disembodied entity moving through the streets of the city".[17] In this way, digital artworks like *Can You See Me Now?* re-centre understandings of globalisation around embodiment and affective subjectivities. In this way, digital art can provide new understandings of globalisation's divergent an at times, contradictory affects.

Justine Cooper: *Transformers*

Justine Cooper's 2002 installation *Transformers* was created after a visit to China, which, the curator Antoanetta Ivanova claims was a culturally confronting experience that made her reconsider the boundaries of culture and identity. Ivanova writes that for Cooper, '[b]eing an outsider to Chinese culture was both a confronting and revelatory experience that prompted her to look deeper into and question how we communicate difference'.[18] Themes of cultural transference, subjectivity, memory and representation pervade the artist's work. Depictions of fingerprints, human faces, English, and Chinese text engage with globalisation's cultural and human surges. Hybrid media such as a projection screen, DVD system, audio channels, and photographic imagery, contribute to the artwork's themes of unification and

---

[13] Rosemary Klich, 'Performing Posthuman Perspective: *Can You See Me Now?*', <http://scan.net.au/scan/journal/display.php?journal_id=91>.

[14] Rosemary Klich, 'Performing Posthuman Perspective: *Can You See Me Now?*', <http://scan.net.au/scan/journal/display.php?journal_id=91>.

[15] Rosemary Klich, 'Performing Posthuman Perspective: *Can You See Me Now?*', <http://scan.net.au/scan/journal/display.php?journal_id=91>.

[16] Rosemary Klich, 'Performing Posthuman Perspective: *Can You See Me Now?*', <http://scan.net.au/scan/journal/display.php?journal_id=91>.

[17] Rosemary Klich, 'Performing Posthuman Perspective: *Can You See Me Now?*', <http://scan.net.au/scan/journal/display.php?journal_id=91>.

[18] Antoanetta Ivanova, '*Transformers*', <http://newmediabeijing.org/md2005/exhibition_display.php?section=2&link_id=8&title=Transformers+%28AU%29&artist_id=8_4>.

Fig. 7.4 Justine Cooper, *Transformers*, 2002. (http://www.adelaidebiennial.com/cocoon/adelaidebiennial/cooper_justine.xml?thing=/adelaidebiennial/xsl_project.xsl)

eclecticism. Through conducting interviews, Justine Cooper collected testimonies and photographs from a diverse range of participants. She deliberately chose immigrants, or individuals who had travelled between different cultures and geographical regions. To support her exploration of memories and experiences, the artist acquired DNA samples of hair strands from the subjects that were then incorporated into the art. Cooper used them as a premise from which to explore genetic differences, leading to arguments about nature and nurture and external impacts upon individual socio-cultural affiliations (Fig. 7.4).

In exploring questions of identity, *Transformers* reveals a concern for the dynamics of information flow, and how ideas about culture and human identity are globally transmitted. Cooper's art also expresses an interest in how scientific data is calculated, shared, and stored. The artist's incorporation of scientific principles such as DNA and X-Ray imaging, challenges the parameters of art and the tendency to cast art as emotional, irrational and abstract, in direct contrast to the sciences. Cooper's integration of qualitative and quantitative concerns, defies binary generalisations. Her practice sheds new light on globalisation, as the sum of its dynamic and differential affects.

Justine Cooper's use of audio-visual montage complements the theme of cultural connectedness and inter-spatiality. Through those strategies, her art poses the questions: can culture be defined? How are local and global allegiances balanced? And, how might we interpret cultural histories and traditions? Cooper's style of biological digital art is apposite to address these questions, through its incorporation of hybrid artistic-scientific principles, practices, and ethics. The physical construction, and discursive themes of *Transformers,* creates new spaces between the universal and the particular, the political and the affective, and traditional notions of the artistic (irrational and abstract), and the scientific (logical and material).

Through integrating individual memories and personal anecdotes, Cooper strengthens these threads. Her integration or 'real' materials such as photo media and hair stands and exploration of human memory and reverie, questions the borderlines between the actual, virtual, imagined and metaphysical. By doing so, the artist provides a new way of perceiving digital art, as a form of expression grounded in the material traditions of art: painting, sculpture, photography, and simultaneously 'un-bound' from the trappings of physical construction and display.

Through *Transformers*, Coopers shows how digital artworks might resist formal categorisations of art, in the same way that globalisation might transcend rigid conceptualisations. The following questions, posed by the exhibition curators, further point to that intent: '[d]oes identity really rest purely in our genetic programming? Is being an individual an oxymoron if we are fated to become what we are? To change our nature do we merely tinker with the human genome? Can genetic determinism really account for the complexity of human consciousness, the beauty of being, the contingency of existence and the randomness of speciation?'[19] Justine Cooper's examination of individual experiences and cultural consciousnesses creates windows from which to explore these fundamentally human questions.

Cooper's presentation of an original Chinese culture might also disrupt fears that local cultures are being completely dominated by North American and Western ideals. In revealing a culture that is assured of its present and past, she depicts a nation that is confident of its own cultural path. While the artist invokes some of the Western idioms that have been embraced, she suggests that the fusion of local-global ideals makes Chinese culture richer. Cooper's subjects are presented as vibrant and contemporary hybridisations, a notion that is replicated in the installation's mosaic construction. As a collage of identities, the artist presents these individuals as cultural works in progress. She claims '[t]here was an observable plasticity in who these people were and what they could become, and an ability to use this plasticity in navigating contemporary society.'[20] In this way, Cooper localises global cultural change.

The narrative of *Transformers* is temporally and sequentially unstructured, and is evocative of iCinema's *T_Visionarium*. The use of audiovisual layers in both works supports the arguable iterations of memory, culture, history, and imagination. In commenting upon this strategy, Ivanova writes: '[f]or Cooper it is about the small and intricate personal details that we uphold as true and meaningful. It is where the incredible beauty and transcended humanity of our difference is to be found'.[21] Digital artists ranging from Golebiewski to PHAT, similarly show the importance of local, private, and particular accounts, in the face of globalisation's potentially subsuming cultural impacts.

---

[19] Antoanetta Ivanova, '*Transformers*', <http://newmediabeijing.org/md2005/exhibition_display. php?section=2&link_id=8&title=Transformers+%28AU%29&artist_id=8_4>.

[20] Antoanetta Ivanova, '*Transformers*', <http://newmediabeijing.org/md2005/exhibition_display. php?section=2&link_id=8&title=Transformers+%28AU%29&artist_id=8_4>.

[21] Antoanetta Ivanova, '*Transformers*', <http://newmediabeijing.org/md2005/exhibition_display. php?section=2&link_id=8&title=Transformers+%28AU%29&artist_id=8_4>.

Fig. 7.5 Marnix de Nijs, *Run Motherfucker Run,* 2004. (http://www.marnixdenijs.nl/ run-motherfucker-run.htm)

Marnix De Nijs: *Run Motherfucker Run*

'You have left a party late at night or in the early hours of the morning and you find yourself in a transformed city. You start to run'.[22] Alex Adriaansen's description of Marnix de Nijs *Run Motherfucker Run* is an apt description of the kind of experience that a user might expect. Constructed in 2004, *Run Motherfucker Run* is composed as a digital installation incorporating a treadmill, interactive sound and video system, and an 8×4 m projection screen. Upon the user's approach, the work's visuals grow and diminish in intensity, tempting the subject onto the larger-than-life 5×2 m treadmill. Marnix de Nijs is renowned for art that explores the contingencies arising from the bodily experience of digital technology. He provides limited instruction on how to approach the art, yet the user soon determines that their bodily position and running speed guides the audio system, sequence of imagery, and its visual intensity. In an explanation of his piece, curator Alex Adriaansens writes, '[t] he distance you run on the conveyor belt is the same distance you will cover in the virtual city in front of you. By quickening your pace, the acceleration of the belt as well as the speed of the image increases and depending on your running behaviour and the directional choices you make, the progress of the film is determined'.[23] The urban imagery projected is formed of 2D and 3D video footage taken from real, global cities. It incorporates images of deserted streets, a night train, and urban obstacles (Fig. 7.5).

Run Motherfucker Run presents the global city as an ominous space. Its streets are deserted and poorly lit: reminiscent of the journey home that night-clubbers or shift workers might make. De Nijs' art reveals a darker side of metropolitan life,

---

[22] Alex Adriaansens, '*RMR—Run Motherfucker Run*', *NewMediaBeijing.org*, <http://newmediabeijing. org/md2005/exhibition_display.php?section=2&link_id=2&title=RMR+-+Run+Motherfucker+Run+ %28NL%29&artist_id=2_1>, 2004, (accessed 1 October 2007). This link is no longer active.

[23] Alex Adriaansens, '*RMR—Run Motherfucker Run*', <http://newmediabeijing.org/md2005/exhibition_display.php?section=2&link_id=2&title=RMR+-+Run+Motherfucker+Run+%28NL%2 9&artist_id=2_1>.

contrasting to the brightness of day, and the optimistic portrayals of global cities, and their human potential. The emptying of the city of inhabitants is reminiscent of Shoba's *Blowing Zen*. The desertion of a usually busy metropolis challenges our expectations of the city as being the product of its people. De Nijs' installation presents the global metropolis as a faceless and generic landscape, hostile to its citizens cast as 'motherfuckers'. In artistic terms, *Run Motherfucker Run* creates intersections between game art, cinema, installation, soundscape, and real-time performance. The artist uses responsive and participatory media to discuss the presence and affect of human bodies within global metropolitan spaces, raising questions of purpose, individuality and identity in a global world. The opportunity to create an original path or history also exists within the work. The interactive video interface and fluctuations of speed and visual display mean that no single journey is the same: each is an individual experience or enactment of urban change. To begin the experience is however, a conscious choice. As Adriaansens explains, 'you must move in order to see the image'.[24] While the user maintains some control, through using their pace to adjust the speed of the belt, a fair level of adeptness is necessary.

In order to function effectively, the installation requires moderate momentum to maintain the brightness and clarity of the visuals. The work's dynamic 'creates a temperamental balance between control and non-control of the situation you voluntarily entered into when you first stepped on the treadmill'.[25] *Run Motherfucker Run* is dangerous art. With a top speed of 30 km/h, there is a high chance of being hurled backwards onto the soft 'catchment' at the base that seems to pre-empt a fall. If the user takes too long to discover that user pace determines the speed of the treadmill, they can be left desperately clutching for the rails. Inevitably, they will be dragged backwards, and the narrative will end. The title of the art acknowledges with mirth, the probability of that outcome: for the user to become a helpless 'motherfucker'.

Run Motherfucker Run presents the global city as a foreboding space, with isolated landscapes and dark and beguiling streets. The installation's disjointed narrative structure—coupled with graphics that rise and diminish in clarity—bewilder and alienate the user. Matrix grids connect this work to early speculative science fiction texts such as Steven Lisberger's 1982 film *Tron*. In countering the notion of the global city as a landscape promising hope and opportunity to its citizens, de Nijs' presents a city that is hostile to its inhabitants. If a user runs too fast, they invariably meet with adversity: as they are hurled backwards, the narrative comes to an end. If they slow their pace, the visuals diminish in clarity and the sound begins to flatline. Either way, an experience of *Run Motherfucker Run* culminates in the death of either the city or metaphorically, the individual.

---

[24] Alex Adriaansens, '*RMR —Run Motherfucker Run*', <http://newmediabeijing.org/md2005/exhibition_display.php?section=2&link_id=2&title=RMR+-+Run+Motherfucker+Run+%28NL%29&artist_id=2_1>.

[25] Alex Adriaansens, '*RMR—Run Motherfucker Run*', <http://newmediabeijing.org/md2005/exhibition_display.php?section=2&link_id=2&title=RMR+-+Run+Motherfucker+Run+%28NL%29&artist_id=2_1>.

The installation generates physical and perceptual responses to a stylised global city. In doing so, it suggests that understandings of global spaces emerge from a nexus between subjective interpretation and bodily response. This reading converses with Marjorie O'Loughlin's sense of 'embodied subjectivity'[26] that "captures a sense of the human being's 'immersion' in places, spaces and environs in which, as gendered subjects, they encounter the world as dwelling place".[27] What we might take from O'Loughlin's claim, is that subjectivity is not 'outside' or detached from the body, but directly informed by corporeal encounters with spaces, and times. As has been suggested in relation to globalisation and digital art, specific contexts, phenomena, and environs significantly shape interpretation and experience. Yet, as shifting and contingent triggers, they generate impacts that can be difficult to define. In this way, responsive and generative forms of digital art might generate new understandings of subjective embodiment and globalisation and art.

Digital art such as de Nijs' Run Motherfucker Run can provide affective and localised understandings of globalisation through haptic, immersive, and responsive technologies that engage with the dynamic realms of human experience and affect. While the artworks might represent the artists' individual perceptions, the use of tactile and responsive digital media directly engage with the body and, in some cases, enable the user to direct the narrative and audiovisual sequencing. If we view subjectivity and experience as malleable constructs, then we might begin to see how digital art can express individual encounters with globalisation. This notion echoes the sense that the individual body is the "glue" that underpins consciousness and connects it with subperceptual sensorimotor processes.[28] This understanding builds upon Hansen's construction which 'wants materially to link the flow of information in the digital image and the body as frame.[29] Hansen claims that by placing the embodied viewer-participant into a circuit with information, the installations and environments they create function as laboratories for the conversion of information into corporeally apprehensible images'.[30]

In his articulation of phenomena, Hansen writes that what digital media 'ultimately yields is less a framed object than an embodied, subjective experience that can only be felt',[31] so that 'as media lose their material specificity, the body takes on a more prominent function as a selective processor of information'.[32] Digital art's emphasis upon sensory affects might shift the focus away from static, 'framed', or universal definitions of subjects such as globalisation. As Hansen elaborates, 'the

---

[26] Marjorie O'Loughlin, 'Intelligent Bodies and Ecological Subjectivities: Merleau-Ponty's Corrective to PostModernism's Subjects of Education', *Philosophy of Education* <http://www.ed.uiuc.edu/EPS/PES-Yearbook/95_docs/o'loughlin.html>, 1995, (accessed 10 December 2007). This link is no longer active.

[27] Marjorie O'Loughlin, 'Intelligent Bodies and Ecological Subjectivities', <http://www.ed.uiuc.edu/EPS/PES-Yearbook/95_docs/o'loughlin.html>.

[28] Mark B.N. Hansen, *New Philosophy for New Media*, p. xxiv.

[29] Mark B.N. Hansen, *New Philosophy for New Media*, p. xxiv.

[30] Mark B.N. Hansen, *New Philosophy for New Media*, p. 11.

[31] Mark B.N. Hansen, *New Philosophy for New Media*, p. 14.

[32] Mark B.N. Hansen, *New Philosophy for New Media*, p. 22.

viewer must participate in the process through which the mediated digital data is transformed into a perceivable image...it is the body—the body's scope of perceptual and affective possibilities—that Kaho Abe & Jung Sin informs the medial interfaces'.[33] In digital artworks, interaction encourages affective response.

Run Motherfucker Run expresses some of the fears associated with globalisation: that individuals will succumb to its over-bearing technologies, floods of information and systems of control, for example. The installation might also be seen to confirm Anna Munster's sense that computerised bodies 'work as differential, qualitative fields within the art work introducing the capacities of bodies, whether social, historical or biological to sustain different speeds and intensities in relation to informatic speeds'.[34] The installation's momentum and displacement of user control, mirrors the sensation of 'surfing the web', the timelessness of digital space and the difficulty of physically detaching ourselves, once we are virtually engaged. As Anna Munster advances, '[d]igital culture provides a stark contrast between different vectors of speed, informatic and organic being the most obvious, and it also multiplies the opportunities for these contrasting vectors to cross each other's paths'.[35] In arguing that '[i]n this way they introduce a break in the machine flows of the information economy and move us in the direction of a computer image capable of producing new affects',[36] Munster might suggest a new way of thinking about the digital art as a generator of differential affects—much like interactive and participatory forms of digital art.

Kaho Abe and Jung Sin: *Haptic Glove*

Haptic Glove, designed by Kaho Abe and Jung Sin, is a set of interactive gloves that responds to users' hand movements. The artists are intrigued by the intersections between art and technology, and their surrounding contexts. Jung Sin studies interactive technology and design. His colleague, Kaho Abe works as a fashion designer, constructing garments that utilise wearable technology. Abe's art explores human applications of technology and the ways in which digital media can generate connection and interaction. Abe and Sin claim that a handshake is a globally understood gesture of trust, friendship and alliance.[37] In building upon this concept, they constructed gloves that could interact with each other and generate sound rhythms. Music is used in the work, because it arguably 'transcends language barriers, creating opportunities for people to communicate even if they do not understand each

---

[33] Mark B.N. Hansen, *New Philosophy for New Media*, p. 22.

[34] Anna Munster, 'Low-res Bleed', pp. 85–86.

[35] Anna Munster, 'Low-res Bleed', p. 90.

[36] Anna Munster, 'Low-res Bleed', pp. 85–86.

[37] Zhang Ga, '*Haptic Glove*', <http://newmediabeijing.org/md2005/exhibition_display.php?section=2&link_id=18&title=Haptic+Glove+%28USA%29&artist_id=18_5>.

Fig. 7.6 Kaho Abe and Jung
Sin, *Haptic Glove, 2005.*
(http://newmediabeijing.org/
md2005/exhibition_display.
php?section=2&link_id=18&
title=Haptic+Glove+%28US
A%29&artist_id=18_5)

other's spoken words'.[38] The gloves explore the boundaries of global contact, where non-verbal, and text-based communication can become as important as verbal communication. By grasping hands, users can create refrains in synchrony. Through encouraging non-verbal means of interaction such as touch, play and sound, the artists instigate a new form of cross-cultural dialogue on globalisation, centred upon human interaction and response (Fig. 7.6).

Through using a simple and globally understood gesture like a handshake, *Haptic Glove* shows how digital media can be familiar, approachable, affective. Through incorporating digital technology into the gloves, the artists may seek to counter trepidation associated with digitisation and perceived affects of immateriality, simulation, and displacement. Through devising a form of digital art that is fun and universally understood, Jung Sin and Kaho Abe's *Haptic Glove* challenge the critique that digital art is hostile, intimidating, and alienating. By using 'soft' and tactile technology, Sin and Abe's art aims to bring individuals humans together in an era of globalisation. The artists strive to create a work that is understandable to young and old, individuals from different cultures, and those with different levels of digital literacy.

Haptic Glove might be understood in terms of Inda and Rosaldo's thesis that in an era of globalisation and digitisation, human connection can be broken into two essential forms: the first characterised by direct, or face-to-face contact, and secondly, by virtual interaction 'made possible by transport and communications systems'.[39] Yet, the artwork arguably goes further in creating a new realm 'in-between'; one that negotiates the separation of physical and virtual space. Through this process, they provide a more nuanced perspective on digitisation, by highlighting the contradictions of human connection and disjuncture. Through centralising the individual in their art, Sin and Abe emphasise the role of the affective body in discourses on global technologies. Although users are restricted by the gloves' boundaries and tones, they can effectively influence and manipulate the pre-existing system. *Haptic Glove* thereby suggests that the individual is a central element in the experience of

[38] Zhang Ga, '*Haptic Glove*', <http://newmediabeijing.org/md2005/exhibition_display. php?section=2&link_id=18&title=Haptic+Glove+%28USA%29&artist_id=18_5>.
[39] Jonathon Xavier Inda and Renato Rosaldo, (Eds.), *The Anthropology of Globalisation*, p. 8.

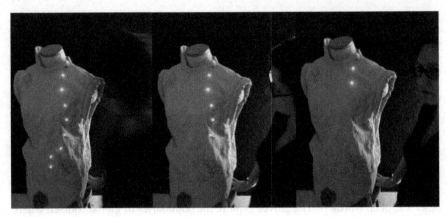

Fig. 7.7 Joanna Berzowska, *Intimate Memory Shirt,* 2005. (Image courtesy of the artist)

global-digital systems. Although this idea is not always explicitly expressed, *Haptic Glove* provides new ways of understanding digitisation and globalisation, as phenomena interpreted by subjectively embodied individuals.

Joanna Berzowska: *Intimate Memory Shirt/Feathery Dresses*

Jung Sin and Kaho Abe's *Haptic Glove* provides a critical framework for contemplating Joanna Berzowska's *Intimate Memory Shirt* and *Feathery Dresses*. Berzowska is a digital artist and Assistant Professor in Design and Computation Arts, at Concordia University. Her academic background informs her conceptualisation of memory and affect in her works of art. Berzowska's memory-rich garments, which recall users' whispers and touches, arguably make sense in terms of affective discourses (Fig. 7.7).

Berzowska's art suggests that the body is part of wider system, influenced by the world and the contexts that surround it. Affect to this end, is seen as 'the active discharge of emotion, the counterattack'.[40] What this understanding gives to Berzowska's art is an awareness of her intent in presenting garments that are intimate, in as much as they 'remember' their histories of touch. Haptic technologies encourage affective and highly personalised responses to digitisation. In doing so, they contest categorical and macro accounts, that overlook the particularities of individual encounters and affects.

The garments counter the contention that "in its obsession with developing a 'machine' aesthetic digital artwork might stand accused of neglecting affective, aes-

---

[40] Anna Munster, 'Low-Res Bleed', p. 87.

Fig. 7.8 Joanna Berzowska, *Feathery Dresses,* 2005. (Image courtesy of the artist)

thetic experience".[41] In contrast to this claim, *Intimate Memory Shirt* and *Feathery Dresses* use tactic and feminine technologies that facilitate intimacy and sensual touch, in dialogue with digitisation. The artist's 'soft' affects privilege bodily responses over political articulations. The application of her approach, to discourses on globalisation and digitisation, might particularise the phenomena, through making them familiar and seemingly within 'reach'. Affect illuminates issues such as the haziness of recollection: the personalisation of memory, and the subtleties of cultural difference.

Berzowska's *Intimate Memory Shirt* and *Feathery Dresses* have the capacity to remember human touches, and the time lapses between interactions. *Intimate Memory Shirt* incorporates a digital microphone, which is sewn into the collar of the garment. The reverberations of voice or breath are recalled, stimulating a pattern of lights that light up from the waste to the collar of the shirt. The symbolic feathers encourage subjects to explore questions about sensual touch and intimacy, animalistic behaviour, and femininity in a digital *oeuvre*. Through using soft, haptic technologies, and feminine emblems such as feathers, flowers and dresses, the garments interrogate the perceived hostility, inoperability and masculinity of digital technologies. By integrating digital technology into wearable examples of art, Berzowska challenges the traditional limits of art production, while opposing constructions of digital change centred upon disconnection, dislocation, dehumanisation or masculinisation. In Joanna Berzowska's art, sensual and affective encounters with digital technology are as important as the politics of any *objet d'art* (Fig. 7.8).

Berzowska's garments have the ability to 'remember' interactions. That recording of events contests the perceived transience of digital events. The garments' 'memories' bind users to their actions, thereby challenging the perceived diminishing of responsibility, anonymous sexualisation of others and concealment of

---

[41] Anna Munster, 'Low-Res Bleed', p. 78.

identity, in a digital age. Within these works, the body becomes a critical platform expression. In making it so, Berzowska draws attention to the themes of localisation, particularisation, and individuality. 'A worn object', the curator Sara Diamond writes, 'carries the evidence of our identity and our history. Digital technologies allow us to shape and edit that evidence to reflect more subtle or more poetic, aspects of our identity and our history'.[42] In this way, Berzowska's digital art encourages physical engagement rather than virtual disembodiment, in an era of digital change.

Berzowska offers contrary accounts of globalisation and digitisation, centred upon the intimacy of touch, emotional connection, sensuality, and subjective interpretation. She uses digital media to re-materialise human connection, while opposing the supposed 'hardness' of the technology. In these ways, Berzowska's art might contest the perceived masculine control of global politics, economy and technology. This is the strength of the artist's work: the disruption of worn assumptions about globalisation's affect that limit its potential to be anything else. Joanna Berzowska's *Intimate Memory Shirt* and *Feathery Dresses* instead, shows how digitisation can enable individuals to grasp globalisation's reins, using its flows of technology to defy totalising assumptions and create spaces for human connection, exchange and liberation.

Conversations on Globalisation

In their eclectic and often divergent treatments of globalisation, the *In the Line of Flight* artists suggest the fallacy of unified approaches to phenomenon. As many of these works illustrate, globalisation does not create simple binaries between the local and global, the particular and universal, but eclectic experiences that move in, and between these constructs. The exhibition's theme is the lynchpin that brings these diverse expressions together. In reflecting upon the themes of globalisation and 'flight', the art 'testifies to a new aesthetic sensibility accentuated by the struggle of city dwellers, proposing new perspectives on contemporary urban conditions from around the world'.[43] As the curators of *In the Line of Flight* propose, 'the exhibition suggests integrity in diversity, possibilities derived from multiplicity'.[44] This is reflected in the variant platforms used, from virtual reality systems to interactive cinema, net.art, robotics, and haptic media. The difference in the artists' approaches to globalisation however, confirms Mark Tribe's sense that '[w]hile in a material sense, the Internet is a globally homogenous network with common tools and pro-

---

[42] Sara Diamond, *'Feathery Dresses', NewMedia.org*, <http://newmediabeijing.org/md2005/exhibition_display.php?section=2&link_id=4&title=Feathery+Dresses+%28CND%29&artist_id=4_2>, 2004, (accessed 1 October 2007).

[43] Zhang Ga, '*In the Line of Flight*—Transcending Urbanscapes', <http://newmediabeijing.org/md2005/exhibition.php?section=2>, NewMedia.org, 2004, (accessed 1 October 2007).

[44] Zhang Ga, '*In the Line of Flight*—Transcending Urbanscapes', <http://newmediabeijing.org/md2005/exhibition.php?section=2>.

tocols, and while it is contributing, perhaps more than any other technology, to the globalisation of economies and cultures…it nevertheless means different things in different parts of the world'.[45] The artists' employment of different media and techniques facilitate diverse experiences, in as much as they provide means to present different perspectives on the globalisation and digitisation of daily life.

Some of the more powerful works examined in this chapter are arguably Justine Cooper's *Transformers* and Joanna Berzowska's *Intimate Memory Shirt* and *Feathery Dresses*. Cooper shows high level of innovation, through weaving human DNA into her installation—literally centralising the individual in her art. To this end, *Transformers* operates as an active critique of globalisation's particular impacts. Similarly, Joanna Berzowska's memory-rich fabrics critically simulate and interrogate, affects such as intimate touch and response. Through these processes, the artist enables the subject to personally experience the global 'technoscape', through focusing upon digital technology's capacities for physical engagement, localisation, personalisation and human connection. By breaking down categorical assumptions about globalisation and digitisation, Berzowska and Cooper show how digitisation can be subjectively experienced.

The artists Leon Cmielewski and Josephine Starrs reveal a different application of digital media. In their installation *Floating Territories,* Cmielewski and Starrs employ 'old school' gaming technologies to construct a contemporary critique of Appadurai's globalisation's flows of politics, people and ideology.[46] The simplicity of the format ironically heightens the gravity of the themes: world domination, colonisation, and corporate takeover. The often disastrous outcomes that result from the user's decision to 'escape', 'defend' or 'petition' present a construction of globalisation that is in some ways sympathetic with the reactive net.art of Ross Mawdsley, ®™ark, and The Yes Men. The artists' portrayal of simplistic toy figures resonates with the Lego-like™ characters in ®™ark's *Etoy* campaign. Cmielewski and Starrs' use of a highly structured grid system ironically sheds light onto perceived spatial, temporal and human disruptions, under globalisation. The title *Floating Territories,* and search options like 'Wander', address themes of diapora, travel, and escape; engaging with globalisation's facilitation of virtual and physical travel across borders. The artists' work creates interplays between ordered and regulated, fluid and democratic space. As discussed in Chap. 7, Cmielewski and Starrs' conflicting spatial and temporal arrangements might emulate the haphazard experiences of online gaming, and traversing global spaces such as the Internet.

While Cmielewski and Starrs' use a mix of new and old formats, Marnix de Nijs employs the latest haptic and kinetic technology to depict the metropolis of *Run Motherfucker Run*. The use of potentially 'hostile' technology, such as a treacherous treadmill, and audiovisuals that seemingly shift of their own accord, portray a dehumanised and indifferent global city. While Cmielewski and Starrs create disjunctures between their media and messages—a tactic that raises awareness through shock—Marnix de Nijs' use of hostile technologies supports his portrayal

---

[45] Mark Tribe, *Foreword*, pp. xi–xii.

[46] Arjun Appadurai, 'Disjuncture and Difference in the Global Culture Economy', pp. 295–310.

of a de-humanised city. In *Run Motherfucker Run*, de Nijs exploits techniques and technologies unique to digital technology. As the central interface, the treadmill is not only interactive, but also responsive to the user's movements in real-time. The installation's visual sequencing and audio frequencies are generated in response to the user's footsteps. In this way, de Nijs illustrates digital art's potential to deconstruct globalisation's spaces and times, and reconfigure these constructs according to individual encounters, bodily rhythms and flows.

To that end, *Run Motherfucker Run* becomes a personal projection of the phenomenon, which while influenced by the artists' selection of audiovisual material, provides scope for the individual to 'choose their own adventure', and construct their own narrative sequence. Like Cmielewski and Starrs, de Nijs' presents an ominous rendering of globalisation. Through the trajectory of the global city, he presents a threatening landscape, composed of dark, labyrinthine streets. The installation's disjointed sequencing adds to this sense. While the cushions at the base of the treadmill seem to pre-empt the user's (down)fall. Like *Floating Territories, Run Mother fucker Run* might stand accused of presenting only one side of globalisation's story, a claim which would align it with more alarmist accounts, associated with some early net.art renderings of globalisation, and speculations on digitisation by Baudrillard.

Conclusion

This chapter has examined digital artworks made by different artists from diverse parts of the globe. It has shown how despite their points of departure different artists are exploring the production and individual experience of digital art in a global age. Through a case study approach, this chapter has revealed how many artists are engaging critical theories and ideas concerning subjectivity, embodiment, cultural identity, the universal and the particular. It has argued that many new digital artworks are conveying heightened levels of criticism and nuance in their engagement with globalisation and digitisation's impacts. Haptic and tactile art it has claimed, can engage with individual bodies and subjectivities and present globalisation as something more layered than a universal construct. Artworks such as Joanna Berzowska's tactile *Feathery Dresses* and *Intimate Memory Shirt* draw out this idea: the notion that as a technological process aligned with globalisation, digitisation is a complex phenomenon that can be personally 'felt'. By engaging with an eclectic array of contemporary works, the richness and diversity of digital artistry and affect has been shown. At the same time, this chapter has revealed how haptic art such as Marnix de Nijs' *Run Motherfucker Run* creates two-way dialogues with the user, by physically responding in real-time and encouraging the individual contemplation of themes such as the global city, rapid digital speed and temporal transcendence. In this way, de Nijs encourages the user to perceive and determine globalisation's affects.

In the Line of Flight's exciting mélange of works suggests the variances and inter-flows of subjective construction, personal experience, particular interpretation and physical response. In exploring these diverse artworks, this chapter has engaged with changing methods in art production and display, in dialogue with globalisation. Each artwork has been analysed in terms of its engagement with the phenomenon, and the artist's cognition of its affects upon the artwork's themes and construction methods. Finally, this chapter has shown how through their negotiations of digital media, digital artists are generating affective messages about globalisation and globalisation. Their practice suggests the need for new conceptualisations about globalisation and digital art, as phenomena that might inform each other. This idea will be explored further in the following chapter, which will discuss artworks made from 2009 on that engage with digital art and social engagement.

Chapter 8
Digital Art and Social Engagement

Introduction

One of the most notable trends since 2009 has been the rise of social activist or 'call to action' works. In an age of digital connectivity, artists are exploiting new levels of access and exposure to launch social and political conversations. Alternative means of financial backing are being exploited, while social media is being used as an inexpensive way to promote works. Artists are increasingly using mobile devices to make art and distribute it online. This chapter examines a number of more recent digital works that reflect these shifts (Fig. 8.1).

Kevin Macdonald: *Life in a Day*

The 2011 film *Life in a Day*, directed by Kevin Macdonald, was created as a crowd-sourced feature. The filmmakers invited people from around the world to film their lives on a single day: 24 July 2010. Participants were given three questions to respond to: 'what do you have in your pocket?' 'who do you love?' and 'what do you fear?' Incredibly, over 80,000 films from 192 countries were received. 400 cameras were also sent out to developing countries to attempt, in Macdonald's words, 'to paint a global picture'. He notes: 'I didn't want a global film that's just about rich people, or Europeans and North Americans.'[1] *Life in a Day* gained vast amounts of attention online. As of January 2013, the film had received 37,785,322 views.[2] The film was shared on *YouTube* and distributed by National Geographic Films, which contributed to the vast amounts of publicity it received.

---

[1] Courtney Boyd Myers, 'YouTube's Life in a Day Movie is a Stunner', *The Next Web*, </http://thenextweb.com/google/2011/06/15/youtubes-life-in-a-day-movie-is-a-stunner/>, 2011, (accessed 1 August 2013).

[2] Kevin Macdonald, '*Life in a Day*', <http://movies.nationalgeographic.com/movies/life-in-a-day/about-the-production/>.

M. Langdon, *The Work of Art in a Digital Age: Art, Technology and Globalisation*,
DOI 10.1007/978-1-4939-1270-4_8, © Springer Science+Business Media New York 2014

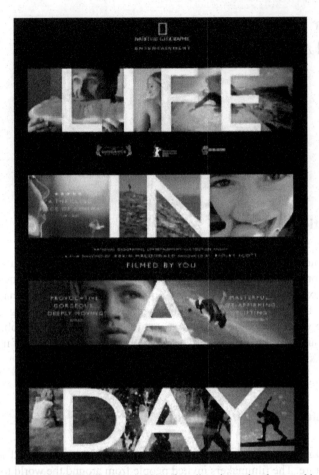

Fig. 8.1. Kevin Macdonald, *Life in a Day*, 2011. (http://movies.nationalgeographic.com/movies/life-in-a-day/about-the-production/)

Social and Political Messages

There are a number of thematic crossovers in *Life in a Day,* with participants frequently addressing topics such as environmental sustainability, economic inequity, social equality and social and political disparities between 'the West and the rest'. To this end, the film converses with recent movements around the world, such as the Occupy Wall Street protests and 2011 Arab Spring. Since 2010, there has been a rise in 'call to action' works, distributed online and designed to generate conversations on current global social and political issues.

Within Life *in a Day,* universal questions are used to structure and frame the film. The filmmakers use universal themes—such as hopes for the future—to create narrative cohesion. In collating and cutting the footage, editor Joe Walker notes how

Fig. 8.2 Kevin Macdonald,
Life in a Day, 2011. (http://
movies.nationalgeographic.
com/movies/life-in-a-day/
about-the-production/)

[o]ne could always rely upon millions of coincidences and rhymes in this material…just because of the sheer volume and range of it. So when we had to move big chunks of the film into a different order, and had to lose connections we'd begun to rely upon, we knew that other connections would swiftly take their place.[3]

Writing for *The Next Web*, Courtney Boyd Myers discusses two scenes in the film where the same question is posed: 'what do you have in your pocket?' In the first scene, a man pulls out a Lamborghini key. A juxtaposing shot features a Haitian man who declares: 'I have nothing.' Similar parallels occur throughout the film, to highlight similarities and differences in the human condition. These thematic crossovers and collisions encourage contemplation of global social and political issues such as poverty, consumption, and socio-political inequity. Boyd Myers claims that when reviewing the footage received, natural patterns began to emerge. She states that '[c]ontributors tended to film either themselves or people known to them. They followed distinct patterns of a daily routine in many cases—waking, washing, walking, and eating.'[4]

Editing plays a key role in *Life in a Day*, given the lack of a conventional narrative. The entire editing process took 7 months due to the submission of more than 4500 hours worth of footage by global contributors. The editor sought natural connections, to progress the film's themes and narrative momentum. Adam Sternbergh writes in *The New York Times* how '[t]he film aims to tell the story of a planet, but it's the vulnerability of these individual moments, contributed as part of a larger project, that lingers.'[5] As a highly emotive work, *Life in a Day* has a strong audience impact (Fig. 8.2).

---

[3] Joe Walker, *'Life in a Day', YouTube/National Geographic Films*, <http://movies.nationalgeographic.com/movies/life-in-a-day/about-the-production/>, (accessed 1 August 2013).

[4] Courtney Boyd Myers, 'YouTube's Life in a Day Movie is a Stunner', </http://thenextweb.com/google/2011/06/15/youtubes-life-in-a-day-movie-is-a-stunner/>.

[5] Adam Sternbergh, 'Around the World in One Day', *New York Times*, <http://www.nytimes.com/2011/07/24/mag-azine/around-the-world-in-one-day-on-youtube.html?_r=0>, (accessed 30 July 2011). Link no longer active.

Global Production

As an online crowd sourced film, *Life in a Day* was created as a global production. In commenting upon the methods used to obtain the footage for the film. Macdonald argues that '[w]hile the concept of a global project like this may not be new, the media in which the elements are laid out—the Internet, and in particular, You-Tube—is certainly groundbreaking.'[6] In addition to exploring universal themes, the film has been made through global crowd sourcing. In commenting upon the film's online distribution, the director argues that the Internet operates as 'a great metaphor for and a creator of connectedness'.[7] Macdonald claims that

> [t]he film is doing something that wouldn't have been possible pre-Internet, specifically pre-YouTube. The idea that you can ask thousands, tens of thousands, maybe hundreds of thousands of people all to contribute to a project and all to communicate about it and learn about it at the same time belongs essentially to this age that we live in.[8]

The production of *Life in a Day* reflects a number of important shifts that have occurred in recent years. As highlighted by the director, this film engages with changes production and distribution. As smart phones have become more affordable—and photo and video capabilities have improved—more people are making and sharing their creative works online. The creators of the film harnessed this new potential for global collaboration by sending mobile devices to developing countries.

Life in a Day also converses changes to viewing habits in a digital age. Increasingly, productions are not being screened in cinemas or released on DVDs, but broadcast on websites like *YouTube,* enabling users to contribute content, engage with conversation threads, watch material anytime and anywhere using smart devices, and re-distribute material. Macdonald sees the film as a metaphor for Internet use, which involves 'clicking from one place to another, in this almost random way…following our own thoughts, following narrative and thematic paths.'[9]

The use of the Internet as a screening platform provides unprecedented levels of access and exposure. *Life in a Day* has attracted more than 37 million viewers, which is a phenomenal result for a non-traditional narrative film. The film also demonstrates how digital artists and filmmakers are seeking alternative sources of finance. While *Life in a Day* received support from the Sundance Institute and National Geographic, it was made on a low budget and relied upon free input from global contributors.

---

[6] Kevin Macdonald, '*Life in a Day*', <http://movies.nationalgeographic.com/movies/life-in-a-day/about-the-production/>.

[7] Kevin Macdonald, '*Life in a Day*', <http://movies.nationalgeographic.com/movies/life-in-a-day/about-the-production/>.

[8] Kevin Macdonald, '*Life in a Day*', <http://movies.nationalgeographic.com/movies/life-in-a-day/about-the-production/>.

[9] Rachel Dodes, 'Life in a Day' Director Aims to Elevate YouTube Videos Into Art', *The Wall Street Journal,* 22 July 2011, <http://blogs.wsj.com/speakeasy/2011/07/22/life-in-a-day-director-kevin-macdonald-aims-to-elevate-youtube-videos-into-art/>, 2011, (accessed 12 August 2013).

In marketing the film, the team used blogs and social media to raise awareness through free word-of-mouth publicity.[10] In these ways, *Life in a Day* highlights new forms of global communications, online collaboration, and the production and sharing of creative works online. Macdonald claims that the film 'could only be made in the last five years because…you can get enough people who will have an understanding of how to shoot something.'[11] This crowd-sourced work reflects new levels of connectivity and understandings of how mobile devices can be used to produce content. *Life in a Day* encourages contemplation of the relationship between globalisation and digitisation, while offering viewers the opportunity to engage with global social and political issues.

Social and Political Effectiveness

The social and political effectiveness of online expression is often questioned. Do they achieve social and political change in the physical world? Or, do they simply begin conversations, but leave problems unresolved? *Life in a Day* clearly encourages contemplation of social justice issues such as economic hardship and political inequity. The juxtaposition of advantage and disadvantage is powerfully highlighted by the variant responses to the question 'what do you have in your pocket?' While the film does not offer solutions or clear means for viewers to take action, it still serves an important function as a conversation starter.

While there may not be clear avenues for viewers to take action on the issues raised, online works such as this can raise awareness, educate viewers, and rally individuals to pursue social and political causes, through sparking conversations that have been excluded or dropped from public discussion. As a creative platform, digital art can also provide some freedom of expression, and the capacity to engage with contentious topics not addressed by governments or the mainstream Press. News agencies and politicians, however, sometimes take up these issues, once creative works have highlighted or public interest. Taskforce 350.org recently criticised MSN NBC and the US government for only tackling the controversial topic of climate change, once the topic was trending online.[12]

---

[10] Tim Partridge, 'Life in a Day', *Google: Official Blog,* 6 July 2010, <http://googleblog.blogspot.com.au/2010/07/life-in-day.html>, 2010, (accessed 11 August 2013).

[11] Rachel Dodes, 'Life in a Day', <http://blogs.wsj.com/speakeasy/2011/07/22/life-in-a-day-director-kevin-macdonald-aims-to-elevate-youtube-videos-into-art/>.

[12] *350.org Facebook Page,* <https://www.facebook.com/350.org>, (accessed 11 August, 2013).

Fig. 8.3 Ibrahim Hamdan,
Images of Revolution, 2011.
(http://www.aljazeera.com/
programmes/aljazeera-
world/2011/10/
2011101974451215541.html)

Ibrahim Hamdan: *Images of Revolution*

A film that more powerfully engages with social and political issues is Ibrahim Hamdan's 2011 documentary *Images of Revolution*.[13] The work was commissioned by news station Al Jazeera. It was broadcast on the agency's website and uploaded on to various websites such as *YouTube* and *Daily Motion*. The film explores the role that everyday people played in exposing the hardships of living under regimes in the Arab world. In the opening sequence of the film, political analyst Ali al-Bouazizi offers the statement that '[i]mages are like weapons. They can help topple a regime.' (Fig. 8.3).[14]

The central premise of Hamdan's film is that films, images and messages that people shared on social media sites impelled the revolutions of the 2011 Arab Spring. In making the film, Hamdan interviewed some of the people whose content was uploaded onto sites such as *Facebook, Twitter* and *YouTube*. Their posts offered the rest of the world glimpses inside countries such as Tunisia and Egypt, as revolutions took place on the streets. The sharing of messages, video and photographs sparked global dialogues and enabled some of those oppressed citizens in other parts of the world to unite and also seek empowerment.

Criticism of Online Campaigns

The effectiveness of digital works and their commentaries is often debated. Some critics claim that the role of social media during the Arab Spring was overstated and misrepresented levels of political discontent. As Ramesh Srinivasan writes in his article 'Taking power through technology in the Arab Spring', one criticism of social

---

[13] Ibrahim Hamdan, '*Images of Revolution*', <http://www.aljazeera.com/programmes/aljazeerawo rld/2011/10/2011101974451215541.html>.

[14] Ibrahim Hamdan, '*Images of Revolution*', <http://www.aljazeera.com/programmes/aljazeerawo rld/2011/10/2011101974451215541.html>.

media is that it 'often "makes real" that which may not exist for most or any'.[15] Online campaigns often only reveal the views of a limited sector of the population, which can give a false sense of popular opinion.

Equally, online campaigns are sometimes as means for venting, rather than platforms for effecting real change in the physical world. In his blog 'Losing Interest in Social Media: There is no there there', George Siemens criticises writers like Jeff Jarvis for suggesting that a hashtag is 'the equivalent of a power movement'.[16] Siemens states:

> [t]he notion that hashtag = power or the no one owns a hashtag appeal to power and fairness is absolute and utter nonsense...Sure, it's a good avenue to vent personal feelings and blow off steam. However, that is not a "movement" and it doesn't influence policy. The notion of the Arab Spring being about social media is similarly misguided.[17]

Siemens argues that while social media enable us to connect and share information, they are essentially secondary media. 'The enormous and complex problems faced by different societies around the world', Siemens writes, 'will not be solved by twitter, G+, or social media.'[18]

Digital Media as a Social Barometer

The extent to which digital media brought about the events of the Arab Spring is debated. While the scale of its influence may be questioned, it arguably still had a role to play. Looking specifically at Egypt, digital media enabled activists to communicate with each other and the rest of the world, and gave everyday people a platform to voice their concerns. According to research conducted by Zeynep Tufekci and Christopher Wilson claim that nearly half of those surveyed found about the demonstrations in Egypt through word-of-mouth communication, with only 28.3% finding out via Facebook. The authors concluded that 'traditional mass media were far less important for information people about the protest than were more interpersonal means of communication (face-to-face, telephone, or Facebook).'[19] In gaining information about the protests, the first participants in the demonstrations relied upon 'interpersonal forms of media over the mass media.'[20]

---

[15] Ramesh Srinivasan, 'Taking power through technology in the Arab Spring', *Al Jazeera,* <http://www.aljazeera.com/indepth/opinion/2012/09/2012919115344299848.html>, (accessed 26 Oct 2012).

[16] George Siemens, 'Losing Interest in Social Media: There is no There There', *eLearnspace,* <http://www.elearnspace.org/blog/2011/07/30/losing-interest-in-social-media-there-is-no-there-there/>, 2011, (accessed 11 August 2013).

[17] George Siemens, 'Losing Interest in Social Media <http://www.elearnspace.org/blog/2011/07/30/losing-interest-in-social-media-there-is-no-there-there/>.

[18] George Siemens, 'Losing Interest in Social Media <http://www.elearnspace.org/blog/2011/07/30/losing-interest-in-social-media-there-is-no-there-there/>.

[19] Zeynep Tufekci and Christopher Wilson, 'Social Media and the Decision to Participate in Political Protest: Observations From Tahrir Square', *Journal of Communication,* Vol. 62., 2012, p. 370.

[20] Zeynep Tufekci and Christopher Wilson, 'Social Media and the Decision to Participate in Political Protest: Observations From Tahrir Square', p. 370.

According to Tufekci and Wilson, digital content production was high during the Egyptian revolutions. Approximately half of those surveyed had made or shared films and photographs of the events online, with Facebook being the main platform for distribution.[21] Almost half of those surveyed made or shared digital content, which made it difficult for the government or state run media channels to conceal information about the demonstrations. Tufekci and Wilson argue that '[i]f that proportion was applied to even the most conservative estimates of total participation in the Tahrir Square demonstrations, it becomes apparent that at least tens, if not hundreds of thousands of people were documenting the protests.'[22]

Social media had an important role to play during the Egyptian revolutions. It enabled everyday people to act as 'citizen journalists'—capturing events occurring on the streets and sharing content with the rest of the world. To this end, digital media operated as a popular barometer that captured levels of discontent, augmented mass protests and helped bring down a regime. Contrary to opposing accounts, Tufekci and Wilson claim that '[i]n the case of protests in Egypt, it appears that social networks, often mediated through the new online platforms in the emergent networked public sphere, played a crucial role.'[23]

Achieving Social and Political Change

Ibrahim Hamdan engages with this idea in his film *Images of Revolution*. As a journalist, he felt it was important to show how during the Arab Spring, everyday citizens captured instances of social and political injustice. In the opening sequence of the film, we are introduced to a young Tunisian woman who captured the shooting of a Syrian man shouting 'the great Tunisian people will never die'[24] down on the street. She claims 'I expected my video to become popular only in Tunisia or on Facebook, I never imagined it would be shown so many times on TV channels.' She talks about her friends' surprise that 'an ordinary person took these extraordinary pictures.' (Fig. 8.4).[25]

As lawyer and activist Abdul Nasser Ouaini states,

the people of Tunisia created their own media tools with their mobile phones and small cameras. They succeeded in publicising their cause and tragedy to the entire world. Those

---

[21] Zeynep Tufekci and Christopher Wilson, 'Social Media and the Decision to Participate in Political Protest: Observations From Tahrir Square', p. 370.

[22] Zeynep Tufekci and Christopher Wilson, 'Social Media and the Decision to Participate in Political Protest: Observations From Tahrir Square', p. 370.

[23] Zeynep Tufekci and Christopher Wilson, 'Social Media and the Decision to Participate in Political Protest: Observations From Tahrir Square', p. 370.

[24] Ibrahim Hamdan, '*Images of Revolution*', <http://www.aljazeera.com/programmes/aljazeerawo rld/2011/10/2011101974451215541.html>.

[25] Ibrahim Hamdan, '*Images of Revolution*', <http://www.aljazeera.com/programmes/aljazeerawo rld/2011/10/2011101974451215541.html>.

Fig. 8.4 Ibrahim Hamdan, *Images of Revolution*, 2011. (http://www.aljazeera.com/ programmes/aljazeera-world/2011/10/ 2011101974451 215541.html)

amateur images became like a news agency supplying international channels with pictures from Tunisia.'[26]

The footage captured by these 'citizen journalists' gave face to the conflict in Syria. Personal testimonies provided the rest of the world with ways of understanding a macro political situation. The photographs, videos and comments posted by every-day people provided visual access to unreachable regions, in places such as Syria. Because much of the footage was shot in a transferable digital format, it enabled content to be re-posted on social media sites and picked up by media agencies around the world. A new relationship emerged between traditional news agencies and citizen journalists.

The sharing of digital content via social media sites also allowed citizens to ad-dress topics that were either too localised or contentious for state run news agencies to address. Many citizen journalists drew attention to social and political injustices, such as the covered up killing of Khaled Mohammed Said by Egyptian police.[27] Through boldly engaging with these contentious topics, they challenged the au-thority of the regime. Srinivasan believes that digital technology enabled citizens to take power in Egypt. [28] Firstly, it allowed people to infiltrate the state-run mass media. He states that while 'domestic corporate media channels are self-serving and

[26] Ibrahim Hamdan, '*Images of Revolution*', <http://www.aljazeera.com/programmes/aljazeerawo rld/2011/10/2011101974451215541.html>.

[27] *Khaled Said Facebook Page,* <https://www.facebook.com/pages/Khaled-Said/100792 786638349>, (accessed 11 August 2013).

[28] Ramesh Srinivasan, 'Taking power through technology in the Arab Spring', <http://www.aljazeera. com/indepth/opinion/2012/09/2012919115344299848.html>.

volatile in their coverage',[29] during the Arab Spring activists posted transferable digital content online, which was then republished by international news agencies. Arguably, Egyptian activists saw the connection between street protests with online action. They showed how when digital media campaigns work well, they augment physical action rather than seeking to replace it.

One of the challenges, however, is to keep abreast of changes to technology and how it can be used. Srinivasan writes that activists 'need to discover new tools that can continue to influence the political environment.'[30] He cites the example of Hossam Hamalawy, an activist and blogger for the Revolutionary Socialists. Hamalawy described to him how a website could function as a means to create networks and organise protests in real-time. However, Srinivasan also notes that '[t]echnologies to spy, hack, and leak are all part of the environment',[31] meaning that digital media is not just a domain for liberal youth or left leaning activists, but militaries, governments and regimes.

Lara Baladi: *Alone, Together…In Media Res*

Lara Baladi, 2012 video installation *Alone, Together…In Media Res* explores the impacts of the Egyptian revolution of 25 January 2011 across three video channels. Baladi is an Egyptian-Lebanese artist that was born in Beirut and spent her childhood in Cairo and Paris. She returned to Egypt in 1997 where she now resides. Her art has been exhibited internationally and features film, photography, collage and tapestries. She takes her influences from international cultures that she has experienced. Baladi's sound installation *Borg el Amal* (translated as *Tower of Hope*), was awarded the 2008/2009 Grand Nile Award at the Cairo Biennale. Baladi also co-founded two projects during the Arab Spring: *Radio Tahrir* and *Tahrir Cinema*. According to the artists, '[b]oth initiatives were inspired and informed by the 18 days that toppled Mubarak's leadership,'[32] with *Tahrir Cinema* enabling citizens to share films that would document the Egyptian revolution (Fig. 8.5).

Alone, Together…In Media Res features three LCD screens, which bombard the viewer with videos from the Egyptian uprising, as well as content from other revolutions. The installation emulates the saturation of imagery that occurred, as news agencies reported on the events and citizen journalists posted content online. As a work in progress, *Alone, Together…In Media Res* effectively captures the flux

[29] Ramesh Srinivasan, 'Taking power through technology in the Arab Spring', <http://www.aljazeera. com/indepth/opinion/2012/09/2012919115344299848.html>.

[30] Ramesh Srinivasan, 'Taking power through technology in the Arab Spring', <http://www.aljazeera. com/indepth/opinion/2012/09/2012919115344299848.html>.

[31] Ramesh Srinivasan, 'Taking power through technology in the Arab Spring', <http://www.aljazeera. com/indepth/opinion/2012/09/2012919115344299848.html>.

[32] Lara Baladi, 'Alone, Together…Tahrir Two Years Later,' <http://creativetimereports. org/2013/01/25/tahrir-revolution-in-media-res/>, *Creative Time Reports,* 25 January 2013, (accessed 11 August 2013).

Fig. 8.5 Lara Baladi, *Alone, Together…In Media Res,* 2012. (3 channel video installation, 42 min, Egypt, 2012 in Dorothea Schoene, 'Beyond The Image: A Project By Lara Baladi', *Contemporary Visual Culture In North Africa and The Middle East,* http://www.ibraaz.org/projects/40#author96)

and uncertainty of Egypt's political situation, while suggesting that the social issues raised by the Tahrir Square protestors still require resolve. Importantly, the installation also functions as a record, documenting and archiving footage that may become lost within the Internet's web, once the revolution was no longer deemed 'newsworthy'. As Dorothea Schoene argues in her critique of Baladi's art, '[w]hile the Internet as an archive is a vast and rich source of information, it is also dangerously ephemeral and unstable: documents, photos or films discovered once, may be deleted the very next moment and lost forever'.[33]

Social and Political Engagement

Alone, Together…In Media Res was borne of the project *Vox Populi (The Voice of the People),* which and collated archived posts, articles, photographs and films uploaded by everyday people during the 2011 Tahrir Square protests. Baladi was motivated to create the installation because two years on, she felt that the aims of the activists remain unfulfilled. Equally, she believes that Tahrir Square has 'lost much of its impact as a public space for changing history.'[34] To this end, the artwork seeks to identify and locate the ways in which citizens have sought freedom, across the course of history. The title: *Alone, Together…In Media Res* means 'in the midst of things' in Latin. It refers to the individual actions of citizens, as well as the senses of solidarity that come from collaborating online and aligning with revolutionary thinkers and actors from other moments in time.

During the revolution, Baladi relied upon the Internet for news and updates, since she did not own a television. Social media sites in particular, enabled everyday

---

[33] Dorothea Schoene, 'Beyond The Image', <http://www.ibraaz.org/projects/40#author96>.

[34] Lara Baladi, 'Alone, Together…Tahrir Two Years Later,' <http://creativetimereports. org/2013/01/25/tahrir-revolution-in-media-res/>.

people to network and organise, share their stories and report on events taking place in their communities. As Rhona Wells asserts, in reference to art from the Middle East, '[s]ocial media, perhaps thanks to the international and domestic hype, has a cache in Egypt that it did not have before the events of 2011. These technologies, seen as Modern and 'liberating, have been embraced by many throughout Egypt's population, including by those without a computer or Internet access.'[35] To this end, they acted as citizen journalists providing up-to-date information on the revolution. In documenting the protests and offering a chronology of events, *Alone, Together… In Media Res* serves a similar role.

In making the film, Baladi searched online sites such as *YouTube* and selected footage that echoed the sentiments of the Egyptian revolution. In her searches, she focussed upon themes such as democracy, violence against women, censorship, brutality and suppression. Baladi also researched messages posted by activists on Twitter using the #Jan25 hashtag, noting that

> [a]s the political tension grew, more and more images and videos of a packed Tahrir Square were uploaded to YouTube and other websites. They echoed footage from other uprisings across the Middle East and North Africa, as well as the sights and sounds of a vast array of past social movements. It was as though Sartre was protesting with us in Tahrir.[36]

Baladi also uses the three video channels to create connections and juxtapositions that provide frameworks for locating the events in broader social and political terms.

Social and Political Effectiveness

In making her installation, Baladi wanted to discover what has motivated people to revolt throughout history. She incorporates a speech by Jean Paul Sartre, for example, which was used to motivate striking car manufacturers in France. She also includes images from other iconic revolutions, as well as banned cartoons, iconic photographs, political graffiti and statements by activist groups such as Greenpeace. To this end, Baladi manages to 'find and define the archetypes within historical processes, which reflect the embedded quality in humans to search for freedom.'[37]

As Baladi searched for content online, she discovered the video Tiananmen-Like Courage in Cairo: Egypt's 25 Jan Protests.[38] The short film was shot on a mobile phone and uploaded onto YouTube, where it went viral. The film features a man standing defiantly in front of a police water cannon, trying to block its path. Dorothea Schoene interviewed the artist and believed that the film was included because

---

[35] Rhona Wells, 'The Future of a Promise', *Middle East,* Issue 428, Dec 2011, p. 60.

[36] Lara Baladi, 'Alone, Together…Tahrir Two Years Later,' <http://creativetimereports. org/2013/01/25/tahrir-revolution-in-media-res/>.

[37] Dorothea Schoene, 'Beyond The Image', <http://www.ibraaz.org/projects/40#author96>.

[38] WilyawilDotCom, 'Tiananmen-Like Courage in Cairo: Egypt's 25 Jan Protests', *YouTube,* <http://www.youtube.com/watch?v=q1m4_q_HP5o>, (accessed 1 February 2013).

'[t]he strong symbolic gestures and iconography in the video successfully paralleled two major uprisings of the last few decades.'[39]

Some critics argue that it is too early to be making art about the Arab Spring. In reflecting upon artworks exhibited at the 2012 Art Dubai fair, Laura U. Marks claimed '[i]t is too soon after Tahrir Square to make art: an indisputable consensus.'[40] She discussed one work in particular, Isak Berbic's 2011 film *Battle for Petra*, in which the artist transformed television footage of the Arab Spring into a *Ben Hur* inspired battle scene. Marks writes that [t]his work, casting protestors and police as gladiators, was so disrespectful it took my breath away.[41]

However, Baladi's, installation neither simplifies of trivialises the events of 25 January 2011, but provides a rich framework for viewers to locate and contextualise the protests in broader social and political terms. She considers her installation as 'documentation of a revolution in the digital age, and watching the virtual world turn into reality'.[42] This is an important statement, as it points to the artist's aware-ness of the need for online campaigns to augment physical action, if they are to effect real social and political change. As the events of the Arab Spring continue to unravel, we might begin to believe in what Wells terms 'the promise of visual cul-ture in an age that has become increasingly disaffected with politics as a means of social engagement.'[43] But for some critics such as Marks, wonder who should have the ability to represent these realities.[44]

Art and Environmentalism

In her article 'The Art of Activism: Painting The Faces of Social and Climate Change', Kimberley Mok writes that '[a]rt can be a powerful tool for social change, disseminating ideas and inspiring people to act together.'[45] She refers to a recent series of works exhibited as part of Oxfam America's exhibition *Climate Change on Campus,* which sought to bring 'art, activism and concern for climate change together for an exhibition at December's UN Conference of Parties meeting in Poznan, Poland.'[46] Increasingly, world artists are engaging with issues of climate

---

[39] Dorothea Schoene, 'Beyond The Image', <http://www.ibraaz.org/projects/40#author96>.

[40] Laura U. Marks, 'Moving Images', *Afterimage,* Vol. 40 Issue 1, 2012, p. 5.

[41] Laura U. Marks, 'Moving Images', p. 5.

[42] Lara Baladi, 'Alone, Together…Tahrir Two Years Later,' <http://creativetimereports. org/2013/01/25/tahrir-revolution-in-media-

[43] Rhona Wells, 'The Future of a Promise', p. 60.

[44] Laura U. Marks, 'Moving Images.'

[45] Kimberley Mok, 'The Art of Activism: Painting The Faces of Social and Climate Change', *Treehugger,* <http://www.treehugger.com/culture/the-art-of-activism-painting-the-faces-of-social-climate-change.html>, (accessed 13 February 2013).

[46] Kimberley Mok, 'The Art of Activism', <http://www.treehugger.com/culture/the-art-of-activ-ism-painting-the-faces-of-social-climate-change.html>.

change, environmental degradation and the impacts upon people living in developed and third world countries. Some are using their art to raise awareness of issues, but to also help bring about change through donating profits from sales to environmental organisations and encouraging online audiences to support worthy causes or support political candidates and agencies addressing climate change.

One such artist is Seattle-based digital photographer, Chris Jordan. The lawyer turned artist has used human detritus—ranging from oil barrels to plastic bottles and discarded Barbie™ dolls—to comment upon the impacts of waste and consumption upon the environment. He uses physical objects to represent concerning and perhaps incomprehensible statistics. Jordan's series include: *Intolerable Beauty: Portraits of American Mass Consumption* (2003–2006), *In Katrina's Wake: Portraits of Loss From an Unnatural Disaster* (2005), *Running The Numbers I: An American Self Portrait* (2006-current), *Running the Numbers II: Portraits of Global Mass Culture* (2009–2010) and *Midway: Message from the Gyre* (2009-current). The provocative titles highlight the artist's concern with human consumption, social inequity and environmental devastation.

Jordan's website provides links to supporting articles and resources, which provides critical contexts for engaging with his works. In an interview with Simon Preuss, Jordan reflects upon audience experiences of his art. He claims that

> seen from a distance, the images are like something else, maybe totally boring pieces of Modern art. On closer view, the visitor has an almost unpleasant experience with the artwork. It's almost like a magic trick; inviting people to a conversation that they didn't want to have in the first place.[47]

Jordan's artworks are deliberately provocative, designed to make real incomprehensible statistics and perhaps motivate audiences to change their habits for the betterment of the environment.

Chris Jordan, *Midway: Message from the Gyre*

One of Jordan's most powerful art series is *Midway: Message from the Gyre*. This series—commenced in 2009 and currently ongoing—documents the devastating effects of Western consumption upon a population of albatrosses. The carcasses of dozens of birds are photographed, with plastic caps and other discarded objects embedded within the remains. What is tragic about this work is that Midway Atoll is more than 2000 miles from any civilisation and is therefore meant to provide a sanctuary to these creatures. Instead, human waste that washes into the atoll is mistaken as food and fed to the chicks. In an article in the *Huffington Post*, Stiv J. Wilson claims that Jordan's images 'were often dismissed by critics as "photoshopped" or

---

[47] Simone Preuss, 'An Interview with Photographic Artist Chris Jordan', *Environmental Graffiti*, 2008, <http://www.environmentalgraffiti.com/featured/interview-photographic-artist-chris-jordan/11408>, (accessed 15 February 2013).

Fig. 8.6 Forest and Kim Starr, *Habit with Laysan Albatross Chicks and Marine Debris,* 2008. (http://www.starrenvironmental.com/images/image/?q=080603-5640&o=plants)

altered' in some way because of the sheer, unbelievable amounts of plastics inside their bodies (Fig. 8.6).[48]

On his website, he writes that 'kneeling over their carcasses is like looking into a macabre mirror'.[49] Like *Unsinkable*, the series *Midway: Message from the Gyre* provides a lens for us to reflect upon our patterns of consumption, and to see their direct impacts upon the environment. As Jordan states,

> These birds reflect back an appallingly emblematic result of the collective trance of our consumerism and runaway industrial growth. Like the albatross, we first-world humans find ourselves lacking the ability to discern anymore what is nourishing from what is toxic to our lives and our spirits.[50]

---

[48] Stiv J. Wilson, 'Dead Plastic Filled Birds', *Huffington Post,* <http://www.huffingtonpost.com/stiv-j-wilson/dead-plastic-filled-birds_b_638716.html>, (accessed 15 February 2013).

[49] Chris Jordan, *Midway: Message from the Gyre,* <http://www.chrisjordan.com/gallery/midway/#about>, (accessed 15 February 2013).

[50] Chris Jordan, *Midway: Message from the Gyre,* <http://www.chrisjordan.com/gallery/midway/#about>.

Jordan is said to have experienced great trauma during his trip, and depression for some time after.[51] He stated: 'I was like Dante, entering hell, but thought eventually I would come out the other side. The problem is, I never came out.'.[52] Jordan emotionally spoke about the Midway Atoll and what he described as the 'problem of unconscious collective behaviour',[53] and during his 2008 TED presentation. He claimed 'we've lost our outrage and our anger and our grief',[54] having become desensitized to such traumatic events. Yet, as Helen Walters observed, ['h]e clearly wasn't wagging his finger or blaming or preaching, rather trying to combat what he described as "the anaesthesia" prevalent in contemporary culture within the United States.[55]

Active Art

Chris Jordan's art offers more than passive viewing experiences. Like *Life in a Day*, Jordan uses his website to foster active engagement and participation, by providing critical contexts as well as means for individuals to comment or take action on the issues presented. Jordan uses his website to provide critical contexts for viewing the works, raise awareness of key issues, establish and report on milestones, and offer avenues for audiences to support the cause.

To complement this art series, Jordan is also working on the film *Midway,* which is due for release in 2013. The film will be a collaborative work involving the artists Bill Weaver, Jan Vozenilek, Victoria Sloan Jordan, and Manuel Maqueda. The film will have limited narration and instead use video, photography and poetry to allow each artist to personally respond. According to a website for the film, the documentary will use limited narration and instead allow spectacular images to show the extent of the degradation of the environment. High-definition cinematography will present 'stunning juxtapositions of beauty and horror, destruction and renewal, grief and joy, birth and death', with the aim being to shift viewer's perspectives on environmental protection and their practices of consumption. Functioning as both 'elegy and warning the film explores the interconnectedness of species, with the

---

[51] Stiv J. Wilson, 'Dead Plastic Filled Birds', <http://www.huffingtonpost.com/stiv-j-wilson/dead-plastic-filled-birds_b_638716.html>.

[52] Stiv J. Wilson, 'Dead Plastic Filled Birds', <http://www.huffingtonpost.com/stiv-j-wilson/dead-plastic-filled-birds_b_638716.html>.

[53] Chris Jordan, 'Turning Powerful Stats into Art', <http://www.ted.com/talks/chris_jordan_pictures_some_shocking_stats.html>, *TED,* 2008, (accessed 5 August 2013).

[54] Chris Jordan, 'Turning Powerful Stats into Art', <http://www.ted.com/talks/chris_jordan_pictures_some_shocking_stats.html>.

[55] Helen Walters, 'First Tears at TED', *Bloomberg Business week,* 28 February 2008, <http://www.businessweek.com/innovate/next/archives/2008/02/first_tears_at.html>, 2008, (accessed 15 February 2013).

albatross on Midway as a mirror of out humanity.'[56] Several times on his website, Jordan refers to the albatross in mythical terms, viewing it as a symbolic metaphor for the environment and man's impact upon it.

The film *Midway* is being financed through private donations and sponsorship from the not-for-profit artist organisation Fractured Atlas, which suggests means for artists to raise the revenue to make art. On the *Midway* website there is a plea for viewers to donate to the project and take action on the environmental issues raised. The film also has a blog, which allows the artists to directly communicate with viewers and encourage them to take action. In addition, *Midway* has its own *YouTube* channel as well as a presence on *Flickr, Facebook, Livestream* and *Twitter.* The project provides multiple means for users to become informed as well as involved in the environmental campaign to save the Midway Atoll.

Conclusion

Increasingly, artists are using digital media to shape social and political agendas. All of the artworks discussed in this chapter seek to effect some kind positive change. *Life in a Day* and *Alone, Together…In Med Res* explore events that were not always covered by the mainstream media. Much of the West's awareness of social and political injustices—such as the murder of Egyptian citizen Khaled Said by police—came from 'citizen journalists' who, like these artists, used connective media to document the events online. While *Images of Revolution* alludes to digital media's role in implementing social and political change, *Alone, Together…In Media Res* goes further in suggesting that digital art serves an important role, as a means for communicating controversial ideas.

While Hamdan and Macdonald use the Internet media to distribute their art, Baladi and Jordan offer modified versions of their works online. To this end, these works engage with online social and political commentary, and serve similar functions themselves: operating as platforms for launching and continuing conversations about issues such as global living conditions, economic disparity, political inequity, censorship and restrictions on freedom, and individual and collective uprising. By virtue of being published online, each of the artworks discussed in this chapter have the capacity to transform passive viewers into active users that can converse with artists and comment upon works, 'liking' or 'disliking' them, and following links posted on accompanying websites to further engage with the topics raised.

This is powerfully shown in *Midway: Message from the Gyre* and *Life in a Day,* which uses associated websites and social media channels to encourage users to support political and environmental campaigns. As a crowd-sourced work, *Life in a Day* also invites enables users to become part of the production process, and personally explore social issues such as poverty and environmental change more

---

[56] Chris Jordan, 'Midway Film', <http://www.midwayfilm.com/about.html>, *Midway Film,* (accessed 18 February 2013).

personally. Equally, the websites for *Midway: Message from the Gyre* and the *Midway* film encourage users to reflect upon their own patterns of consumption. These sites provide links to supporting articles, affiliated organizations and current campaigns, and invite users to become involved in the conversations broached by their art.

However, the question remains: can digital art effect social and political change in the physical world? Certainly, only those with digital access and literacy, a social media presence, and an interest in the topics presented will engage with the artists' campaigns. But the advantage of online action is that it allows for the wider spread of ideas, beyond local contexts. The sharing of art online enables dialogues to not just be initiated but continued, through facilitating two-way communication channels between makers and users.

Arguably, when online campaigns work well, they complement and augment physical action. This can be achieved through linked websites, blogs or social media sites that encourage audiences to join rallies, lobby governments, donate money to worthy causes, sign petitions, change their behaviours or opinions, or push for international agreements on issues such as climate change or child poverty. To bring about actual changes in the physical world, however, arguably artists need to provide something more than a passive viewing experience. As this chapter has shown, the most powerful works are harnessing the connective and participatory tools of digital media to transform passive spectators into active users.

In the digital age, the notion of social responsibility takes on new meaning. With new opportunities for information sharing and global action, those with social and political empowerment might use digital media to try and bring positive change. The globalisation of media offers users unprecedented levels of access to different part of the world. Yet, as we become aware of the difficulties faced by others, we are faced with new questions regarding our social responsibility. Do those of us with political freedom and social empowerment have an obligation to lend our support? As some by all of the artists in this chapter, surely the answer is 'yes'.

Chapter 9
Conclusion: Digital Art as a Platform of Articulation

Introduction

This book has shown how digital art can enable globalisation to be experienced on an individual level. Through an examination of diverse case studies, it has revealed how digital art can act as a critical voice that encourages dialogues centred on individual experience and response. Through iterative conversations, this text has explored how globalisation and digital art can 'speak' to each other, and provide ways of seeing each phenomenon as an experiential, particular and essentially human construct (Fig. 9.1).

A concern about universal and binary articulations of globalisation seemed to necessitate a more particular approach. While not discounting the value of macro analyses for general studies, positivist articulations can be problematic, particularly when applied to the realm of experience. Deterministic frameworks can negate the dynamic, contingent and ephemeral elements of human response. As discussed in Chap. 2 with reference to macro accounts of globalisation, and in Chap. 3 with regards to technological determinist constructions of digital art, positivist affirmations tend to be at the expense of particular difference. The contrary responses to globalisation expressed by the digital artists explored in this book, seem to negate the value and applicability of universal discourses.

From the radical art of ®™ark and the Yes Men through to Chris Jordan's *Midway: Message from the Gyre,* this book has shown how artists are using different tools and techniques to convey globalisation's impacts. Works such as iCinema's *T_Visionarium* and de Nijs' *Beijing Accelerator* illuminate the fluid and indeterminate qualities of globalisation, while challenging the traditional limits and conventions of art. In generating affective experiences centred upon touch, interaction and response, these artists offer new means of articulating globalisation and art, as evolving, experiential constructs.

To make this text more approachable, each chapter approached globalisation and digital art in terms of particular themes. In Chap. 5, for example, spatial, temporal and kinetic impacts were discussed. In Chap. 6, globalisation was explored in terms of specific urban sites. The arrangement of case studies also reflected an historical

M. Langdon, *The Work of Art in a Digital Age: Art, Technology and Globalisation,*
DOI 10.1007/978-1-4939-1270-4_9, © Springer Science+Business Media New York 2014

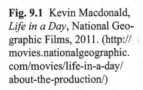

Fig. 9.1 Kevin Macdonald, *Life in a Day*, National Geographic Films, 2011. (http://movies.nationalgeographic.com/movies/life-in-a-day/about-the-production/)

progression in the production of digital art. The ordering was designed to illuminate shifts in the thinking about globalisation, as well as stylistic developments within the field of digital art. From the discussion of reactionary net.art in Chap. 4, to the critique of individuating technology in Chap. 5, and the affective *Metropolis* films explored in Chap. 6, this book has conversed with new levels of nuance and gradation in evolving digital art practice and criticism. In reflecting upon the socially engaged artworks discussed in Chap. 8, it is predicted that future artists will take advantage of emerging haptic, mobile, analytical and locational technologies, to create new commentaries that locate digital art in terms of its times.

Digital Art as Art

A further objective of this book was to provide grounds for locating and understanding digital artworks as art. It contended that digital art *is* art by virtue of its innovative re-orientations of media and messages in dialogue with cultural contexts and external phenomena like globalisation. Some of the pieces explored explicitly questioned the nature of art, and tested its limits. Chapter 2 for example, discussed digital art in terms of attention economies. In Chap. 4, Ross Mawdsley and ®™ark's critique of commercialisation was examined, as was their satirical description of themselves as a corporate entity rather than a group of artists.[1] The chapter also engaged with The Yes Men's radical campaigns, described as 'hijinks'. Their resistance to established concepts of art reveals, as Stallabrass observes, that 'the very notions of greatness and of timeless masterpieces do not sit comfortably with an art so dependent upon and responding to fast-changing technology'.[2]

As discussed in Chap. 2, the denial of digital art as 'art' has much to do formal notions of artistry, originality and authorship. We might question why digital art-

---

[1] Julian Stallabrass, *Internet Art*, p. 137.

[2] Julian Stallabrass, *Internet Art*, p. 143.

ists continue to align themselves with the field of art. Critics might argue that this is purely a pragmatic move, and claim that due to funding rules there is a need for digital works to be deemed 'artistic' to gain revenue and exposure through gallery acquisition. As Geert Lovink notes, 'political climates in Western countries wildly vary. Whereas e-culture funding in the Netherlands has gone up over the past years, the situation in Berlin, Paris and London, for instance, remains bleak'.[3]

Looking to the future there remain unresolved questions about the formal display and acquisition of digital art. These are complicated by the fact that many digital works change their meaning or function when exhibited in gallery spaces. This was the case with the works *Can You See Me Now* and *Haptic Gloves*, for example, which lost some of their functionality when displayed at *In the Line of Flight*. Clearly, the modification of an artwork to suit the physical, technical or economic constraints of a gallery can force artists to make adverse alterations. There is also the issue of galleries deliberately modifying works to make them more 'understandable' to mass audiences.

In seeking to locate digital art, Chap. 3 revealed how the articulation of the globalisation in positivist terms might limit its affects. It explored the fluid discourses of Appadurai, Enwezor, Augé, and Sassen, which challenge singular, universal and alarmist accounts. In opposing the claim that globalisation's 'technoscapes' are hostile or desensitizing, this text explored works by artists such as Justine Cooper, who uses digital media to generate soft and 'feminine' affects.

With reference to the work of iCinema, this book contemplated how global technologies could contribute to new forms of collaboration, production, display and distribution. It revealed how digital technology could provide new opportunities for artistic exchange, and lead to global exhibitions such as *Metropolis* and *In the Line of Flight*. With art becoming increasingly globalised—supported by new flows of information, ideology, finance, technology, and people—it was shown how traditional senses of art drawn from Modern Western traditions, may be losing their relevance or applicability. Reiterating claims established in the Introduction, this book argued for the expansion of the category to accommodate new expressive forms.

While digital art's technical elements are unique, it has also been shown demonstrated how new works converse with earlier art forms dialogues. Chapter 2 discussed earlier interventions in art and technology, and contextualised digital art in terms of precedent styles such as Modern cinema. A case was made for viewing digital expressions as 'art', and acknowledging its strong capacity to offer cultural critiques of phenomena, such as globalisation.

Many of the uncertainties related to the conceptualisation, location, acquisition and display of digital works, suggest a lack of understanding of how it relates to the broader field of art. In his text *Interzone,* Darren Tofts reflects upon some of the perceived issues with digital art, particularly the technological requirements, which are not always fully accommodated by traditional galleries. Yet, rather than apply-

---

[3] Geert Lovink,'New Media, Art and Science: Explorations Beyond the Official Discourse', <http://laudanum.net/geert/files/1129753681/2005>, *Laudanum*, 2005, (accessed 16 December 2007). Link is no longer active.

ing the same expectations to analogue and digital works, Tofts suggest that different approaches are required, as well as broader public education on how digital works can function and be understood as art.[4] While new spaces dedicated to digital art are emerging—ranging from institutions such as the Australian Centre for the Moving Image to forums such as *Rhizome*[5] dedicated to the theorising of digital art and media.

Digital Media as a Humanising Technology

While there have been many attempts to 'popularise' and delimit globalisation—by writers like Naomi Klein and Thomas Friedman[6]—there still remains the sense as Mark K. Smith expresses, that '[m]uch of the talk of 'globalization' is confused and confusing'.[7] Similarly, as has been discussed, understandings of digital art's terminology, boundaries and location are also limited. However, alarmism and fear have often reduced the understanding of globalisation and digitisation, with each being variously described as alienating or as Sukomal Sen writes, 'de-humanising to the core'.[8]

However, throughout this book, universal and binary articulations of globalisation have been questioned. Technological Determinist and Alarmist approaches were challenged on the grounds that they simplistically reduced the phenomenon. To the contrary, many of the artists explored have shown how it is possible to have contradictory reactions to globalisation, so that in one context it may be seen as liberating, while in another viewed as oppressive. For example, Joanna Berzowska's tactile and sensory art that promotes intimacy and touch, revealed the limitations of Baudrillard and Virilio's thesis that new technologies de-humanise and disconnect. *T_Visionarium* also revealed how digital works could converse with individual bodies and senses, through immersive, interactive, and particular technologies. The artists uncovered digital art's sensual, connective and tactile qualities, challenging Baudrillard's claims that simulatory media is de-sensitising.[9] Finally, Lara Baladi's installation Alone, Together…In Media Res offered a conflicted account of global technologies, in showing how the Internet could both liberate and repress individuals.

---

[4] Darren Tofts, *Interzone*, p. 133.

[5] Rhizome, <http://www.rhizome.org>, (accessed 23 September 2007).

[6] No author, 'Thomas Friedman on Globalisation', *The Economist*, 31 March 2005, <http://www.economist.com/books/displaystory.cfm?story_id=3809512>, 2005, (accessed 3 November 2008).

[7] Mark K. Smith, 'Definitions of Globalization', *Informal Education Organisation,* <http://www.infed.org/biblio/defining_globalization.htm>, (accessed 3 November 2008).

[8] Sukomal Sen, 'The Fantasy of 'Fair Globalisation'', *Counter Currents*, 15 July 2008, <http://www.countercurrents.org/gl-sen150704.htm>, 2008, (accessed 4 November 2008).

[9] See: Baudrillard's writings on digitisation's simulation of reality in Jean Baudrillard, 'From 'Simulcra and Simulations''.

In terms of cultural commentary, it was argued that digital art could challenge our perceptions of globalisation, as well as our sense of what art might be. Digital art has the potential to offer unique articulations, through exploring and generating differential responses and events. Chapter 6, for example, explored how Tom Otterness uses simple animation in *Nine Eleven* to express complex feelings of trauma and despair, in the wake of 11 September 2001. This difficult subject might have been communicated far less powerfully, if it was not articulated through the emotive platform of film. Human feelings cannot always be conveyed in linear text. Hyper, sensory and non-linear formats can offer what Peter W. Foltz terms 'associative retrieval paths',[10] which are 'similar to the way retrieval is performed from human memory'.[11]

In presenting digital art as an individual form of cultural commentary, this book has also engaged with affective response. As a sensory, subjective, and expressive form of articulation, it highlighted how digital art can provide new means of expressing 'felt' responses. In relation to *T_Visionarium* and *Beijing Accelerator*, it was shown how digital art can spatially, temporally and kinetically emulates globalisation's perceived impacts, and generate conflicting experiences. Feelings, for example, that the world is closer or more dispersed; that life has sped up or slowed down; that linear time has become more or less relevant in a global world. Artworks that juxtaposed or contradicted one another were deliberately chosen. In Chap. 7, for example, Jung Sin and Kaho Abe's tactile *Haptic Glove* was discussed alongside Starrs and Cmielewski's *Floating Territories,* which featured hard gaming infrastructure and controls. Through offering contrary expressions, this text problematises universal approaches to globalisation and art.

The artworks presented in this book were historically, culturally and technically diverse. Despite the diversity of formats explored, each case study offers a unique understanding of what globalisation might mean, to individual people in particular places or times. They highlighted the richness and variability of reactions to globalisation, while suggesting the value of digital art as an affective means of articulation. While de Nijs' treadmill in *Run Motherfucker Run* directly responds to users' movements, ®™ark's forms of revolt encouraged users to take physical action. While the *Metropolis* films lacked this level of interactivity, the focus upon personal testimony in pieces such as Golebiewski's *This Is Where I Live* re-centred discussions of globalisation around individual memories, encounters and responses. In focussing upon the local and private spaces of a global city, the artist offered a particularised account. Equally, the dark and intimate theatre of the *Metropolis* exhibition emulated the mental realm, drawing attention to the roles that memory, recollection and reverie play in the formation of responses to globalisation.

---

[10] Peter W. Foltz, 'Comprehension, Coherence, and Strategies in Hypertext and Linear Text', in Jean-François Rouet (Ed.), *Hypertext and Cognition*, Mahwah, Lawrence Erlbaum Associates, 1996, p. 110.

[11] Peter W. Foltz, 'Comprehension, Coherence, and Strategies in Hypertext and Linear Text', p. 110.

A progressive ordering of case studies, revealed more complex and nuanced critiques of globalisation's affects within digital works. Chap. 4 focussed upon early net.art examples, which provided ominous accounts of globalisation, and used less subtle techniques. The use of 'hard' and non-tactile technologies produced limited understandings of its variant affects. In Chaps. 5–8, however, it was shown how new works were engaging with individual bodies and consciousnesses and in doing so, generating more intricate responses to globalisation. With the benefit of time, advancements in technology, and new critical understandings, Janet Murray's prediction that 'a new narrative art will come into its own expressive form'[12] was being realised.

Looking Forward

In addressing the question posed in the Introduction of: what understandings of globalisation can digital art provide?, this text has argued that digital art has the capacity to offer affective expressions of globalisation, and promote understandings of its physical and cognitive shifts. By creating a dialogue between globalisation and digital art, this book has shown the difficulty of categorising human experiences. This focus upon globalisation's micro impacts provided new ways of 'accessing' a phenomenon that is often viewed as confounding. Through a close engagement with diverse case studies, new means for locating the self in terms of globalisation and digital art were explored. The works raised different questions concerning cultural identity, territory, connection, empowerment, individualism and morality.

This book has revealed how digital art can offer dynamic and polychromic expressions of globalisation through affective, responsive and immersive media. The flexible languages afforded by digital art, connected with fluid constructions of globalisation. Appadurai's description of it as a series of human, ideological, media, financial and technological flows, for example, framed the book's approach. It has emphasised the value of difference and divergence in the contextualisation of art and globalisation, and revealed how digital art could overcome the constraints of formal or schematic approaches. From the discussion of *T_Visionarium*'s interactive narrative, through to the exploration of socially conscious works in Chap. 8, this text has revealed digital art's capacity to raise human and ontological questions.

Just as this work prompts consideration of globalisation, it also encourages contemplation of what art is or may be, in a digital age. By using the term 'digital art', digital expressions have been located within the realm of art, with their capacity to be 'artistic' firmly acknowledged. While the disruption of traditional principles has been discussed—particularly aura, originality, authorship and display—it has shown how their reinterpretation or rejection, is often part of what 'constitutes' them as art. The subversion of Formalist ideals through replica, misappropriation and crowd sourcing converses with earlier styles, such as Situationist art. Chapter 2

---

[12] Janet Murray, *Hamlet on the Holodeck*, p. 93.

illustrates how Post-Structuralist cinema and Modernist experiments in art and technology, similarly re-defined and expanded the category of art.

In conclusion, the aim of this text was to show how individual experience, interpretation and affect are central to our understandings of art and globalisation. When approached in these ways, both may be seen as phenomena defined by their experiencers. Digital art in particular, is technically and discursively apposite to both engage with and generate, sensory and particular responses. The conversations created between digital art and globalisation throughout this work, have revealed how both concepts can be accessed through affective understandings. As one of the most important platforms of this age, digital art has the capacity to not just articulate—but also generate—individual responses to globalisation.

Selected Bibliography

Print Texts

ALVAREZ, S. *et al.*, 'The Cultural and Political in Latin American Social Movement', in *Cultures of Politics and Politics of Culture: The Cultural and the Political in Latin American Social Movements*, Boulder, Westview Press, 1998, pp. 1–23.

ANGELIL, M. *On Architecture, the City and Technology*, Cambridge, Mass., Butterworth, 1990.

APPADURAI, A. 'Disjuncture and Difference in the Global Culture Economy, *Theory, Culture, and Society*, Vol. 7, 1990, pp. 295–310.

APPADURAI, A. *Modernity at Large: Cultural Dimensions of Globalization*, Minneapolis, University of Minnesota Press, 1996.

APPADURAI, A. (Ed.) 'Grassroots Globalization and the Research Imagination', *Public Culture*, Vol. 12, No. 1, Winter Ed., 2000, pp. 1–20.

ARENDT, H. (Ed.), *Illuminations*, Fontana, Fontana Press, 1970.

ARISTOTLE. *Constitution of the Athenians*, (Trans. P.J. Rhodes), Vol. 12, London, Penguin, 1984.

ARISTOTLE. *Politics*, (Trans. E. Barker), Oxford, Oxford University Press, 1998.

AUGÉ, M. *Non-Places: Introduction to an Anthology of Supermodernity*, (Trans. J. Howe), London, Verso, 1995.

AUGÉ, M. *The War of Dreams*, (Trans. L. Heron), London, Pluto Press, 1999.

BAILEY, J.B. and MCKNIGHT, L. (Eds.), *Internet Economics*, Cambridge, Mass., MIT Press, 1997.

BARTHES, R. *Image, Music, Text*. (Trans. S. Heath), New York, Hill, and Wang, 1977.

BARTRAM, R. 'Visuality, Dromology and Time Compression: Paul Virilio's New Ocularcentrism, *Time & Society*, September 2004 vol. 13, no. 2–3, pp. 285–300.

BAUDRILLARD, J. *Simulations*, New York, Semiotext(e), 1983.

BAUDRILLARD, J. 'From 'Simulcra and Simulations', in P. Brooker (Ed.), *Modernism/Postmodernism*, London, Longman, 1992, pp. 151–162.

BAUDRILLARD, J. 'The Order of Simulcra', (Trans. I.H. Grant) *Symbolic Exchange and Death*, London, Sage, 1993.

BAUDRILLARD, J. *Simulacra and Simulation*, Ann Arbor, University of Michigan Press, 1994.

BENJAMIN, W. 'The Work of Art in the Age of Mechanical Reproduction', in H. Arendt (Ed.), *Illuminations: Walter Benjamin*, New York, Schocken Books, *1968*, pp. 217–253.

BENJAMIN, W. *Charles Baudelaire: A Lyric Poet in the Era of High Capitalism*, (Trans. H. Zohn), London, New Left Books, 1973.

BENJAMIN, A. and NORRIS, C. *What is Deconstruction?* London and New York, Academy Editions/St Martin's Press, 1988.

BENNETT, J. 'Face-to-Face Encounters: Testimonial Imagery and the South African Truth and Reconciliation Commission', in *Australian and New Zealand Journal of Art*, Vols. 2–3, 2001–2002, pp. 33–60.

M. Langdon, *The Work of Art in a Digital Age: Art, Technology and Globalisation,*
DOI 10.1007/978-1-4939-1270-4, © Springer Science+Business Media New York 2014

BERGER, J. *Ways of Seeing*, London, Penguin Books, 1989.

BEY, H. *T.A.Z: The Temporary Autonomous Zone, Ontological Anarchy, Poetic Terrorism*, Brooklyn, Autonomedia, 1991.

BIJVOET, M. 'How Intimate Can Art and Technology Really Be? A Survey of the Art and Technology Movement of the 1960s', in P. Hayward (Ed.), *Culture, Technology and Creativity in the Late Twentieth Century*, London, John Libbey Press, 1991, pp. 15–38.

BLAIS, J. and IPPOLITO, J. *At the Edge of Art*, London, Thames and Hudson, 2006.

BOGARD, W. *The Simulation of Surveillance*, Cambridge, Cambridge University Press, 1996.

BOLTER, J.D. and GROMALA, D. *Windows and Mirrors: Interaction Design, Digital Art and the Myth of Transparency*, Cambridge, Mass., MIT Press, 2003.

BOLTER, J.D. and GRUSIN, R. *Remediation: Understanding New Media*, Cambridge, Mass., MIT Press, 1999.

BORSOOK, P. *Cyberselfish: A Critical Romp Through the Terribly Libertarian Culture of High Tech*, New York, Little, Brown and Company, 2000.

BOURDIEU, P. *Distinction: A Social Critique of the Judgement of Taste*, (Trans. R. Nice), Cambridge Mass., Harvard University Press, 1984.

BOURDIEU, P. 'The Field of Cultural Production', in A. Giddens *et al.*, *The Polity Reader in Cultural Theory*, Cambridge, Polity Press, 1994.

BOURDIEU, P. (Ed.), *Acts of Resistance: Against the New Myths of Our Time*, Cambridge, Polity Press, 2001.

BRADSHAW, A. 'The Alienated Artist and the Political Economy of Organised Art', *Consumption Markets & Culture*, Vol. 9, Issue 2, June 2006, pp. 111–117.

BROOKER, P. (Ed.), *Modernism/Postmodernism*, London, Longman, 1992.

BROWN, N. et al., 'Interactive Narrative as a Multi-Temporal Agency', in J. Shaw and P. Weibel (Eds.), *Future Cinema: The Cinematic Imaginary After Film*, Massachusetts, MIT Press, 2003, pp. 312–315.

BROWN, N. *et al. 'T_Visionarium*: The Aesthetic Transcription of Televisual Databases', in *Present Continuous Past[s] – Media Art. Strategies of Presentation, Mediation and Dissemination*, Bremen, Hochschule fur Kunste University of the Arts, Springer, 2004, pp. 132–141.

BURROWS, R and FEATHERSTONE, M. (Eds.), *Cyberspace, Cyberbodies, Cyberpunk: Cultures of Technological Embodiment*, London, Sage Publications, 1996.

CASTELLS, M. *The Rise of the Network Society*, Cambridge, Mass., Blackwell Publishers, 1996.

CHARMAZ, K. *Constructing Grounded Theory: A Practical Guide Through Qualitative Analysis*, Thousand Oaks, California, Sage Publications, 2006.

CLARKE, T.J. *Image of the People: Gustave Courbet and the 1848 Revolution*, London, Thames and Hudson, 1973.

CLARKE, D. *The Cinematic City*, London, Routledge, 1997.

CRANDALL, J. and SCHOLDER, A. (Eds). *Interaction: Artistic Practice in the Network*, New York, Distributed Art Publishers Inc, 2001.

CRANG, M. (Ed.), *Thinking Space*, London, Routledge, 2000.

CRARY, J. (Ed.), *Techniques of the Observer: On Vision and Modernity in the Nineteenth Century*, Cambridge, Mass., MIT Press, 1990.

DARLEY, A. *Visual Digital Culture: Surface Play and Spectacle in New Media Genres*, London, Routledge, 2000.

DAVIS, D. 'The Museum of the Third Kind', in *Art in America*, Vol. 93, Issue 6, 2005, pp. 75–81.

DEBORD, G. *The Society of the Spectacle*, Detroit, Black and Red, 1983.

de CERTEAU, M. *The Practice of Everyday Life*, (Trans. S. Rendall), Los Angeles, University of California Press, 1984.

de KERCKHOVE, D. *Connected Intelligence: The Arrival of the Web Society*, London, Kogan Page, 1998.

DE LANDA. M, *A Thousand Years of Nonlinear History*, New York, Swerve Editions, 1997.

DELEUZE, G. *Cinema 1: The Movement Image*, (Trans. B. Haberjam and H. Tomlinson), Minneapolis, University of Minnesota Press, 1986.

DELEUZE, G. *Cinema 2: The Time Image*, (Trans. R. Galeta and H. Tomlinson), London, Athlone Press, 1989.

DELEUZE, G. and GUATTARI, F. *A Thousand Plateaus: Capitalism and Schizophrenia*, Minneapolis, University of Minnesota Press, 1987.

DELEUZE, G. and GUATTARI, F. *What is Philosophy?* (Trans. G. Burchill and H. Tomlinson) London, Verso, 1994.

DEL FAVERO, D. 'Expanded Cinematic Forms of Narration', in D. Del Favero and J. Shaw (Eds.), *(dis)LOCATIONS*, Karlsruhe and Sydney, University of New South Wales, 2001, pp. 8–9.

DERRIDA, J. 'Deconstruction and the Other', in R. Kearney, *States of Mind: Dialogues with Contemporary Thinkers*, Washington, New York University Press, 1995, pp. 120–126.

DESCARTES, R. *Meditations on the First Philosophy*, Cambridge, Cambridge University Press, 1986.

DIETZ, S. 'Why Have There Been No Great Net Artists?', in V. Cosic, *Net.Art Per Me*: *Catalogue for the Slovenian Pavillion*, 49th Venice Biennale, Venice, MGLC, 2001, pp. 56–65.

DODGE, M. and KITCHIN, R. *Mapping Cyberspace*, London, Routledge, 2000.

DONALD, J. 'Metropolis: The City as Text', in A. D. King (Ed.), *Re-Presenting the City: Ethnicity, Capital and Culture in the 21st-Century Metropolis*, Washington Square, New York University Press, 1996, pp. 417–461.

DU GAY, P. and S. Hall, (Ed.) *Questions of Cultural Identity*, London, Sage Publications, 1996.

DURING, S. (Ed.), *The Cultural Studies Reader*, London, Routledge, 1993.

ECO, U. *The Limits of Interpretation*, Bloomington, Indiana University Press, 1990.

ECO, U. 'Postscript to *the Name of the Rose*: Postmodernism, Irony, The Enjoyable', in Charles Jencks (Ed.), *The Post-Modern Reader*, London, Academy Editions, 1992.

ECO, U. *Apocalypse Postponed*, Bloomington, Indiana University Press, 1994.

ELKINS, J. *On Pictures and the Words That Fail Them*, Cambridge, Cambridge University Press, 1998

ENWEZOR, O. 'Global Tendencies: Globalism and the Large-Scale Exhibition', in *Art Forum International*, Vol. 42, No. 2, November 2003a, pp. 152–163.

ENWEZOR, O. 'The Postcolonial Constellation: Contemporary Art in a State of Permanent Transition', in *Research in African Literatures*, Vol. 34, Issue 4, 2003b, pp. 57–82.

FANON, F. *The Wretched of the Earth*, New York, Grove Press, 1968.

FATHY, T.A. *Telecity: Information Technology and its Impact Upon City Form*, New York, Praeger, 1994.

FERGUSON, J. and GUPTA, A. 'Beyond 'Culture': Space, Identity and the Politics of Difference' in X. Inda and R. Rosaldo (Eds.), *The Anthropology of Globalisation: A Reader*, Malden, Blackwell Publishing, 2002, pp. 65–80.

FOLTZ, P.W. 'Comprehension, Coherence, and Strategies in Hypertext and Linear Text', in Jean-François Rouet (Ed.), *Hypertext and Cognition*, Mahwah, Lawrence Erlbaum Associates, 1996, pp. 109–136.

FOUCAULT, M. *Discipline and Punish: The Birth of the Prison*, (Trans. A. Sheridan), Harmondsworth, Penguin, 1979.

FRAMPTON, K. and RICOEUR, P. 'Towards a Critical Regionalism: Six Points for an Architecture of Resistance', in H. Foster (Ed.), *The Anti-Aesthetic: Essays on Postmodern Culture*, Seattle, Bay Press, 1983. pp. 16–30.

FRIEDRICH, C.J. *The Philosophy of Kant: Immanuel Kant's Moral and Political Writings*, New York, The Modern Library, 1949.

FRIEDMANN, J. 'The World City Hypothesis', in *Development and Change*, Vol. 17, No 1, 1986, pp. 69–83.

FRY, R. *Vision and Design*, Oxford, Oxford University Press, 1981.

FUSCO, C. 'The Unbearable Weightness of Beings: Art in Mexico after NAFTA', *The Bodies that Were Not Ours: And Other Writings*, London, Routledge, 2001.

GIBSON, W. *Neuromancer*, New York, Ace Publications, 1984.

GOTTDIENER, M. *Postmodern Semiotics: Material Culture and the Forms of Postmodern Life*, Oxford, Blackwell, 1995.

GREEN, R. *Internet Art*, World of Art Series, London, Thames and Hudson, 2004.

GREENBERG, C. *Art and Culture: Critical Essays*, Boston, Beacon Press, 1961.

GROSSBERG, L. *Dancing in Spite of Myself: Essays on Popular Culture*, Durham, Duke University Press, 1997.

GROSZ, E. *Space, Time and Perversion: The Politics of Bodies*, London and New York, Allen and Unwin, 1995.

HADJINICOLAOU, H. *Art History and Class Struggle*, London, Pluto Press, 1999.

HAKKEN, D. *Cyborgs @ Cyberspace: An Ethnographer Looks to the Future*, New York, Routledge, 1999.

HALL, S. (Ed.), *Representation: Cultural Representations and Signifying Practices*, London, Sage Publications, 1997.

HALL, S. 'Globalisation and the World Cities', in F-C Lo and Y-M Yeung (Eds.), *Globalisation and the World of Large Cities*, Tokyo, United Nations University Press, 1998.

HANNERZ, U. 'Notes on the Global Ecumene', in X. Inda and R. Rosaldo (Eds.), *The Anthropology of Globalisation: A Reader*, Malden, Blackwell Publishing, 2002, pp. 37–45.

HANSEN, M.B.N., *New Philosophy for New Media*, Cambridge Mass., MIT Press, 2004.

HARRAWAY, D. *Simians, Cyborgs and Women: The Reinvention of Nature*, New York, Routledge, 1991.

HARRIES, D (Ed.), *The New Media Book*, London, British Film Institute, 2002.

HARVEY, D. *The Condition of Postmodernity: An Enquiry into the Origins of Cultural Change*, Oxford and Mass., Blackwell, 1990.

HAUG, W.H. 'Critique of Commodity Aesthetics', in A. Giddens (Ed.), *et al.*, *The Polity Reader in Cultural Theory*, Cambridge, Polity Press, 1994.

HAUSER, A. *The Philosophy of Art History*, New York, Knopf, 1959.

HAYLES, N.K. *How We Became Post-Human: Virtual Bodies in Cybernetics, Literature, and Informatics*, Chicago, University of Chicago Press, 1999.

HEIM, M. *Virtual Realism*, New York, Oxford University Press, 1998.

HENRI, A. *Total Art: Environments, Happenings, and Performance*, New York, Praeger, 1974.

HUTCHEON, L. 'Telling Stories: Fiction and History', in P. Brooker (Ed.), *Modernism/Postmodernism*, London, Longman, 1992, pp. 229–242.

HUYSSEN, A. 'Mapping the Postmodern', in C. Jencks (Ed.), *The Post-Modern Reader*, London, Academy Editions, 1992, pp. 40–72.

HUYSSEN, A. 'Back to the Future: Fluxus in Context', in E. Armstrong *et al.*, *In the Spirit of Fluxus*, Minneapolis, Walker Art Center Press, 1993, pp. 140–152.

INDA, J.X. and ROSALDO, R. (Eds.) *The Anthropology of Globalisation: A Reader*, Malden, Blackwell Publishing, 2002.

JACKSON, T.A. 'Towards a New Media Aesthetic', in D. Trend (Ed.), *Reading Digital Culture*, Oxford, Blackwell, 2001, pp. 347–353.

JACOBS, J. *Edge of Empire: Postcolonialism and the City*, London, Routledge, 1996.

JAMESON, F. 'Postmodernism and Consumer Society', in H. Foster (Ed.), *The Anti-Aesthetic: Essays on Postmodern Culture*, Seattle, Bay Press, 1983. pp. 16–30., pp. 111–125.

JAMESON, F. and MIYOSHI, M. (Eds.), *The Cultures of Globalisation*, Durham, Duke University Press, 1998.

JORDAN, T. *Cyberpower: The Culture and Politics of Cyberspace and the Internet*, London, Routledge, 1999.

KELLNER, D. *Media Culture: Cultural Studies, Identity and Politics Between the Modern and Postmodern*, London, Routledge, 1995.

KIM, J. 'Phenomenology of Digital-Being', *Human Studies*, Vol. 24, 2001, pp 104–108.

KING, A.D. *Culture, Globalisation and the World-System: Contemporary Conditions for the Representation of Identity*, Binghampton, State University of New York Press, 1991.

KINNVALL, C. and JONSSON, K. (Eds.), *Globalisation and Democracy in Asia: The Construction of Identity*, London, Routledge, 2002.

KIRKUP, G. *The Gendered Cyborg: A Reader*, London, Routledge, 2000.

KLEIN, N. *No Logo: No Space, No Choice, No Jobs*, New York, Picador, 2002a.

KLEIN, N. *Fences and Windows: Dispatches From the Front Lines of the Globalization Debate*, New Delhi, Leftword, 2002b.

KLEINROCK, L. 'Information Flow in Large Communication Nets', *RLE Quarterly Progress Report*, Cambridge Mass., MIT Press, July, 1961, pp. 1–35.

KNOX, P. *Urbanization: An Introduction to Urban Geography*, New Jersey, Prentice Hall, 1994.

KOOISTRA, A. 'Speaking into Sight: Articulating the Body Personal with the Body Politic', *Explorations in Anthropology*, Vol. 8, No. 1, 2008, pp. 1–17.

KOSACK, S. *et al.*, *Globalization and the Nation State: The Impact of The IMF and The World Bank*, London, Routledge, 2006.

KRAUSS, R. *The Originality of the Avant Garde and Other Modernist Myths*, Cambridge, Mass., MIT Press, 1985.

KRISTEVA, J. 'Strangers to Ourselves: The Hope of the Singular', in R. Kearney (Ed.), in *States of Mind: Dialogues with Contemporary Thinkers*, Washington, New York University Press, 1995, pp. 6–13.

KUHN, A. *The Power of the Image: Essays on Representation and Sexuality*, London, Routledge, 1985.

KUPER, A. (Ed.), *Conceptualizing Society*, London, Routledge, 1992.

KURZWEIL, E. The Age of Structuralism, New York, Columbia University Press, 1980.

LEFEBVRE, H. *The Production of Space*, Oxford, Blackwell, 1992.

LENOIR, T. 'Foreword', in M.B.N. Hansen, *New Philosophy for New Media*, Cambridge Mass., MIT Press, 2004, p. xiii.

LEVINSON, P. *Digital McLuhan: A Guide to the Information Millennium*, London, Routledge, 1999.

LO, F-C. and YEUNG, Y-M. (Eds.), *Globalisation and the World of Large Cities*, Tokyo, United Nations University Press, 1998.

LOVINK, G. *Dark Fiber: Tracking Critical Internet Culture*, Cambridge, Mass., MIT Press, 2002.

LUNENFIELD, P (Ed.), *The Digital Dialectic: New Essays on New Media*, Cambridge Mass., MIT Press, 1999.

LYOTARD, J.F. 'Answering the Question: What is Postmodernism?', in P. Brooker (Ed.), *Modernism/Postmodernism*, Longman, London, 1992, pp. 139–150.

MANOVICH, L. *The Language of New Media*, Cambridge, Mass., MIT Press, 2001.

MARX, K. *et al.*, *Capital: A Critique of Political Economy*, Vol. 1, (Trans. B. Fowkes), London, Penguin Classics, 1976.

MASSEY, D. *Space, Place and Gender*, Polity Press, Cambridge, 1994.

MASSEY, D. (Ed.), *A Place in the World: Places, Cultures and Globalisation*, Oxford, Oxford University Press, 1995.

McEVILLEY, T. *Art and Otherness: Crisis in Cultural Identity*, New York, Documentext, McPherson and Company, 1992.

McEVILLEY, T. *Art and Discontent: Theory at the Millennium*, Documentext, New York, McPherson and Company, 1991.

McLUHAN, M. *Understanding Media: The Extensions of Man*, London, Routledge & Kegan Paul, 1964.

McLUHAN, M. and POWERS, B.R., *The Global Village: Transformations in World Life and Media in the 21st Century*, New York, Oxford University Press, 1989.

McNEILL, D. (Ed.), *Art Since 1990: Theories of Meanings/Meanings of Theories*, Paddington, UNSW College of Fine Art Course Reader, 2000.

MERLEAU-PONTY, M. *The Phenomenology of Perception*, (Trans. C. Smith), Routledge, London, 1962.

MIRZOEFF, N. (Ed.), *Visual Culture Reader*, London and New York, Routledge, 1998.

MITCHEL, W.J. *The Reconfigured Eye: Visual Truth in the Post-Photographic Era*, Cambridge, Mass., MIT Press, 1992.

MITCHELL, W.J. *City of Bits: Space, Place, and the Infobahn*, Cambridge, Mass., MIT Press, 1995.

MITCHELL, W.J. *E-topia: Urban Life, Jim – But Not As We Know It*, Cambridge, Mass., MIT Press, 1999.

MIYOSHI, M. ' "Globalization", Culture and the University', in F. Jameson and M. Miyoshi (Eds.), *The Cultures of Globalisation*, Durham, Duke University Press, 1998, pp. 247–272.

MORAN, D. *Introduction to Phenomenology*, London, Routledge, 2000.

MORSE, M. *Virtualities: Television, Media, Art and Cyber Culture*, Bloomington, Indiana University Press, 1998.

MULVEY, L. *Visual and Other Pleasures*, Indiana, Macmillan, 1988.

MUMFORD, L. *The Culture of Cities*, New York, Harcourt, Brace and Co., 1938.

MUMFORD, L. *The City in History*, Harmondsworth, Penguin, 1961.

MUNSTER, A. 'New Media as Old Media: Strategies of Dislocation and Relocation', in *(dis) LOCATIONS*, Karlsruhe, ZKM Center for Art and Media, 2001, pp. 22–31.

MUNSTER, A. 'Low-Res Bleed: Congealed Affect and Digital Aesthetics', in 'Affect and Sensation', *Australian and New Zealand Journal of Art*, Vols. 2–3, 2001–2002, pp. 77–95.

MURPHIE, A. and POTTS, J. *Culture and Technology*, New York, Palgrave MacMillan, 2003.

MURRAY, J. *Hamlet on the Holodeck: The Future of Narrative in Cyberspace*, Cambridge, Mass., MIT Press, 1997.

NUNES, M. *Cyberspaces of Everyday Life*, Minneapolis, University of Minnesota Press, 2006.

PATTON, P. (Ed.), *Deleuze: A Critical Reader*, Oxford, Blackwell, 1996.

PETIT, P. 'Cybermonde: The Politics of Degradation' in *Open City – Alphabet City Six: Culture Theory Politics*, Toronto, House of Anansi Press Ltd, 1998, pp. 192–203.

PLANT, S. *The Most Radical Gesture: The Situationist International in a Postmodern Age*, London, Routledge, 1992.

POSTER, M. (Ed.), *Selected Writings by Jean Baudrillard*, Stanford, Stanford University Press, 2001.

POSTER, M. 'Everyday (Virtual) Life', *New Literary History*, Vol. 33, No. 4, 2002, pp. 743–760.

PRATT, G. and SAN JUAN, R.M. 'Virtual Cities: Film and the Urban Mapping of Virtual Space', *Screen*, Vol. 43, No. 3, 2002, pp. 250–270.

PRINZE, J. *Art Discourse/Discourse in Art*, New Brunswick, Rutgers University Press, 1991.

PROBYN, E. *Sexing the Self: Gendered Positions in Cultural Studies*, London, Routledge, 1993.

PROBYN, E. *Outside Belongings*, London, Routledge, 1996.

RALEY, R. 'Statistical Material: Globalization and the Digital Art of John Klima', *The New Centennial Review*, Vol. 3.2, 2003, pp. 67–89.

RICHTER, G. 'Aesthetic Theory and Nonpropositional Truth Content in Adorno', *New German Critique*, Vol. 33, 2006, pp. 119–135.

RIDLESS, R. *Ideology and Art: Theories of Mass Culture from Walter Benjamin to Umberto Eco*, New York, Taschenbuch, 1984.

RITZER, G. *The McDonaldization of Society*, Revised New Century Ed., Thousand Oaks, Pine Forge Press, 2004.

ROBERTSON, R. and WHITE, K.E. *Globalization: Critical Concepts in Sociology*, London, Routledge, 2003.

RORTY, R. *Truth, Politics and 'post-modernism'*, Amsterdam, Van Gorcum Ltd, 1997.

RUSH, M. 'Media and Performance', *New Media in Late Twentieth Century Art*, London, Thames and Hudson, 1999.

SASSEN, S. 'The Impact of the New Technologies and Globalisation on Cities', in F-C LO and Y-M. YEUNG, (Eds.), *Globalisation and the World of Large Cities*, Tokyo, United Nations University Press, 1998, pp. 391–409.

SASSEN, S. 'Globalisation and the Formation of Claims', in J. Copjec and M. Sorkin (Eds.), *Giving Ground: The Politics of Propinquity*, London, Verso, 1999, pp. 86–105.

SASSEN, S. *Cities in a World Economy, Sociology for a New Century*, Second Ed., Thousand Oaks, Pine Forge Press, 2000.

SCHNEIDER ADAMS, L. *The Methodologies of Art: An Introduction*, Boulder, Westview Press, 1996.

STALLABRASS, J. *Internet Art: the Online Clash of Culture and Commerce*, London, Tate Publishing, 2003.

STILWELL, F. 'Going Global? Australian Cities and the Challenges of Globalisation', *Transnational Corporations Research Project*, Sydney, University of Sydney, 1998, pp. 1–30.

SUKENICK, R. *Narralogues*, Albany, State University of New York Press, 2000.

SWIFT, J. *Gulliver's Travels*, New York, Oxford University Press, 1998.

TAYLOR, L. (Ed.), *Socially Relevant Policy Analysis: Structuralist Computable General Equilibrium Models for the Developing World*, Cambridge Mass., The MIT Press, 1990.

TAYLOR, P. 'Australian 'Newwave' and the 'Second Degree',' in *Art + Text*, Vol. 1., 1981, pp. 23–32.

TOFTS, D. *Interzone: Media Arts in Australia*, Melbourne, Craftsman House, 2005.

TRIBE, M. 'Foreword', in L. Manovich, *The Language of New Media*, Cambridge, Mass., MIT Press, 2001.

TURKLE, S. *Life on the Screen: Identity in the Age of the Internet*, New York, Simon and Schuster, 1995.

VALÉRY, P. *Aesthetics: The Conquest of Ubiquity*, (Trans. R. Manheim), Bollingen Series, New York, Pantheon Books, 1964.

WALKER, J.A. *Art in the Age of Mass Media*, Third Ed., London, Pluto Press, 1983.

WARK, M. *Celebrities, Culture and Cyberspace: The Light on the Hill in a Postmodern World*, Annandale, Pluto Press, 1999.

WELLS, R. 'The Future of a Promise', *The Middle East Magazine*, Issue 428, Dec 2011, p. 60.

WENT, R. *The Enigma of Globalisation: A Journey to a New Stage of Capitalism*, London, Routledge, 2002.

WHITELAW, M. *Metacreation: Art and Artificial Life*, Cambridge, Mass., MIT Press, 2004.

WILSON, S. *Information Arts: Intersections of Art, Science, and Technology*, Cambridge, Mass., MIT Press, 2002.

WOLF, M.J.P. *Abstracting Reality: Art, Communication, and Cognition in the Digital Age*, Lanham, University Press of America, 2000.

WOLFF, J. *The Social Production of Art*, Second Ed., London, Macmillan, 1993.

WOLFF, J. *Aesthetics and the Sociology of Art*, Second Ed., Michigan, University of Michigan Press, 1999.

WOOLEY, B. *Virtual Worlds*, London, Blackwell, 1992.

YIN, A.K. *Case Study Research: Design and Methods*, 3rd Ed., Sage Publications, Newbury Park, 2002.

YOUNGBLOOD, G. 'A Medium Matures: Video and Cinematic Enterprise', in T. Druckrey (Ed.), *Ars Electronica: Facing the Future*, Cambridge, Mass., MIT Press, 1999, pp. 43–50.

Online Texts

ADRIAANSENS,A.'*RMR–RunMotherfuckerRun*',*NewMediaBeijing.org*,<http://newmediabeijing.org/md2005/exhibition_display.php?section=2&link_id=2&title=RMR+-+Run+Motherfucker+Run+%28NL%29&artist_id=2_1>, 2004, (accessed 1 October 2007).

ALEXA, C. '*10-Second Couples*', National Gallery of Victoria, <http://www.ngv.vic.gov.au/metropolis/resources/rb_metropolis.pdf>, 2004, (accessed 10 December 2006). This link is no longer active.

AMERIKA, M. 'Excerpts From 'Portrait of The VJ', *Fibreculture*, <http://www.journal.fibreculture.org/issue7/issue7_portraits_amerika.pdf>, 2005, (accessed 23 March 2007). This link is no longer active.

ANON. 'Electronic Civil Disobedience Against the RNC', *The Hacktivist*, <http://thehacktivist.com/modules.php?op=modload&name=News&file=article&sid=413&mode=thread&order=0&thold=0>, 2004a, (accessed 15 July 2004). This link is no longer active.

ANON. 'What is Electronic Civil Disobedience?', *The Hacktivist*, <http://thehactivist.com/ecd.php>, 2004b, (accessed 15 July 2004). This link is no longer active.

ANON. 'Digital Art User', *New Media Beijing*, <http://newmediabeijing.org/md2005/exhibition.php?section=2>, 2004, (accessed 22 September 2007).

BALADI, L. *Alone, Together...In Media Res*, 2012 in Dorothea Schoene, 'Beyond The Image: A Project By Lara Baladi', Contemporary Visual Culture In North Africa and The Middle East, *Ibraaz*, <http://www.ibraaz.org/projects/40#author96>, (accessed 30 January 2013).

BALADI, L. 'Alone, Together…Tahrir Two Years Later,' *Creative Time Reports*, January 25 2013, <http://creativetimereports.org/2013/01/25/tahrir-revolution-in-media-res/>, 2013, (accessed 11 August 2013).

BBC NEWS. 'Globalisation: Capitalist Evil or a Way Out of Poverty?' *BBC News: Talking Point*, 6 February 2002, <http://news.bbc.co.uk/1/hi/talking_point/1791105.stm>, 2002, (accessed 12 October 2007).

BE, K. and SIN, J. *'Haptic Glove', NewMediaBeijing.org*, <http://newmediabeijing.org/md2005/exhibition.php?section=2>, 2004, (accessed 22 September 2007).

BELL, A. *'Metropolis* Exhibition Brochure', *National Gallery of Victoria*, <http://www.ngv.vic.gov.au/metropolis/resources/rb_metropolis.pdf>, 2004, (accessed 10 December 2006).

BELLO, W. 'Globalization in Retreat', *Foreign Policy in Focus*, <http://www.fpif.org/fpiftxt/3826>, 2006, (accessed 11 December 2007). This link is no longer active.

BOYD MYERS, C. "YouTube's Life in a Day Movie is a Stunner', *The Next Web,* </http://thenextweb.com/google/2011/06/15/youtubes-life-in-a-day-movie-is-a-stunner/>, 2011, (accessed 1 August 2013).

BROWN, N. *et al.*, *'Placeworld'*, *iCinema*, <http://www.icinema.unsw.edu.au/projects/prj_placeworld.html>, 2004a, (accessed 17 December 2007). This link is no longer active.

BROWN, N. *et al.*, *'Web of Life'*, *iCinema*, <http://www.icinema.unsw.edu.au/projects/prj_wol.html>, 2004b (accessed 16 September 2007). This link is no longer active.

BROWN, N. *et al.*, *'T_Visionarium II Promotional Still, iCinema*, <http://www.icinema.unsw.edu.au/projects/prj_tvis_II.html>, 2008 (accessed 16 September 2009). This link is no longer active.

BROWN, N. *et al.*, *'T_Visionarium II',* 2008 in Sara Kolster, *'T_Visionarium II', Sarako*, 25 November, 2010, <http://sarako.net/work/tvisionarium-century-of-the-city/>, 2010 (accessed 5 April 2013).

CERF, V.G. *et al.*, 'A Brief History of the Internet', *Internet Society*, <http://www.isoc.org/internet/history/brief.shtml>, (accessed 06 December 2007).

CONFERENCE SECRETARIAT. *Controlling Bodies/Controlling Spaces Conference*, <http://www.h-net.org/announce/show.cgi?ID=138286&keyword=media>, 2004, (accessed 01 November 2004).

COOPER, J. *'Transformers', New Media Beijing*, <http://newmediabeijing.org/md2005/exhibition.php?section=2>, 2004, (accessed 22 September 2007).

DALZIEL, J. 'New Masters of Flash: The 2002 Annual', *Flash Magazine*, <http://www.flashmagazine.com/468.htm>, 2001, (accessed 23 March 2007).

De NIJS, M. *'Run Motherfucker Run'*, *New Media Beijing*, <http://newmediabeijing.org/md2005/exhibition.php?section=2>, 2004, (accessed 23 March 2007).

DEVA, S. 'From 3/12 to 9/11: Future of Human Rights?', *Social Science Research Network*, <http://papers.ssrn.com/sol3/papers.cfm?abstract_id=644882>, 2004, (accessed 16 December 2007).

DIAMOND, S. *'Feathery Dresses'*, *New Media Beijing*, <http://newmediabeijing.org/md2005/exhibition_display.php?section=2&link_id=4&title=Feathery+Dresses+%28CND%29&artist_id=4_2>, 2004, (accessed 1 October 2007).

DODES, R. 'Life in a Day' Director Aims to Elevate YouTube Videos into Art', *The Wall Street Journal*, 22 July 2011, <http://blogs.wsj.com/speakeasy/2011/07/22/life-in-a-day-director-kevin-macdonald-aims-to-elevate-youtube-videos-into-art/>, 2011, (accessed 12 August 2013).

GA, Z. *'Haptic Glove'*, *NewMedia.org*, <http://newmediabeijing.org/md2005/exhibition_display.php?section=2&link_id=18&title=Haptic+Glove+%28USA%29&artist_id=18_5>, 2004a, (accesses 1 October 2007).

GA, Z. *'In the Line of Flight* – Transcending Urbanscapes', <http://newmediabeijing.org/md2005/symposium.php?section=2>, *NewMediaBeijing.org*, 2004b, (accessed 22 September 2007).

GA, Z. 'Section One: New Media Art as Global Cultural Alchemy', <http://newmediabeijing.org/md2005/symposium.php?section=3>, *NewMediaBeijing.org*, 2004c, (accessed 22 September 2007).

GA, Z. 'Symposium', <http://newmediabeijing.org/md2005/symposium.php?section=3>), *New Media Beijing*, 2004d, (accessed 22 September 2007).

GORDON, T. 'Biography 2', <http://www.marshallmcluhan.com/gordon.html>, *Marshall McLuhan*, 2002, (accessed 16 September 2007). This link is no longer active.

HOPE, A.D. *'Financial District Infiltration: Everybody is Somebody's Terrorist'*, <http://www. ngv.vic.gov.au/metropolis/resources/rb_metropolis.pdf>, *National Gallery of Victoria*, 2004, (accessed 10 December 2006). This link is no longer active.

IVANOVA, A. *'Transformers'*, <http://newmediabeijing.org/md2005/exhibition_display. php?section=2&link_id=8&title=Transformers+%28AU%29&artist_id=8_4>, *NewMediaBeijing.org*, 2004a, (accessed 1 October 2007).

IVANOVA, A. *'Floating Territories'*, <http://newmediabeijing.org/md2005/exhibition_display. php?section=2&link_id=8&title=Floating+Territories+%28AU%29&artist_id=8_3>, *NewMediaBeijing*, 2004b, (accessed 22 September 2007).

JACOBSEN, T. 'Where Do Art & Fashion Meet Hi-Tech?', <http://rhizome.org/fp.rhiz?id=3246>, *Rhizome.org*, 2007, (accessed 23 March 2007).

JORDAN, C. 'Midway Film', <http://www.midwayfilm.com/about.html>, *Midway Film*, (accessed 18 February 2013).

JORDAN, C. 'Turning Powerful Stats into Art', <http://www.ted.com/talks/chris_jordan_pictures_some_shocking_stats.html>, *TED*, 2008, (accessed 5 August 2013).

JUDGE, C.S. 'Hegemony of the Heart: American Cultural Power Threatens Old Orders Worldwide,' <http://www.hoover.org/publications/policyreview/3462301.html>, *Hoover Institution Policy Review*, No. 110, Vol. December 2001-January 2002, (accessed 12 October 2008). This link is no longer active.

KLICH, R. 'Performing Posthuman Perspective: *Can You See Me Now?'*, <http://scan.net.au/scan/ journal/display.php?journal_id=91>, *Scan Journal of Media Arts Culture*, Vol. 4, No. 1, 2007, (accessed 11 December 2007).

KLOSTER, S. 'T_Visionarium', *Sarako*, 25 November, 2010, <http://sarako.net/work/tvisionarium-century-of-the-city/>, (accessed 5 April 2013).

KLUITENBERG, E. 'New Media Art Mythologies: Cool Media Hot Talk Show', <http://www.nettime.org/Lists-Archives/nettime-nl-0705/msg00076.html>, *nettime*, 28 May 2007, (accessed 4 November 2008).

KNIGHT, W. 'Hacktivists Launch Virtual Demo While Streets Blocked', <http://www.thehacktivist.com/archive/news/2001/Hacktivistsvirtualdemo-ZDNET-2001.pdf>, *ZDNet UK*, 2001, (accessed 23 October 2004). This link is no longer active.

LICHTY, P. 'Alpha Revisionist Manifesto', *Nettime*, <http://www.nettime.org/Lists-Archives/ nettime-bold-0105/msg00391.html>, 2001, (accessed 23 June 2007).

LOVINK, G. 'New Media, Art and Science: Explorations Beyond the Official Discourse', <http:// laudanum.net/geert/files/1129753681/2005>, *Laudanum*, 2005, (accessed 16 December 2007). This link is no longer active.

LOVINK, G. and MUNSTER, A. 'Theses on Distributed Aesthetics. Or, What a Network is Not', <http://www.journal.fibreculture.org/issue7/issue7_munster_lovink.html>, *Fibreculture*, 2005, (accessed 15 January 2007).

LOVINK, G. and SCHNEIDER, F. 'A Virtual World is Possible: From Tactical Media to Digital Multitudes', <http://n5m.new.zope.nl/n5m/essays/n5mJournalEntry.2003-09-13.2845> *Next Five Minutes*, 2004, (accessed 14 July 2004). This link is no longer active.

MACDONALD, S.M. 'Book Review: Closer: Performance, Technologies, Phenomenology', <http://liminalities.net/5-1/rev-closer.html>, *Liminalities*, 2007, p. 385, (accessed 16 March 2012). This link is no longer active.

MANOVICH, L. 'The Death of Computer Art', <http://www.thennetnet.com/schmeb/schmeb12. html>, *The Net Net*, 2007, (accessed 03 June 2004). This link is no longer active.

MAWDSLEY, R. *'Journey Into Darkness'*, <http://www.simian.nu>, *Simian*, 2000, (accessed 06 February 2001). This link is no longer active.

MAWDSLEY, R. *'Revolt'*, <http://www.simian.nu>, *Simian*, 2000, (accessed 06 February 2001). This link is no longer active.

MAWDSLEY, R. *'Tokyo Love Hotel Mistake'*, <http://www.simian.nu>, *Simian*, 2000c, (accessed 06 February 2001). This link is no longer active.

MILTON-SMITH, M. 'Creative Resistance in Digital Art', <http://ijh.cgpublisher.com/product/ pub.26/prod.574/index_html?manage_tabs_message=Product+added+to+order>, *International Journal of the Humanities*, Vol. 2, Issue 3, 2004, (accessed 17 December 2007).

MOK, K. 'The Art of Activism: Painting The Faces of Social and Climate Change', <http:// www.treehugger.com/culture/the-art-of-activism-painting-the-faces-of-social-climate-change. html>, *Treehugger*, (accessed 13 February 2013).

MORIWAKI, K. 'Joey Berzowska Interview by Katherine Moriwaki', <http://rhizome.org/thread. rhiz?thread=16921&page=1#322592007>, *Rhizome*, 2005, (accessed 20 March 2007).

NATIONAL GALLERY OF VICTORIA. *'Metropolis* Exhibition Brochure', <http://www.ngv.vic. gov.au/metropolis/resources/rb_metropolis.pdf>, *National Gallery of Victoria*, 2004, (accessed 10 December 2006). This link is no longer active.

NO AUTHOR, 'What is Globalisation?', <http://www.globalisationguide.org/01.html>, *Globalisation Guide*, 2001, (accessed 12 October 2008). This link is no longer active.

NO AUTHOR. 'Capital Bonanzas: Does Wall Street's meltdown show financial globalisation itself is part of the problem?', *The Economist*, 25 September 2008, <http://www.economist. com/research/articlesBySubject/displaystory.cfm?subjectid=423172&story_id=12304702>, (accessed 12 October 2008).

NO AUTHOR. 'Thomas Friedman on Globalisation', *The Economist*, 31 March 2005, <http:// www.economist.com/books/displaystory.cfm?story_id=3809512>, (accessed 3 November 2005). This link is no longer active.

NO AUTHOR, <http://www.aljazeera.com/programmes/aljazeeraworld/2011/10/201110197445121 5541.html>, *Al Jazeera*, 19 October 2011, (accessed 11 August 2013). This link is no longer active.

NO AUTHOR, *Strozzina Gallery Website*, <www.strozzina.org/asap/e_index.php>, (accessed 30 September 2010).

NOVA, 'Sona8', TagR.tv, 7 July 2008, <http://tagr.tv/tag/beijing-accelerator/>, (accessed 4 April 2013).

NYE, J. 'Globalization and its Discontents', <http://209.85.173.104/search?q=cache:IykpeyGIkw J:unpan1.un.org/intradoc/groups/public/documents/APCITY/UNPAN005944.pdf+sped+up+ti me+globalization&hl=en&ct=clnk&cd=3&gl=au>, *UN*, 2001, (accessed 15 December 2007). This link is no longer active.

O'LOUGHLIN, M. 'Intelligent Bodies and Ecological Subjectivities: Merleau-Ponty's Corrective to Postmodernism's "Subjects" of Education', <http://www.ed.uiuc.edu/eps/pes-yearbook/95_ docs/o'loughlin.html>, *Philosophy of Education*, 1995, (accessed 10 December 2007).

OTTERNESS, T. *'Nine Eleven'*, <http://www.ngv.vic.gov.au/metropolis/resources/rb_metropolis. pdf>, *National Gallery of Victoria*, 2004, (accessed 10 December 2006). This link is no longer active.

PARTRIDGE, T. *'Life in a Day'*, <http://googleblog.blogspot.com.au/2010/07/life-in-day.html>, *Google: Official Blog*, 6 July 2010, (accessed 11 August 2013).

PHAT, *'Harlem: The Ghetto Fabulous'*, <http://www.ngv.vic.gov.au/metropolis/resources/rb_me-tropolis.pdf>, *National Gallery of Victoria*, 2004, (accessed 10 December 2006). This link is no longer active.

PICASSO, P. *'Guernica'*, <http://www.mala.bc.ca/~lanes/english/hemngway/picasso/guernica. htm>, *Malaspina*, 1937, (accessed 1 October 2007). This link is no longer active.

PICHLER, C. *'Territorism II'*, <http://newmediabeijing.org/md2005/exhibition_display. php?section=2&link_id=21&title=Territorism+II+%28AT%29&artist_id=21_5>, *NewMedia-Beijing.org*, 2004, (accessed 22 September 2007).

PREM Economic Policy Group and Development Economics Group. 'What is Globalization', http://www1.worldbank.org/economicpolicy/globalization/ag01.html>, *The World Bank*, 2000, (accessed 1 October 2007). This link is no longer active.

PREUSS, S. 'An Interview with Photographic Artist Chris Jordan', *Environmental Graffiti*, 2008, <http://www.environmentalgraffiti.com/featured/interview-photographic-artist-chrisjor-dan/11408>, (accessed 15 February 2013).

RICHARDS, R.L. 'Review of Dan Harries (Ed.), *The New Media Book'*, <http://muse.jhu.edu/ journals/the_moving_image/v004/4.1edwards.html>, *The Association of Moving Image Archivists*, 2004, (accessed 28 April 2006).

®™ARK. *'Promotional Still'*, <http://rtmark.com/ads.html>, ®™*ark*, 2007, (accessed 17 December 2007).

SALTZMAN, L. 'Marketing Modernism in Fin-de-Siecle Europe – Book Review', <http://findarticles.com/p/articles/mi_m0422/is_n4_v78/ai_19178144/pg_6>, *Find Articles*, 1996, (accessed 18 April 2007).

SEN, S. 'The Fantasy of "Fair Globalisation"' <http://www.countercurrents.org/gl-sen150704.htm>, *Counter Currents*, 15 July 2008, (accessed 4 November 2008).

SHOBA, *'Blowing Zen'*, <http://www.ngv.vic.gov.au/metropolis/resources/rb_metropolis.pdf>, *National Gallery of Victoria*, 2004, (accessed 10 December 2006). This link is no longer active.

SIEMENS, G. 'Losing Interest in Social Media: There is no There There', <http://www.elearnspace.org/blog/2011/07/30/losing-interest-in-social-media-there-is-no-there-there/>, *eLearnspace*, (accessed 11 August 2013).

SMITH, K. 'Rewarding the Viuser: A Human-Televisual Data Interface Application', <http://72.14.253.104/search?q=cache:s3oXhII19jUJ:www.icinema.unsw.edu.au/pdf/rewarding_viuser.pdf+Keir+Smith+'Rewarding+the+Viuser:+A+Human-Televisual+Data+Interface+Application'&hl=en&ct=clnk&cd=1&gl=au>, *iCinema*, 2003, (accessed 01 January 2005).

SMITH, M.K. 'Definitions of Globalization', <http://www.infed.rg/biblio/defining_globalization.htm>, *Informal Education Organisation (infed.org)*, (accessed 3 November 2008). This link is no longer active.

SORENSEN, R. 'Ain't No Sunshine When the Grants are Gone', <http://www.theaustralian.news.com.au/story/0,,22875256-16947,00.html>, *The Australian*, 2007, (accessed December 06 2007). This link is no longer active.

SRINIVASAN, R. 'Taking power through technology in the Arab Spring', <http://www.aljazeera.com/indepth/opinion/2012/09/2012919115344299848.html>, *Al Jazeera*, (accessed 11 August 2013).

STERNBERGH, A. 'Around the World in One Day', New York Times (in italics), <http://www.nytimes.com/2011/07/24/mag-azine/around-the-world-in-one-day-on-youtube.html?_r=0>, (accessed 30 July 2011). Link no longer active.

THE YES MEN. 'Promotional Still', <http://www.theyesmen.org> *The Yes Men*, 2000, (accessed 17 December 2007).

TOFTS, D. 'Forward and Beyond: Anticipating Distributed Aesthetics', <http://www.journal.fibreculture.org/issue7/issue_7tofts.html>, *Fibreculture*, 2005, (accessed 23 March 2007). This link is no longer active.

Zeynep Tufekci and Christopher Wilson, 'Social Media and the Decision to Participate in Political Protest: Observations From Tahrir Square', *Journal of Communication,* Vol. 62., 2012, pp. 363–379.

VICKERS, R. 'From 'Hello World' To Global Gallery: The Internet for Exhibition and Dissemination of Visual Artifacts and Interactive Work', <http://72.14.253.104/search?q=cache:OOSBRuYEGIAJ:newmedia.yeditepe.edu.tr/pdfs/isimd_04/08.pdf+simian+mawdsley&hl=en&ct=clnk&cd=6&gl=au>, *Yeditepe University*, 2006, (accessed 23 March 2007). This link is no longer active.

WALKER, J. 'Life in a Day', *YouTube/National Geographic Films,* <http://movies.nationalgeographic.com/movies/life-in-a-day/about-the-production/>, (accessed 1 August 2013).

WALTERS, H. 'First Tears at TED', *Bloomberg Business week,* 28 February 2008, <http://www.businessweek.com/innovate/next/archives/2008/02/first_tears_at.html>, 2008, (accessed 15 February 2013).

WE ARE EVERYWHERE. 'Hacktivism: A Week of Electronic Disruption during the Republican National Convention', <http://www.thehacktivist.com/archive/news/2004/RNC-ECD-Indymedia-2004.pdf>, *Indybay*, 2004, (accessed 08 September 2005). This link is no longer active.

WEILAND, S. 'Sense, Memory and Media', <http://www.digitalartsource.com/content/featur/feat17/feat17p1.html>, *Digital Art Source*, 2004, (accessed 14 May 2004). This link is no longer active.

WELLS, R. 'The Future of a Promise', *Middle East,* Issue 428, Dec 2011, p. 60.

WILLIAMS, A. *'YES'*, <http://www.ngv.vic.gov.au/metropolis/resources/rb_metropolis.pdf, *National Gallery of Victoria*, 2004, (accessed 10 December 2006). This link is no longer active.

WILSON, S.J. 'Dead Plastic Filled Birds', *Huffington Post,* <http://www.huffingtonpost.com/stiv-j-wilson/dead-plastic-filled-birds_b_638716.html>, (accessed 15 February 2013).

WILYAWILDOTCOM, 'Tiananmen-Like Courage in Cairo: Egypt's 25 Jan Protests', <http://www.youtube.com/watch?v=q1m4_q_HP5o>, *YouTube,* (accessed 11 August 2013).

WRAY, S. 'On Electronic Civil Disobedience', <http://www.thing.net/~rdom/ecd/oecd.html>, *Thing.net,* 1998, (accessed 23 March 2007).

WU, I. 'Wired on the Runway', <http://rhizome.org/news/story.rhiz?timestamp=20070202>, *Rhizome. org,* 2007, (accessed 23 March 2007).

Websites

<http://www.blast.org>, *Blast Theory,* (accessed 15 June 2004). This link is no longer active.

<http://www.cybertown.com>, *Cyber Town,* (accessed 05 May 2002). This link is no longer active.

<http://www.etoy.com>, *Etoy,* (accessed 11 February 2004).

<http://www.etoys.com>, *eToys,* (accessed 9 February 2004).

<http://www.ehum.edu.au/>, *E-humanities,* (accessed 16 December 2007).

<www.subtle.net/empyre/>, *Empyre,* (accessed 23 September 2007).

<https://www.facebook.com/350.org>, *350.org Facebook Page,* (accessed 11 August, 2013).

<http://www.fibreculture.org>, *Fibre Culture,* (accessed 23 March 2007).

<http://www.GWBush.com>, *GWBush,* (accessed 11 February 2004). This link is no longer active.

<http//www.hactivist.com>, *Hactivist,* (accessed 14 February 2004). This link is no longer active.

<http://www.happyhacker.org>, *Happy Hacker,* (accessed 05 May 2001).

<http://www.hishambizri.com/artistic.html>, *Hisham M. Bizri Website,* (accessed 07 December 2004).

<http://www.h-net.org>, *H-Net,* (accessed 17 September 2005).

<http://www.icinema.unsw.edu.au>, *iCinema,* (accessed 11 December 2005).

<http://www.ikda.co.uk>, *Ikda,* (accessed 03 May 2001). This link is no longer active.

<http://www.indymedia.org>, *Indy Media,* (accessed 23 April 2003).

<https://www.facebook.com/pages/Khaled-Said/100792786638349>, *Khaled Said Facebook Page,* (accessed 11 August 2013).

<http://www.marshallmcluhan.com/main.html>, *Marshall McLuhan,* (accessed 16 September 2007).

<http://www.myspace.com>, *MySpace,* (accessed 23 February 2007).

<http://www.nettime.org>, *nettime,* (accessed 23 September 2007).

<http://www.nologo.org>, *No Logo,* (accessed 22 March 2007). This link is no longer active.

<http://www.rhizome.org>, *Rhizome,* (accessed 05 March 2007).

<http://www.rtmark.com/rtcom/protester>, *®™ark,* (accessed 10 May 2007). This link is no longer active.

<http://www.rtmark.com>, *®™ark,* (accessed 03 November 2005).

<http://www.september11news.com/AttackImages.htm>, *September 11 News,* (accessed 16 December 2007).

<http://www.simian.nu>, *Simian,* (accessed 06 February 2001). This link is no longer active.

<http://www.skype.com>, *Skype,* (accessed 23 February 2007).

<http://www.thehacktivist.com/>, *The Hactivist,* (accessed 15 July 2004). This link is no longer active.

<http://www.thenetnet.com>, *The Net Net,* (accessed 03 June 2004).

<http://www.theyesmen.org>, *The Yes Men,* (accessed 23 February 2005).

<http://www.tomotterness.net/>, *Tom Otterness,* (accessed 16 December 2007). This link is no longer active.

<http://www.undergroundnews.com>, *Underground News,* (accessed 01 May 2001).

<http://www.worlds.com>, *Worlds,* (accessed 06 March 2001). This link is no longer active.

<http://www.youtube.com>, *You Tube,* (accessed 23 February 2007).

Audiovisuals

ABE, K. and SIN, J. *'Haptic Glove'*, <http://newmediabeijing.org/md2005/exhibition_display. php?section=2&link_id=18&title=Haptic+Glove+%28USA%29&artist_id=18_5>, NewMedia.org, 2004, (accessed 1 October 2007).

ALEXA, C. *'10-Second Couples'*, black and white video with sound, 6'38" on a loop, Image courtesy of the artist, 2000.

AMMER, W. *'Globalization 2', Michigan State University*, <https://www.msu.edu/user/hillrr/louisville%20talk_files/image002.jpg>, 2002, (Accessed 15 July 2013).

BALADI, L. *'Alone, Together...In Media Res'*, 3 channel video installation, Image courtesy of the artist, 2012.

BERZOWSKA, J. *'Intimate Memory Shirt'*, Image courtesy of the artist, 2005.

BERZOWSKA, J. *Feathery Dresses*, Image courtesy of the artist, 2005.

CMIELEWSKI, L. and STARRS, J. *'Floating Territories'*, Image courtesy of the artists, 2004.

COOPER, J. *'Transformers'*, <http://justinecooper.com/transformers.html>, Justine Cooper Website, 2002, (accessed 6 December 2008).

DE NIJS, M. *'Beijing Accelerator'*, <http://www.marnixdenijs.nl/beijing-accelerator.htm>, Marnix de Nijs, 2004a, (accessed 17 July 2013).

DE NIJS, M. *'Run Motherfucker Run'*, <http://www.marnixdenijs.nl/run-motherfucker-run.htm>, Marnix de Nijs, 2004b, (accessed 17 July 2013).

DIAZ HOPE, A. *Financial District Infiltration: Everybody is Somebody's Terrorist*, Image courtesy of the artist, 2004.

GOLEBIEWSKI, N. *'This is Where I Live'*, Image courtesy of the artist, 2003.

HAMDAN, I. *'Images of Revolution'*, *Al Jazeera*, <http://www.aljazeera.com/programmes/aljazeeraworld/2011/10/2011101974451215541.html>, 2011, (accessed 1 August 2013).

HENRY, D.P., *Image 003 v.2*, Image courtesy of Elaine O'Hanrahan, Manchester, 1961.

MACDONALD, K. *Life in a Day*, Youtube/National Geographic Films, <http://movies.nationalgeographic.com/movies/life-in-a-day/about-the-production/>), 2012, (accessed 1 August 2013).

MOELLER, C. and SAUTER, S. *'Networked Skin'*, <http://www.christian-moeller.com/display. php?project_id=46, Networked Skin>, Christian Moeller Website, 1994, (accessed 18 July 2013).

OTTERNESS, T. 'Painting for *Nine Eleven*', Image courtesy of the artist, 2003.

PUBLIC ENEMY. *It Takes a Nation of Millions to Hold us Back*, New York, Def Jam/Columbia Records, 1988.

STARR, F. and K. *'Habit with Laysan Albatross Chicks and Marine Debris'*, *Starr Environmental*, <http://www.starrenvironmental.com/images/image/?q=080603-5640&o=plants>, 2008, (accessed 21 August 2013).

WILLIAMS, A. *'YES'*, <http://www.bellwethergallery.com/artindivid02.cfm?PageNum_artc=26&fid=322>, Bellwether Gallery, 2002, (accessed 18 July 2013).

Conversations

ALEXA, C. 'Email conversation', 18 July 2013.

Printed in the United States
By Bookmasters